D1608201

THE
CRISIS OF
CHINESE CONSCIOUSNESS

RADICAL ANTITRADITIONALISM IN THE MAY FOURTH ERA

中國意識的危機

林毓生著

臺靜農題

THE
CRISIS OF
CHINESE CONSCIOUSNESS

RADICAL ANTITRADITIONALISM IN THE MAY FOURTH ERA

LIN YÜ-SHENG

THE UNIVERSITY OF WISCONSIN PRESS

Published 1979
The University of Wisconsin Press
Box 1379, Madison, Wisconsin 53701
The University of Wisconsin Press, Ltd.
1 Gower St., London WC1E 6HA, England

First printing
Printed in the United States of America
For LC CIP information see the colophon
ISBN 0-299-07410-2

Publication of this book was made possible in part
by a grant from the Andrew W. Mellon Foundation

TO THE MEMORY OF
MY FATHER

LIN FU-CHIH 林孚治
(1898–1970)
AND
MY TEACHER

YIN HAI-KUANG 殷海光
(1919–1969)

CONTENTS

FOREWORD

BENJAMIN I. SCHWARTZ

During the nineteenth century China was often regarded in the West as the very paradigm of frozen traditionalism. By the midtwentieth century China had become for many the land of revolution—a society which had effected a total, fundamental break with the entire cultural and social order of the past. When one reflects on why China in particular had been the symbol of unchanging tradition, one senses that this attitude was tied to the perception that China had managed to maintain intact a totally integrated social-cultural-political order presided over by a class which managed to embody within itself both the political and the spiritual authority of the society. The endurance of tradition seemed to be a function of its all-encompassing wholeness. With the rise of the Communists to power, one was acutely aware that the ideology of the leaders was of foreign origin, and that it was an ideology which explicitly demanded a total revolutionary break with the "feudalistic" society and culture of the past.

It must be added that students of modern Chinese intellectual history were also deeply impressed long before the victory of the Communists by the degree to which some of the leading intellectual figures of modern China had become converts to what Professor Lin Yü-sheng calls "totalistic iconoclasm." Totalistic iconoclasm, in essence, involves two assumptions—one, that the social-cultural-political order of the past must be treated as a whole, and two, that it must be rejected as a whole. Like Professor Lin, most students of twentieth-century intellectual history have been struck by the dominance during that episode of modern Chinese history known as the "May Fourth movement" of an attitude of "totalistic iconoclasm." They have also been deeply impressed by the degree to which this attitude continued to be held by some of the most influential figures in Chinese intellectual life during all the decades which followed. They have thus often seen the Chinese Communist leadership as the children of the May Fourth movement.

Now, it is quite clear that as an over-all description of the complex history of modern China, the neatly dialectic picture of a total rupture with a totalistic tradition is highly defective, however real and powerful the iconoclastic impulse in twentieth-century China and however real the actual integration of the political and cultural orders in the past. Much has been written in recent decades which drastically corrects this stark image of a total break with the past. The complexity of the traditional culture and the diversity of strains within it are being fruitfully explored. The unconscious or unacknowledged continuities with the culture of the past on every level of life in contemporary China are being thoroughly examined.

In the face of this corrective revisionism—much of which is justified—it must be pointed out that Professor Lin is by no means attempting in this subtle and closely reasoned work to reassert the original image. He by no means claims that traditional China was *in fact* an unproblematic whole made up of inseparable parts. He is, by no means, attempting to assert that the People's Republic has in fact marked a total rupture with all aspects whether good or bad of traditional Chinese culture. Indeed, at the heart of his own analysis is the view that certain attitudes deeply imbedded in certain Chinese cultural predispositions have profoundly shaped the views of the iconoclasts themselves.

What he does assert is that in spite of the extraordinary actual diversity of traditional Chinese culture, in spite of the conflicting tendencies within that culture, the notion of the integral wholeness of culture, the notion that every aspect of society and culture could somehow be controlled through the political order, and the notion that conscious ideas could play a decisive role in transforming human life formed a powerful, widely shared syndrome of ideas within the cultural tradition. He further contends that in many subtle ways these cultural propensities have shaped even those who most decisively rejected the past.

I shall not attempt to restate Professor Lin's subtle and nuanced argument. I would simply point out that whatever its other merits, it serves to focus our attention once more on the remarkable phenomenon of what he calls "totalistic iconoclasm" in twentieth-century China at a time when an excessive "revisionism" may be tending to blur it. When all the qualifications have been made—and no one is more aware of these qualifications than Professor Lin himself—the fact is that the attitudes which he describes have played a profound role in both the intellectual history and the political history of modern China. Thus in spite of all the ambivalence and complexities which we discern in the attitude of the People's Republic to the cultural heritage of the past, as of the present it is still wedded to an official doctrine of fundamental rejection. To be sure, by its unilinear interpretation of Marx's philosophy of history, it is able to assimilate the bad past of China to the more universal bad past of all the higher civilizations. It has been able to praise the material accomplishments of the past without reservation. It has been able to adopt more or less favorable attitudes to various aspects of the high and popular culture of the past but always in terms of a foreign conceptual scheme which denies them present value. However much one may sense a chafing at the constrictions imposed by the Marxist-Leninist frame of reference, however much the Chinese continue to be engrossed in their own past, the "totalistic" aspect of the official ideology has not disappeared.

The significance of the themes stressed by Professor Lin becomes particularly clear when we contrast the modern intellectual and political experience of China to that of some of the other non-Western-culture areas such as India and the Moslem world. To be sure, there are radical iconoclasts in those worlds, and there may be more in the future, just as there are notable "neo-traditionalist" thinkers in modern China. It may also be urged that the commitments of many intellectuals in India and in the Moslem world to Hinduism and Islam are often shallow and inauthentic. Yet the fact remains that in those societies intellectuals have often tended to discern compatibilities rather than stark antitheses between Islam and socialism, Hinduism and democracy, etc. No state has as yet arisen there which has presumed to carry out a frontal assault on the traditional beliefs of the masses. Professor Lin's analysis would suggest that whatever other factors may be at work, the collapse of the old political orders has not had the totalistic implications for those cultures which the collapse of China's political order may have had for China. His analysis also suggests that the intellectual elites of those societies may not share the Chinese faith in the power of such elites (the bearers of what he calls the "cultural-intellectualistic approach") to carry out the total cultural transformation of their societies.

It is to the enormous credit of Professor Lin that he has not simply presented his theses as abstractly argued propositions. He has instead chosen the more difficult path of testing them out by examining the thought of three of China's most eminent "May Fourth" figures—Ch'en Tu-hsiu, Hu Shih, and Lu Hsün. These men are immensely different from each other, and the mental worlds of all three are complex and full of ambivalences. It is nevertheless Professor Lin's conviction that in spite of their many differences, they share some of the basic predispositions with which he is concerned. Quite apart from the cogency of his argument, his analysis of these three figures provides us with new perspectives on all of them. Beyond this, his theses lead him to raise profound and fruitful questions about the Chinese cultural heritage itself. This book is a most thoughtful and suggestive contribution not only to our efforts to understand modern China but also to our efforts to wrestle with some of the most difficult problems of the modern world.

ACKNOWLEDGMENTS

This book has developed from a doctoral dissertation that was undertaken a number of years ago under the auspices of the Committee on Social Thought of the University of Chicago. To my teachers there, especially Professors Friedrich A. von Hayek, John U. Nef, David Grene, James Redfield, and the late Professor Hannah Arendt, as well as to Professor Leopold H. Haimson, formerly of Chicago and now of Columbia University, I am deeply grateful for their intellectual guidance and generous encouragement in my years of graduate training.

I should like to express my profound gratitude to Professor Benjamin I. Schwartz for his incisive comments on various versions of the manuscript, from which I benefited immeasurably, for his kind encouragement throughout the years, and for his willingness to preface this book with his own reflections. In the course of the research for and the writing of this book I have received valuable advice and unfailing support from Professor Maurice Meisner and Professor John K. Fairbank, to both of whom I wish to convey my sincere appreciation.

For offering criticism of certain portions of the manuscript, for helping me to improve the expression of my ideas, for lending me or leading me to important source materials, or for giving me encouragement at critical junctures of my research, I wish to thank Professor David Arkush, Mr. Steven C. Davidson, Professor Charlotte Furth, Professor Jerome B. Grieder, Professor Chang Hao, Professor Stephen N. Hay, Mr. Jeffery D. Hermanson, Professor John Israel, Professor Leo Ou-fan Lee, Professor K. C. Liu, Mrs. Geri McCormick, Professor Frederick W. Mote, Professor Sandra Siegel, Professor Thomas E. Skidmore, Professor T. H. Tsien, Professor Ezra F. Vogel, Mr. Max Woolpy, and Dr. Eugene Wu.

I owe a particular debt of gratitude to Mrs. Elizabeth A. Steinberg, Chief Editor at the University of Wisconsin Press, and Mrs. Jan H. Blakeslee for their painstaking editing of the manuscript, and to Mrs. Steinberg for her many other kindnesses. I should also like to express my appreciation to Professor T'ai Ching-nung, one of the most eminent artists in Chinese calligraphy in the world today, who honors this book with his inscription of its Chinese title and the name of its author. I wish to thank Mr. Ch'en Ch'iu-k'un and Mr. Thomas C. Pierson for their help in preparing the manuscript for the Press. To the Volker and Relm Foundations, the Elinor Castle Nef Fund, the Joint Committee on Contemporary China of the Social Science Research Council and the American Council of Learned Societies (whose grant enabled me to spend a year as a research fellow in the East Asian Research Center at Harvard University), and the Research Committee of the University of Wisconsin, Madison, my thanks are due for financial support toward the completion of this study.

I owe more than I can say to my wife, Tsu-gein, who has shared with me the anxiety, hardship, and joy of this intellectual venture. In the years while this work has been in progress our children, Albert and Winifred, have been born. She provides a stabilizing center in the family without which it is hard to imagine that this book could ever have been completed.

To the memory of my father, Lin Fu-chih, whose unyielding sense of perseverance in the face of difficulty has been a chief source of inspiration to my life, and the memory of my teacher, Professor Yin Hai-kuang of National Taiwan University, whose moral courage and enlightened intellect exemplify the best of the spirit of the May Fourth movement, this book is affectionately dedicated.

LIN YÜ-SHENG

Madison, Wisconsin
June 1978

THE
CRISIS OF
CHINESE CONSCIOUSNESS

RADICAL ANTITRADITIONALISM IN THE MAY FOURTH ERA

ABBREVIATIONS USED IN THE NOTES

HCN   *Hsin ch'ing-nien* (New youth)

HSWT *Hu Shih wen-ts'un* (Collected essays of Hu Shih), 1st collection, 4 chüan. Shanghai, Ya-tung t'u-shu-kuan, 1921; 2nd collection, 4 chüan, 1924; 3rd collection, 4 chüan, 1930.

LHCC *Lu Hsün ch'üan-chi* (Complete works of Lu Hsün), 10 vols. Peking, Jen-min wen-hsüeh ch'u-pan she, 1956.

THWT *Tu-hsiu wen-ts'un* (Collected essays of Ch'en Tu-hsiu), 3 chüan. Shanghai: Ya-tung t'u-shu-kuan, 1922.

SPPY   Ssu-pu pei-yao (Essentials of the four libraries)

SPTK   Ssu-pu ts'ung-k'an (Four-library series)

1

INTRODUCTION

One of the most striking and peculiar features of the intellectual history of twentieth-century China has been the emergence and persistence of profoundly iconoclastic attitudes toward the cultural heritage of the Chinese past. Despite the success of the Communist revolution in transforming state and society, the relationship of the new order to the traditional historico-cultural legacy remains uncertain and deeply ambiguous. Rather than promoting a purely nationalist celebration of the traditions of old China, the leaders of Communist China have been more preoccupied with uprooting those traditions, traditions which they perceive as threats to the present and barriers to the realization of their visions of a socialist future.

The immediate historical roots of this contemporary cultural ambivalence can be traced to the particular nature of the origins of the modern Chinese intelligentsia at the turn of this century, and especially to the specific intellectual tendencies that characterized the May Fourth movement of 1915–27. It is by no means fortuitous that the calls for "cultural revolution," which were so dominant in the May Fourth era, have been heard again during the history of the People's Republic, and most dramatically in the "Great Proletarian Cultural Revolution" of 1966–69. In both cases the demand for "cultural revolution" has been characterized by a virulently iconoclastic stance toward traditional ideas and values. And in both cases the demand for "cultural revolution" has been based on an underlying assumption that the basic precondition for meaningful political and social change is a wholesale transformation of the values and the spirit of the people. Such a transformation is further assumed to require a radical rejection of the prevailing traditions of the Chinese past.

The idea of cultural revolution has long occupied a prominent place in the Maoist revolutionary mentality, and in recent years it has become formalized as an essential component of Maoist revolutionary theory. The Maoist notion of cultural revolution cannot be understood simply in terms of political power struggles or as a function of the processes of political and social revolution. Power struggles of course have occurred frequently in the history of Chinese Communism, but they possess no inner logic that necessitates "cultural revolution." And political and social revolutions are not inevitably dependent upon cultural revolutions, nor do they necessarily give rise to them.

Moreover, the enormous Maoist emphasis on "cultural revolution" does not derive from the Marxist-Leninist tradition. However much a voluntarist interpretation of original Marxist theory might stress the role of human consciousness in history and the importance of the transformation of human nature in the revolutionary process, these "subjective" factors, according to Marxist theory, are ultimately conditioned by "objective" socioeconomic realities. Mao, by contrast, attributed to human consciousness a decisive role in the making of revolutions and the shaping of historical reality, and from this belief there flows the central Maoist concern with the question of "cultural revolution." Lenin, of course, was also very much of a voluntarist, particularly in his emphasis on the need for an intellectual elite to impose its superior "consciousness" on the "spontaneity" of the masses. But the Leninist stress on the conscious factors in history bears only a superficial resemblance to the Maoist emphasis. The views of Lenin and Mao are similar when they speak of the crucial function of culture and education in enabling a backward nation to advance to socialism and when they express the belief that the proper proletarian consciousness will not automatically be produced by the development of the forces of production. However, Lenin's view of the scope and focus of this consciousness reflects a technocratic proclivity which is incongruous with the ideas of Mao. Education is of importance for both of them; but the Leninist emphasis is on organizational education, specialist education, and political education, whereas Maoist education (although not excluding the above types) emphasizes instilling into the masses the appropriate and requisite social and moral ideas and values in order to bring about their intellectual and spiritual transformation.

Mao Tse-tung's persistent and emphatic demand for "cultural revolution," accompanied by his insistence on a radical rejection of the old culture as its prerequisite, was in fact one of the most distinctive features of the Maoist variant of Marxism-Leninism, which reflects qualitative departures from the premises of both Marxism and Leninism. While this is not the place to inquire into the complex problem of the origins and character of the Maoist conception of "cultural revolution," it is worth suggesting that it may well be fruitful to view the contemporary Maoist notion in the light of the radical ideas of the May Fourth intelligentsia, ideas which so crucially influenced Mao during the formative years of his intellectual life.[1]

In view of the strong currents of cultural iconoclasm[2] which run throughout

1. When Mao Tse-tung was a student at the First Provincial Normal School in Changsha he was fond of reading *New Youth*. According to Li Jui's authorized biography of the young Mao, Mao and his friends "read infatuatedly (*tsui-hsin yüeh-tu*) the anti-Confucianist essays of Ch'en Tu-hsiu and Wu Yü, and Li Ta-chao's essays 'Spring' and 'Now'." They used to copy out the important paragraphs of these essays and then write their comments in their notebooks and diaries. Li Jui, *Mao Tse-tung t'ung-chih ti ch'u-ch'i ke-ming huo-tung* (Peking, 1957), p. 28. Mao later told Edgar Snow that in his student days he "admired the articles of Hu Shih and Ch'en Tu-hsiu very much. They became for a while my models." With regard to Ch'en Tu-hsiu in particular, Mao said, "I had first met him in Peking, when I was at Peking National University, and he had influenced me perhaps more than anyone else." Edgar Snow, *Red Star over China*, 1st rev. and enlarged ed. (New York, 1968), pp. 148, 154. To Lu Hsün's contribution to China's cultural revolution Mao paid the highest, and now well-known, tribute: "Lu Hsün was the greatest and the most courageous standard-bearer of this new cultural force. The chief commander of China's cultural revolution, he was not only a great man of letters but a great thinker and revolutionary. Lu Hsün was a man of unyielding integrity, free from all sycophancy or obsequiousness; this quality is invaluable among colonial and semi-colonial peoples. Representing the great majority of the nation, Lu Hsün breached and stormed the enemy citadel; on the cultural front he was the bravest and most correct, the firmest, the most loyal and the most ardent national hero, a hero without parallel in our history. The road he took was the very road of China's new national culture." Mao Tse-tung, "On New Democracy," in *Selected Works of Mao Tse-tung* (Peking, 1961-65), 2:372; or "Hsin min-chu chu-i lun," in *Mao Tse-tung hsüan-chi* (Peking, 1966), 2:658.

2. I shall use "iconoclasm" and "antitraditionalism" interchangeably. "Iconoclasm" is used here in its broader sense—the ideological rejection of a tradition—*not* in the narrower sense of the rejection of the outward forms—the images—of a tradition.

the history of twentieth-century China, and which find contemporary expression in the enormous Maoist emphasis on the necessity of cultural revolution, the significance of understanding the radical antitraditionalism of the May Fourth era can hardly be overemphasized. The radical May Fourth revolt against the traditional Chinese cultural heritage was a turning point in post-traditional Chinese history, and the scope and depth of this antitraditionalism were probably unique in modern history in general.[3] It was a revolt that reflected a profound crisis of cultural identity in the consciousness of the twentieth-century Chinese intelligentsia. And it was the harbinger of later cultural and intellectual developments. For expressions of cultural iconoclasm in the decades which followed took the antitraditionalism of the May Fourth period as their points of departure; indeed, even many conservative ideas and ideologies that were put forth later showed the influence, to varying degrees, of the iconoclasm of the May Fourth era.

This book is primarily a study of the origins and nature of antitraditionalism in the May Fourth period. It was an antitraditionalism so radical that it can justifiably be described as totalistic.[4] In terms of our knowledge of movements for social and cultural change, this iconoclastic demand for a complete destruction of the past was in many respects an unprecedented historical phenomenon. To be sure, iconoclastic impulses frequently emerge during periods of fundamental sociohistorical change. As the grasp of new norms and values makes visible and intolerable many precepts and practices traditionally taken for granted, there often arise demands for their destruction. But there are many kinds of "destruction" of tradition and many varieties of iconoclasm. One may attack what are perceived to be the baneful elements of a tradition without necessarily condemning the past in toto. To uproot the anachronistic and pernicious elements of a tradition usually need not imply a complete rejection of the cultural heritage. If the transformative potential of a tradition is great, under favorable historical circumstances traditional symbols

---

3. Some French *philosophes* in the Enlightenment accused the *ancien régime* of being an embodiment of total evil. But they could not possibly have conceived their radical condemnation of church and state in a way which included the whole cultural heritage of the Western tradition, since they recognized their debts to the Renaissance and classical antiquity, especially ancient Rome.

4. The word "totalistic" is here used strictly to describe an ideological commitment to a cause of total rejection of Chinese social and cultural tradition; it has nothing to do with a "totalitarian" connotation. While the May Fourth iconoclasts *desired* on ideological grounds the total rejection of Chinese tradition, their totalistic iconoclasm, as this study will show, resulted in part from their inability to totally reject the influence of that tradition.

and values can be reformulated and reconstructed so as to provide propitious "seeds" for change and at the same time maintain a sense of cultural identity in the course of change. In that case, the establishment of a viable modern society is facilitated rather than impaired by cultural elements drawn from the past. Totalistic iconoclasm is by no means inherent in the process of modernization or in striving for modernity.[5]

Although there have been times when either individuals or groups have believed that everything in the past was useless or worthless, in the history of no other society has there occurred a movement of totalistic iconoclasm which proved so lasting and exerted so profound a historical impact. Thus the study of the origins and nature of the iconoclasm that arose in China during the May Fourth era is a particularly challenging task for historians to undertake. In attempting to understand recent Chinese history, it is crucial to take this peculiar historical experience into account.

In order to convey some sense of the intellectual diversity of the iconoclastic movement of the May Fourth period, while avoiding the superficiality and repetitiousness that would be inherent in any general survey of the ideas of all the iconoclasts, this book will take the form of a comparative study of the origins and nature of the iconoclastic consciousness of the three most celebrated leaders of the May Fourth intelligentsia: Ch'en Tu-hsiu, Hu Shih, and Lu Hsün.[6] In the early phase of the May Fourth era, these men shared similar iconoclastic tendencies and joined the antitraditional movement launched by the *New Youth* magazine. Yet the qualities of their iconoclastic thought were profoundly different, as were their personalities and political proclivities. By

5. Cf. Max Weber, *The Protestant Ethic and the Spirit of Capitalism,* tr. Talcott Parsons (New York, 1958); S. N. Eisenstadt, "The Protestant Ethic Thesis in an Analytical and Comparative Framework," in S. N. Eisenstadt, ed., *Protestant Ethic and Modernization* (New York, 1968), pp. 3–45, and his *Modernization: Protest and Change* (Englewood Cliffs, N.J., 1966), and "Transformation of Social, Political and Cultural Orders in Modernization," *American Sociological Review,* 30.5:650–73 (October, 1965); Robert Bellah, "Epilogue" in Robert Bellah, ed., *Religion and Progress in Modern Asia* (New York, 1965), pp. 168–225.

6. Ch'en Tu-hsiu (1879–1942) was the founder and a chief editor of *The Youth Magazine,* later called the *New Youth (Hsin ch'ing-nien* or *La Jeunesse),* China's leading journal of radical opinion in the May Fourth era. He was dean of the School of Letters at National Peking University from 1917 to 1919. With Li Ta-chao, Ch'en founded the Chinese Communist Party in 1921. He was head of the party from 1921 to 1927.

Hu Shih (1891–1962) was generally regarded as the leading spokesman of Chinese liberalism in the May Fourth era. From 1917 to 1927 he was professor of philosophy and later chairman of the department of English literature at National Peking University. From 1930 to 1937 he was dean of the College of Letters and from 1945 to 1949 president of that university. Hu was

comparing their ideas, I hope to bring out the unity as well as the diversity of May Fourth iconoclasm.

In analyzing the ideas and the intellectual development of Ch'en Tu-hsiu, Hu Shih, and Lu Hsün, I shall not be restricted by the rather arbitrary and mechanical dates—1915–27—which conventionally demarcate the May Fourth period. The iconoclastic movement which these three men pioneered reached its peak in the early (1915–19) and middle (1919–23) phases of the May Fourth era. But the impulses toward totalistic iconoclasm persisted in the writings of Lu Hsün that were published well after this period. Although Hu Shih participated in the totalistic assault against Chinese tradition during the May Fourth movement, he did not spell out his argument explicitly until 1934. His later iconoclastic writings, however, did not fundamentally depart from the basic themes of his earlier iconoclastic thought, and they will be included in the analysis despite the fact that they extend past the era of the May Fourth movement as such.

Since this study is not intended to be an aggregate of intellectual biographies, only a limited amount of biographical data is provided. Attention will be focused primarily on the general concerns and iconoclastic thought of Ch'en, Hu Shih, and Lu Hsün. They have been selected for study partly

---

ambassador to the United States from 1938 to 1942, and served as the president of Academia Sinica in Taiwan from 1958 until his death in 1962.

Lu Hsün (1881–1936), the pen name of Chou Shu-jen, was the greatest Chinese writer in the May Fourth era. He served on the staff of the Ministry of Education from 1912 to 1926, with a brief interruption in 1925. He was lecturer in Chinese literature at National Peking University from 1920 to 1926, professor of Chinese literature at Amoy University in 1926 and at Sun Yat-sen University, Canton, in 1927. From 1927 until his death in 1936 Lu Hsün lived in Shanghai, devoting himself to writing and translation.

For concise biographical accounts of these three figures, see articles in Howard L. Boorman, ed., *Biographical Dictionary of Republican China* (New York, 1967–71), 1:240–48, 416–24, 2:167–74, for Ch'en Tu-hsiu, Lu Hsün, and Hu Shih respectively. For detailed biographical information about Hu Shih, see Jerome B. Grieder, *Hu Shih and the Chinese Renaissance* (Cambridge, Mass., 1970). A comprehensive biography of Lu Hsün up to the time he left Peking in 1926 is provided by William A. Lyell, Jr., *Lu Hsün's Vision of Reality* (Berkeley, 1976). All attempts at biographies of Ch'en Tu-hsiu suffer from the scarcity of primary sources for the period before 1915, but see Thomas C. Kuo, *Ch'en Tu-hsiu (1879–1942) and the Chinese Communist Movement* (South Orange, N.J., 1975); Yü-ju Chih, "Ch'en Tu-hsiu: His Career and Political Ideas," in Chün-tu Hsüeh, ed., *Revolutionary Leaders of Modern China* (London and New York, 1971), pp. 335–66; Richard C. Kagan, "Ch'en Tu-hsiu's Unfinished Autobiography," *China Quarterly*, 50:295–314 (April–June, 1972) and his "The Chinese Trotskyist Movement and Ch'en Tu-hsiu: Culture, Revolution, and Polity" (Ph.D. diss., University of Pennsylvania, 1969).

because they were the acknowledged leaders of the May Fourth movement and partly because of the striking differences in their personalities, their politics, and their intellectual histories. Ch'en Tu-hsiu, who eventually became a Marxist and the first leader of the Chinese Communist Party, was known as a man of intense moral passion, combative in temperament and fearlessly individualistic. His mind was more forceful than subtle; he was not greatly concerned with the nuances of meaning or the complexities involved in social and cultural issues. Hu Shih, on the other hand, was a Deweyan liberal and eventually became an ambivalent supporter of the Kuomintang. He was a well-rounded and self-content personality, affable and urbane, and not without a touch of vanity. He possessed an alert mind, and was superficially lucid in his manner of expression, but he did not involve himself in social and cultural issues at their more difficult levels and never probed deeply into the problems with which he was concerned. Lu Hsün, by contrast, was an extremely complex person, with a sharp wit and a sensitive, subtle, and creative mind. He was known for his sardonic humor and mordant sarcasm. Outwardly, he was distant and cold; inwardly, deeply pessimistic and melancholy—but with a genuine warmth and moral passion which enabled him to express the agony of China's cultural crisis with great eloquence. Politically, he was highly sympathetic to the Communists in his later years, but he eschewed formal party ties and firm ideological commitments.

As we shall see, the differences among these men in personality, politics, and intellectual proclivities influenced the qualities of their iconoclasm. Yet all of them arrived at the same basic conclusion: an intellectual and cultural revolution which required a total rejection of the Chinese past was the fundamental prerequisite for modern social and political change. Thus the problem of understanding the totalistic nature of May Fourth iconoclasm cannot be explained in terms of psychological, political, or sociological generalizations. It is a historical problem which must be considered in the broader context of the dialectic of social and intellectual change and continuity in twentieth-century China. It is to this broader historical background that we first must turn.

2

THE ORIGINS OF
TOTALISTIC ANTITRADITIONALISM
IN THE MAY FOURTH ERA—I

Behind the radical iconoclasm of the May Fourth movement as, indeed, behind many other intellectual phenomena in the last one hundred forty years of Chinese history, stands one dominant fact: the intrusion of Western civilization. Its presence, in various forms, undermined the stability and coherence of traditional culture and generally influenced the direction of intellectual and cultural change in modern China.

Acceptance of Western ideas and values was by and large predicated on Chinese nationalism, which in turn emerged as a direct response to the challenge of Western intrusion. Chinese nationalism had brought forth a new hierarchic order of values, "where the commitment to the preservation and advancement of the societal entity known as the nation takes priority over commitment to all other values and beliefs, where other values and beliefs are judged in terms of their relevance to this end rather than vice versa."[1] Hence

---

1. Benjamin Schwartz, *In Search of Wealth and Power: Yen Fu and the West* (Cambridge, Mass., 1964), p. 19. I am grateful to Professor Ezra F. Vogel for his permission to use material in

at the most fundamental level, it was primarily nationalistic goals and aspirations that demanded cultural and sociopolitical changes. In the early years of the May Fourth era those changes were urged in terms of Western democratic and scientific ideas and values (as they were then understood in China), mainly, although not exclusively, because they were thought to be conducive to the preservation and reconstruction of the Chinese nation-state.

Nationalistic impulses also transformed social Darwinian terminology and concepts then prevalent into an ideology of change which prompted many intellectuals to scorn the institutions, ideas, and values of the past.[2] But the totalism of the May Fourth iconoclastic movement cannot be explained by Chinese nationalism, by Chinese social Darwinian concepts of change, or by the acceptance of Western liberal and scientific ideas and values, although these were general background factors in that phenomenon. For the origins of its distinctive nature, we must look into the *interaction* between deep-rooted historical forces and the immediate political events—an interaction that exercised a decisive influence upon the iconoclasts themselves.

DISINTEGRATION OF TRADITIONAL SOCIOPOLITICAL AND CULTURAL-MORAL ORDERS

After celebrating the collapse of the Ch'ing empire, Chinese intellectuals soon came to realize that the founding of the republic, instead of making China a modern nation-state, was merely the culmination of the process of disintegration of the traditional sociopolitical and cultural-moral orders. In the last years of the Ch'ing, these had been weakened by the intrusion of the Western powers and ideologies, by the new nationalistic sentiments held by an emerging modern intelligentsia, and by internal bureaucratic corruption and moral decay, but the survival of the throne had prevented the sociopolitical and cultural-moral orders from breaking down completely.

To understand the reasons for the final breakdown of both the sociopolitical order and the cultural-moral order as a result of the collapse of universal kingship, and the reasons for the development of totalistic antitraditionalism in the May Fourth era as one of its consequences, we must examine first the

---

my "Radical Iconoclasm in the May Fourth Period and the Future of Chinese Liberalism," in Benjamin I. Schwartz, ed., *Reflections on the May Fourth Movement* (Cambridge, Mass.: East Asian Research Center, Harvard University, 1972) in this and other chapters of the book.

2. Nationalism is an elusive concept; so is social Darwinism. They deserve fuller discussion at a later point. I shall deal with the relationship of nationalism and social Darwinism in chapter 4 in the context of Ch'en Tu-hsiu's iconoclastic thought.

implications of the enduring stability and dominance of universal kingship in traditional China, and second, the significance of its function in integrating the sociopolitical and cultural-moral orders.

The evidence of the Shang oracle inscriptions suggests that the notion of universal kingship had already begun taking its distinctive shape at the time of China's earliest records. The king of the Shang was a unique figure who called himself "I, the One Man" *(Yü I-Jen)*—a practice followed by the king of the Chou (1122?–256 B.C.). The supreme deity of the Shang, Ti, who made his impartial will known by his approval and assistance of the king's activities, or sometimes by sending down calamities or even ordering enemy attacks, was perceived as according a special and unique attention to the king's person and thereby legitimizing, at least potentially, his rule in a universal sense.[3] Certainly, by the time of the Chou the idea that the world should be universally governed by a king entrusted with the Mandate of Heaven was deeply embedded in the minds of the people. The king was the proprietor of all territory and the highest sovereign over all people. In addition to his

---

3. Quite a number of the Shang oracle inscriptions show that the king called himself "I, the One Man," for example, Ch'ü Wan-li, *Hsiao-t'un (ti-erh-pen): Yin-hsü wen-tzu chia-pien k'ao-shih* (Taipei, 1961), p. 264, plate 2123. My account of the emergence of universal kingship in the Shang has benefited from David N. Keightley's as yet unpublished "Legitimation in Shang China" for the Conference on Legitimation of Chinese Imperial Regimes, Asilomar, June 15–24, 1975. On pp. 45–47 of his paper Keightley writes, "The very rarity of inscriptions which suggest that Ti was ordering an enemy attack indicates either that enemy attacks were seldom sufficiently threatening to be associated with Ti or that Ti was rarely thought to be hostile to Shang interests; the two possibilities are not exclusive. But these few 'Ti orders harm' inscriptions are of great significance, for they suggest that Ti was potentially a T'ien-like figure capable of harming and destroying the dynasty. . . . In short, I would suggest that Ti was a general, universal power, not the exclusive power of a particular lineage. It is by no means certain that the ancestors of other lineages and tribes were not conceived of as also appealing to Ti in similar ways. Such a possibility would accord well with both the impartiality of Ti for the Shang cause, and the genesis of the mandate of heaven doctrine in western Chou. The claim that Ti (or T'ien) had ordered them to conquer the Shang would thus not have been a new invention of Chou political theory, but a logical extension from the theology of Shang times. It is possible, therefore, that the tribes surrounding Shang hoped for Ti's assistance, just as the Shang did. . . . The king's person was the special concern of Ti. Ti was thought capable of protecting the king, assisting the king, giving his approval to the king, harming the king, etc., just as the ancestors did, but the distinguishing feature was that Ti focused his powers on no other living individual in the same way. This unique attention presumably emphasized the king's special status as 'I the one man.' " I am grateful to Professor Keightley for sending me a copy of his paper. For a survey of the usage of "I, the One Man" by the king of Shang and Chou in the Shang oracle inscriptions, Western Chou bronze inscriptions, the *Book of Documents (Shang-shu)*, the *Tso-chuan*, the *Kuo-yü*, etc., see Hu Hou-hsüan, "Shih 'Yü I-Jen'," *Li-shih yen-chiu*, no. 1:75–78 (1957).

temporal power and authority, the king, perceived as the link between the cosmos and the people, also exercised a religio-spiritual authority.[4]

In the late Chou period, when political division had weakened the symbol and the institution of universal kingship, most schools of ancient Chinese thought still took them for granted, however different their conceptions of the origins and the role of the universal king. Generally recognized as among these schools were classical Confucianism, Moism, and Legalism.[5] But it is very revealing that classical Taoism must also be included. Within the spectrum of classical Chinese thought, Taoism, especially the *Chuang-tzu*, appears in many ways to have taken a more critical stance toward the prevailing conventions; presumably, it had a greater potential for breaking through the confinement of Chinese tradition. Yet the many passages of advice to the king on nonaction in the *Lao-tzu* postulated the legitimacy of universal kingship.[6] The radical relativism of the *Chuang-tzu*, to be sure, makes any effort to pin down a message extremely difficult and perhaps ultimately futile. One may argue

---

4. Many passages from the *Book of Documents* and the *Book of Odes* (*Shih-ching*) can be cited to illustrate this point. "Chao-kao," *Shang-shu*, SPPY ed., 8:12b–13b: "Oh, august Heaven, God on High, has changed his principal son (i.e., chosen the 'Son of Heaven' from another house), and this great state Yin's mandate. Now that the king has received the mandate, unbounded is the grace, but also unbounded is the solicitude. Oh, how can he be but careful! . . . , May the king come and (continue =) take over the work of God on High, and himself manage (the government) in the centre of the land. I, Tan, say: having made the great city, he shall (governing) from there be a counterpart to august Heaven. He shall carefully sacrifice to the upper and lower (Spirits), and from there centrally govern. The king, in case of his fulfilling his mandate, in governing the people will now have the (heavenly) grace." "To-shih," *Shang-shu*, SPPY ed., 9:8a: "[The King is quoted by the Duke of Chou as having said:] If you can be reverently careful, Heaven will give you favour and pity you. If you cannot be reverently careful, not only will you not have your lands, I [the King] shall also apply Heaven's punishment to your persons." "To-fang," *Shang-shu*, SPPY ed., 10:10b: "The king has said: . . . If you are licentious and perverse, and greatly deviate from the king's commands, then your numerous regions will draw upon yourselves Heaven's severity. I will then apply Heaven's punishment, and remove you far from your lands." Bernhard Karlgren, tr., *The Book of Documents* (Stockholm, 1950), pp. 48–49, 56, 65. Ode No. 249 "Chia-lo," *Mao-shih*, SPPY ed., 17:8b: "Greatly happy be the lord; illustrious is his good virtue; he orders well the people, he orders well the men; he receives blessings from Heaven; it protects and helps, and appoints him; from Heaven [comes the favour] that keeps him in power." Bernhard Karlgren, tr., *The Book of Odes* (Stockholm, 1950), p. 205.

5. E.g., the *Lun-yü*, VIII.19, XV.4; the *Meng-tzu*, VA.4, VA.5; the *Hsün-tzu*, IX, XII; the *Mo-tzu*, VIII, XI, XXVI; the *Han-fei-tzu*, II.8.

6. In the *Lao-tzu* the term *sheng-jen* ("sage") occurs more than twenty times, and often refers to the ideal ruler of the *t'ien-hsia* ("world"; lit., "under heaven"), i.e., the universal king, who knows and practices the *tao* of *wu-wei* ("nonaction"). For instance: Chap. 22: "Therefore the 'sage' embraces the One and is the model for the *t'ien-hsia*. He does not show himself, and so is

that its radical relativistic metaphysics renders absurd any deliberation on the form of human society and that, metaphysically speaking, the symbol and the institution of universal kingship are irrelevant to the individual's attainment of freedom. But there are passages in the inner, outer, and miscellaneous chapters of the *Chuang-tzu* that take up problems in human society in a manner which assumes the legitimacy and necessity of universal kingship; insofar as it recognizes the necessity for a certain social and moral order (for a recluse who becomes asocial the matter is, of course, categorically different), that order is to be achieved in the form of universal kingship, whose ideal ruler will follow the advice on nonaction.[7]

Clearly, the idea of universal kingship had roots deep within classical Chinese culture. It survived challenges presented by the political divisions and intellectual diversities of the late Chou period. Reinforced by the establishment of the Chinese empire in 221 B.C., it remained intact throughout later periods of barbarian assaults, political divisions, and the cultural dominance of Buddhism.

---

luminous. He does not justify himself and so is illustrious. He does not brag, and so has merit. He does not boast, and so endures." Chap. 49: "The 'sage' in reigning over the *t'ien-hsia* refrains from imposing his subjective viewpoint upon his people. His mind forms a harmonious whole with that of his people. They all lend their eyes and ears, and he treats them all as infants." Chap. 57: "Govern the state by being straightforward; wage war by being crafty; and win the *t'ien-hsia* by engaging in no activity." Ch'en Ku-ying, *Lao-tzu chin-chu chin-i* (Taipei, 1972), pp. 107–8, 170, 189. Other statements—e.g. chaps. 7 and 81—imply that the principle of *wu-wei* for the "sage" is based upon or analogous to the Way of Heaven. Since the book took its present form in the late period of ancient Chinese feudal society, there are passages addressed to feudal lords rather than the ideal ruler of the *t'ien-hsia*. This in no way conflicts with my understanding of its basic assumption that the ideal form of the human world is the universal kingship. In translating the above passages I have consulted a number of commentaries and Wing-tsit Chan, tr., *The Way of Lao Tzu* (Indianapolis, 1963) and D. C. Lau, tr., *Lao Tzu Tao Te Ching* (Harmondsworth, 1963).

7. Among many examples in the *Chuang-tzu* the following, from chap. 7 (an inner chapter), can be cited: "Yang Tzu-chü, much taken aback, said, 'May I venture to ask about the government of the enlightened king?' Lao Tan said, 'The government of the enlightened king: His achievements blanket the world but appear not to be his own doing. His transforming influence touches the ten thousand things but the people do not depend on him. With him there is no promotion or praise—he lets everything find its own enjoyment. He takes his stand on what cannot be fathomed and wanders where there is nothing at all.' " Kuo Ch'ing-fan, ed., *Chiao-cheng Chuang-tzu chi-shih* (Taipei, 1962), 1:296; Burton Watson, tr., *The Complete Works of Chuang Tzu* (New York, 1968), p. 94. Certain relativistic notions in the *Chuang-tzu* imply that the assumption that society as such is worthwhile may well be unfounded. Here, however, I am not concerned with the ultimate worth of society but with the social and moral order that the *Chuang-tzu* discusses, assuming society is to be retained.

In accounting for the persistence of Chinese universal kingship Benjamin Schwartz points out that it was not simply that China in premodern times encountered no challenge from the emergence in its immediate vicinity of "any universal state whose claims it felt obliged to take seriously in cultural terms," though this fact reinforced the absolute faith of the Chinese in the universality of their kingship.[8] Chinese views, Professor Schwartz has perceptively observed, may well have been founded on a much firmer religio-cosmological base than were those of some other cultures. In the Middle East the gods emerged as anthropomorphized divine beings with well-marked personalities. The universal kings in Mesopotamia were agents of various ascendant deities such as Marduk or Ashur. The sheer multiplicity of deities as sources from which different kings had derived legitimacy and authority militated against their absolute claims to supremacy and universality. "In China, during the Chou period, something like the concept of an impersonal order, a *tao,* had already emerged; this was a cosmic-social order within which the kingship occupied a well-established, permanent, and pivotal locus."[9]

The permanency of universal kingship was buttressed by the incorporation of the *yin-yang* and "five elements" theories into Confucianism, a process which was greatly facilitated by the establishment of the Chinese empire, and which culminated during the second century B.C. in the works of Tung Chung-shu. In Tung's organismic cosmology the universal king was regarded as the *yang,* and the relationship of the subjects and their king as that of *yin* and *yang.*[10] The *yang* would always exist in the cosmos, the universal king in the world. Through universal kingship, which linked the cosmic order to the social order,[11] divine authority sanctioned society's moral order—the Three

8. Benjamin I. Schwartz, "The Chinese Perception of World Order, Past and Present," in John K. Fairbank, ed., *The Chinese World Order* (Cambridge, Mass., 1968), p. 281.

9. Ibid., p. 283.

10. Tung Chung-shu, *Ch'un-ch'iu fan-lu,* SPTK ed., 12:7a–b.

11. Tung Chung-shu, 11:6b: "Those who in ancient times invented writing drew three [horizontal] lines which they connected through the center [by a vertical stroke], and then called this 'King'. These three lines represent Heaven, Earth, and man, while the connecting of them through the center represents the [king's] penetration of their [interrelated] principles. Who, indeed, if not a [true] king, could take the central position between Heaven, Earth, and man, so as to act as the connecting link between them? Therefore the king models himself on Heaven. He takes its seasons as his model and gives them completeness. He models himself on its commands and causes the people to follow them. He models himself on its numerical [categories] and uses them when initiating affairs. He models himself on its course and thereby brings his administration into operation. He models himself on its will and with it attaches himself to *jen.*" Translations are taken, with minor revisions, from Fung Yu-lan, *A History of Chinese Philosophy,* tr. Derk Bodde (Princeton, 1953), 2:46–47.

Bonds (*san-kang*).[12] Said Tung Chung-shu: "The Three Bonds, comprising the Way of the King, may be sought in Heaven."[13]

So dominant was the institution of the kingship that few dissenting views exist, and those are inconsequential. There was, for example, one notable dissenter—Pao Ching-yen, a literatus of probably the late third and early fourth centuries A.D.—who argued that the Mandate of Heaven was a myth: the kingship had arisen from strife in which the strong and cunning established himself as ruler over the weak and innocent.[14] But challenging a myth was one thing; creating an alternative theory of political legitimacy was another. Pao offered no realistic substitute and could do no more than retreat to a no less mythical image, that of an age of golden antiquity in which no sociopolitical hierarchy existed and everyone enjoyed the bliss of primordial harmony.[15] As for how to deal with the existing sociopolitical situation, he was entirely silent. Sociopolitical, economic, and cultural conditions in third- and fourth-century China did not provide room for Pao's criticisms to become a stimulating source of new ideas of political legitimation. His potentially subversive criticism of universal kingship was a lone voice, with virtually no impact on later Chinese culture and society.[16]

Two points are suggested by the preceding discussion. First, the establishment of the empire and the elaborate organismic cosmology which went into the making of imperial Confucianism reinforced the idea and the institution of universal kingship. Thus, the kingship as the link integrating the sociopolitical and the cultural-moral orders was henceforth greatly strengthened and solid-

12. *Kang* literally means a principal cord in a net, to which all the other strings are attached. The Three Bonds are those binding the minister to the king, the son to the father, the wife to the husband.

13. Tung Chung-shu, 12:8a.

14. Ko Hung, *Pao-p'u tzu*, SPPY ed., wai-p'ien, 48:1a: "The Confucian literati say: 'Heaven gave birth to the people and then set the ruler over them.' But how can High Heaven have untiringly said this? Is it not rather that interested parties make this their pretext? The fact is that the strong oppressed the weak and the weak submitted to him; the cunning tricked the innocent and the innocent served him. It was because there was submission that the relation of ruler and subject arose, and because there was servitude that the people, being powerless, could be kept under control. Thus servitude and mastery result from the struggle between the strong and the weak and from the comparison between the cunning and the innocent. Heaven has nothing whatsoever to do with them." The translation is adopted with revisions from Etienne Balazs' translation of Pao Ching-yen's writings preserved by Ko Hung in his *Chinese Civilization and Bureaucracy*, tr. H. M. Wright (New Haven, 1964), p. 243.

15. Ko Hung, wai-p'ien, 48:1a-2a; Balazs, pp. 244-46.

16. This is also true of Liu Tsung-yüan's evolutionary idea of ancient Chinese "feudalism." See below, pp. 53-54.

ified. Secondly, universal kingship was a most thoroughly embedded assumption, taken for granted across the boundaries of many divergent schools of thought, dominant in China since her written record began. Traditional Chinese civilization had few resources for breaking free of it. More generally, this continuity of universal kingship implies that the integrated structure of Chinese culture and society had existed through time without generic change.

The history of the erosion and final collapse of the idea and the institution of universal kingship has been extensively discussed by others and I shall not dwell on the subject here.[17] Ironically, when it came to its end, the time-honored and deep-rooted universal kingship had been so corroded that it was overthrown with comparative ease. But this should not lead us to overlook the historic significance of its fall. Its continuity over the centuries and its integrative function in Chinese society meant that the collapse had particularly devastating consequences.

Precisely because the universal kingship was the necessary link that held the sociopolitical order and the cultural-moral order together in a highly integrated fashion, the breakdown of the former as a result of the collapse of the universal kingship inevitably undermined the latter. This is not to say that the sociopolitical and cultural-moral disintegration of China after 1911 was simply and suddenly caused by the collapse of the throne. It was a long and complex process which covers Chinese history from the 1840s to 1911. Over a long period, the gate of a dike may be eroded away; when it finally bursts, nothing can hinder the thrust of the flood that spreads ruin and destruction in the natural order beyond. Just so did the dissolution of the throne—the final collapse of the gate—bring destruction to the traditional order of things in China.

I do not mean that among the Chinese all sense of traditional ideas or values was lost in the cultural and moral breakdown; rather, that the clusters of ideas and values fashioned in the integrated order of the past were either eroded or dislocated. In other words, the framework of traditional culture and morality had become disintegrated. Those who wanted to hold or defend traditional ideas and values were forced to look for new justifications. Since nothing in the content of traditional Chinese thought could still safely be assumed, all aspects of it were liable to be questioned or attacked. This wholesale disintegra-

17. See, e.g., Schwartz, "The Chinese Perception of World Order," pp. 276–88, and his *In Search of Wealth and Power: Yen Fu and the West;* Joseph R. Levenson, *Liang Ch'i-ch'ao and the Mind of Modern China* (Cambridge, Mass., 1959); Hao Chang, *Liang Ch'i-ch'ao and Intellectual Transition in China, 1890–1907* (Cambridge, Mass., 1971).

tion provided the *structural possibility* for the May Fourth iconoclasts to use a traditionally derived mode of thinking (I shall describe it in the next chapter) as a weapon for their totalistic attack on Chinese tradition. In other words, had the traditional culture been structured in such a way that its framework could not have been totally undermined by the breakdown of the traditional political order, some traditional ideas and values would have still been moored to the existing cultural order rather than becoming totally disengaged.[18] Then, the May Fourth iconoclasts could not have conceived an organismic view of the traditional Chinese culture, to be accepted or rejected in toto. On the contrary, a certain differentiation in their perception of Chinese tradition would have been possible—hence, they could have rejected those evil and/or useless elements of the tradition without necessarily arguing for totalistic antitraditionalism. However, their arguments were couched in terms of an organismic nature for Chinese tradition, although they did not actually refer to the integrating function and persistent dominance of the universal kingship itself.[19]

18. The defenders of Chinese tradition were also, in their own way, deeply influenced by its disintegration. Profoundly shocked by the breakdown of traditional culture and morality, many members of the first generation of Chinese intelligentsia—such men as K'ang Yu-wei, Yen Fu, Liang Ch'i-ch'ao, who reached intellectual maturity before the collapse of the Chinese cultural order—went to great extremes in seeking new justifications, some almost absurd, for a tradition that could no longer even be clearly defined. For an account of the strain of the cultural and moral disintegration, as it was manifested in the thought of a non-elite intellectual who desperately tried to preserve the Chinese moral tradition, see Lin Yü-sheng, "The Suicide of Liang Chi: An Ambiguous Case of Moral Conservatism," in Charlotte Furth, ed., *The Limits of Change: Essays on Conservative Alternatives in Republican China* (Cambridge, Mass., 1976), pp. 151–68.

19. I have presented the devastating effects of the collapse of universal kingship on Chinese culture with a heuristic and expository intent—as an "ideal-type" analysis in which relevant elements of the historical reality are constructed into a logically coherent conception. My analysis falls in with Max Weber's "individualizing ideal type" rather than "generalizing ideal type." Max Weber, *The Methodology of the Social Sciences,* tr. Edward A. Shils and Henry A. Finch (New York, 1949), pp. 89–112. A clarification of these two subcategories of Weber's concept of "ideal type" was made by Alexander von Schelting and followed by Talcott Parsons. Talcott Parsons, *The Structure of Social Action* (Glencoe, Ill., 1949), pp. 601–10. Precisely because this analysis possesses, I hope, logical clarity, it approximates but does not mirror the actual situation. I do not claim that all aspects of traditional Chinese culture and morality lost their credibility among all radical Chinese intellectuals immediately after the abdication of the Ch'ing emperor on February 12, 1912 (the 25th of the 12th moon in the *hsin-hai* year). The effects of the breakdown of the sociopolitical and cultural-moral orders after the collapse of the throne spread at varying rates among Chinese intellectuals, depending on a wide variety of social and geographic circumstances. Hu Shih, for instance, remote from Chinese society in the United States, still talked in 1914 about reforming Confucianism because he still assumed it should have some validity and value. See chapter 5, pp. 87–88. His personal rejection of Chinese tradition occurred after he returned to China in 1917.

YÜAN SHIH-K'AI AND CHANG HSÜN, AND THE ABUSES OF TRADITION

The nominal republic established after the dissolution of the empire could provide neither a new, comprehensive world view nor a viable political system. In a time of bewilderment and chaos, when political and cultural norms no longer existed, only a "strong man" proved capable of "ruling." A chaotic China readily yielded to the military power of Yüan Shih-k'ai. When he failed, no one was again strong enough to rule the country single-handedly. China succumbed to warlordism and internecine wars. Since there was no longer a Mandate of Heaven to justify political power, and new political ideologies were beyond their reach, the warlords could only thrash about without meaningful goals or aspirations.

The period of Yüan's domination formed an immediate political background for the rise of the May Fourth intelligentsia in general and the iconoclastic attack on Chinese tradition in particular. But before examining the implications of the rule of Yüan Shih-k'ai, it is necessary to consider a crucial event in the sphere of foreign affairs, one which greatly intensified nationalist sentiment among the intellectuals as well as the populace at large: the Twenty-one Demands issued on January 18, 1915, by the Japanese government to Yüan Shih-k'ai. Quick to see opportunity to take advantage of the chaotic situation in China, knowing that China did not have the strength to resist their aggression, and anticipating that Yüan would be too cunning to jeopardize his own position by following a policy of resistance, the Japanese in these secret demands in effect called for colonization of most of the key economic areas of China, and clearly anticipated depriving China of her sovereignty in domestic affairs as well. After negotiations lasting little more than three months, the Japanese minister to China, on May 7, delivered his government's ultimatum, requiring China to accept all the demands except the fifth group, which was left for future negotiation.[20] Yüan yielded two days later, thus concluding one of the most humiliating episodes in Chinese diplomatic history.

During the negotiations, Yüan's government made known to the press the nature of the demands in order to elicit public support. The response of the

20. This fifth group comprised seven demands which included China's agreeing to employ influential Japanese as advisers in political, financial, and military affairs and to have the police departments of important places jointly administered with the Japanese and granting rights for Japan to build two railways and to become China's lender of foreign capital. Yüan Shih-k'ai attempted to have them canceled, and the Imperial Japanese government finally agreed that they would be "postponed for later negotiation" as part of the terms of China's acceptance of groups one through four. Jerome Ch'en, *Yuan Shih-k'ai,* 2nd ed. (Stanford, 1972), pp. 152–58.

Chinese people was extremely sharp and indignant. Money flowed in to finance military resistance; public meetings in many cities called on the government to reject the demands; boycotts of Japanese goods, organized first in Shanghai, soon spread rapidly to other cities; and in Hunan some young men even committed suicide in protest.[21]

Upon receiving the news of the Twenty-one Demands, about four thousand Chinese students left Japan en masse for their homeland, protesting against the Japanese government. Later, in the summer of 1915, one of the three major figures of this study, Ch'en Tu-hsiu, who was to found *New Youth* in Shanghai, also came back from Japan.[22] Upon his return, he found Yüan Shih-k'ai's monarchical movement, for which members of Yüan's entourage had been stirring up agitation since about December, 1914, about to be formally launched.

In assessing the implications which Yüan's rule and his monarchical movement held for the rise of May Fourth iconoclasm, we must first ask one pertinent question. If the traditional Chinese political and cultural orders had broken down as a result of the collapse of universal kingship, why did the post-1911 iconoclasts find it necessary to attack so violently a tradition which had already disintegrated? The breakdown of the traditional Chinese sociopolitical and cultural-moral orders did not, of course, make the old evils disappear from Chinese society. On the contrary, after the framework in which they had been embedded could not itself be taken for granted, they were more visible and less tolerable in the ensuing chaos and demoralization. Moreover, from the immediate perspectives of the iconoclasts, who were not concerned with scholarly analysis but rather were deeply involved in the burning issues of the day, the old evil forces, which they felt were embodied in Yüan Shih-k'ai's unscrupulous manipulations, were more virulently active because they were unleashed from their traditional restraints. Attacks against them and, more important, against their roots were, therefore, all the more necessary and urgent.

Demoralization in China at this time was widespread, and generally recognized. Such a phenomenon is not uncommon in a situation of cultural and political disintegration when the charisma in society has been disrupted and the established norms of social conduct are undermined. The central locus of

21. *Li Ta-chao hsüan-chi* (Peking, 1959), p. 32.

22. Ch'en Tu-hsiu had joined Po Wen-wei, the governor of Anhwei, against Yüan Shih-k'ai in the Second Revolution in 1913. He fled to Japan after it failed. See Chow Tse-tsung, *The May Fourth Movement* (Cambridge, Mass., 1960), pp. 33, 42–43.

ultimate charisma in Chinese society was destroyed when the throne collapsed. In this situation many people lost the medium through which they had kept in touch with a transcendent order. They found themselves disengaged from civil bonds because these bonds were no longer held to be legitimate, and their moral sensibility was so bewildered after the loss of the authoritative agent of ordering—the throne—that they could hardly aspire to cultivate civility.[23] Social and moral anomie prevailed; a clear definition of ends was no longer possible. Some sought sensual pleasure, regardless of principles; others tilted at windmills. Most people existed in a state of appalling confusion.[24]

---

23. By civility I mean the virtue of the citizen. The old meaning of this word has been resurrected by Edward Shils, who observes that "civility has meant more than good manners, and it is an impoverishment of our vocabulary as well as a sign of the impoverishment of our thought on political matters that this word has been allowed to dwindle to the point where it has come to refer to good manners in face-to-face relationships." Edward Shils, "Ideology and Civility," in his *The Intellectuals and the Powers and Other Essays* (Chicago, 1972), p. 60.

24. My analysis of the effects of the destruction of the central locus of charisma in Chinese society is influenced by Edward Shils, who in his analysis of the relationship between charisma and order has made a major advance in sociological theory. The term "charisma" (the gift of grace) is taken from the vocabulary of early Christianity. Max Weber extended and reformulated it in connection with his elucidation of different types of authority. He used charisma to refer to certain extraordinary qualities of innovative personalities which are regarded by them and/or their followers as having either been endowed with divine power or made contact with what is most vital, most powerful, and most authoritative in the universe or in society. The manifestation of charismatic qualities is usually intense. But Weber also analyzed the routinization or institutionalization of charisma through kinship, heredity, and office. It is a process through which charismatic characteristics are transformed into a more continuous social organization and institutional framework. Nevertheless, Weber believed that the embodiment of genuine charisma in individuals and institutions is incompatible with secular institutionalization and hence had become diminished in the course of increasing rationalization and bureaucratization in the modern social and political order.

By taking issue with this last point of Weber's, while using the Weberian analysis of charismatic authority as his point of departure, Shils has provided a more comprehensive perspective of the charismatic phenomenon in society. He points out that charisma in society is not necessarily deduced from the creativity of the charismatic individual. It is "the quality which is imputed to persons, actions, roles, institutions, symbols, and material objects because of their presumed connection with 'ultimate,' 'fundamental,' 'vital,' order-determining powers." Edward Shils, "Charisma," in his *Center and Periphery: Essays in Macrosociology* (Chicago, 1975), p. 127. It is therefore able to order various dimensions of human experience. In other words, "the charismatic propensity" Shils observes, "is a function of the need for order." Edward Shils, "Charisma, Order, and Status," ibid., p. 261. Charisma informs the center, or the central value system, of society. "Society has a center. There is a central zone in the structure of society.... The center, or the central zone, is a phenomenon of the realm of values and beliefs. It is the center of the order of symbols, of values and beliefs, which govern the society. It is the center because it is the ultimate and irreducible; and it is felt to be such by many who cannot give explicit articulation to its irreducibility. The central zone partakes of the nature of the sacred.... The

Furthermore, Chinese political and cultural disintegration had some peculiar sequelae. First, the "national leader," Yüan Shih-k'ai, instead of trying to restore stability and harmony, exacerbated China's demoralization by his unscrupulous manipulations both before and after his decision to become emperor.[25] Secondly, his activities were buttressed by an appeal to Confucianism and an attempt to return to the obsolete political patterns of the past. Late in 1914, Yüan began to deploy a variety of traditional devices to legitimize his claim that he was the heir of the imperial system. On December

---

existence of a central value system rests, in a fundamental way, on the need which human beings have for incorporation into something which transcends and transfigures their concrete individual existence. They have a need to be in contact with symbols of an order which is larger in its dimensions than their own bodies and more central in the 'ultimate' structure of reality than is their routine everyday life." Edward Shils, "Center and Periphery," ibid., pp. 3, 7. Thus, people need to be related to the center of society so that they can make contact with a transcendent order and thereby partake of charisma which gives order to their existence. The destruction of the central locus of charisma in Chinese society had therefore its corollaries of cultural anomie and widespread demoralization. For an appreciation of Professor Shils's ideas on charisma and order in the context of the development of sociological thought, see S. N. Eisenstadt, "Introduction: Charisma and Institution Building, Max Weber and Modern Sociology," in S. N. Eisenstadt, ed., *Max Weber on Charisma and Institution Building* (Chicago, 1968), pp. ix–lvi, especially xxii–xxxii; and his "The Development of Sociological Thought," *International Encyclopedia of the Social Sciences* (New York, 1968), 15:35.

25. Before Yüan's death in 1916, for example, Liang Ch'i-ch'ao observed: "Yüan does not know the difference between a man and a beast. He thought that it was human nature to tremble before a flashing knife and to go wild for gold, both of which weapons he used to rule the country, and by means of which he thought everything could be done. For four years there was nothing that might be called administration in the Peking government except the ghostly shadows of a knife and a piece of gold. . . . Yüan occupies the highest position of the nation, yet, day in and day out, he has enticed people on by waving a piece of gold in front of their eyes and threatened them with a knife at their back. He wanted to enslave all the people either by soft bribery or by hard terror. Few who lacked strong will could escape from these two weapons. For four years, there has been a steady demoralization among the elite of our country. It cannot be denied that seven or eight out of ten of them are now thoroughly corrupt and rotten. . . . Yüan has perceived a common weakness of human beings and he devoted himself to encouraging and using this weakness for his own personal benefit. Those who could overcome this common weakness and refused to be utilized by Yüan were murdered, driven away, or oppressed so severely that they could no longer survive. Before the collapse of the Ch'ing dynasty, when Yüan was in charge of state affairs, he already employed this policy for securing his power. The corrupt and filthy atmosphere of Chinese political circles actually originated at that time. When he came to be President of the Republic, he once again strengthened this policy and spread this atmosphere." Liang Ch'i-ch'ao, *Yin-ping-shih ho-chi* (Shanghai, 1936), *Chuan-chi,* 9:108–9. Here Liang Ch'i-ch'ao, writing as an emotion-charged champion against Yüan's monarchical movement, placed a rather heavy causal weight upon Yüan's manipulations, which we may now see as exacerbating, not causing, China's demoralization.

23, 1914, he rode in an armored car to the Temple of Heaven to perform the antiquated rite of worshipping Heaven, a prerogative reserved for the traditional emperor alone.[26] Two months later, he appeared as the guardian of the Confucian faith in a ceremony dedicated to the memory of Confucius—a rite performed by most emperors since the Han dynasty.[27]

But Yüan was well aware that he could not realize his ambition merely by reviving traditional ceremonies and rituals. He had always been quick to use the most ruthless means to secure his ends, as shown in the assassination of Sung Chiao-jen.[28] And now, in addition to his efforts to create an imperial aura around him, he employed brutal methods to eliminate his foes and to prevent the formation of an opposition. Chou Tso-jen recalled:

> It is still not possible to count how many were arrested and how many disappeared when Peking was under the tyrannical control of Lu Chien-chang, the Superintendent of the Police Department in Yüan's government, as the monarchical movement was in full swing. Civil service officials regardless of their positions were all closely watched, lest they should dissent.[29]

On December 12, 1915, Yüan declared, in answer to a "petition" drawn up by his henchmen, that he was willing to accept the throne. Preparations for his enthronement on January 1, 1916, which had been secretly in train since September, were publicly set under way. A few days before the first of January, however, the National Protection Army commanded by General Ts'ai O launched its anti-Yüan expedition from Yunnan. Under the combined pressure of that army—later joined by a number of other provincial forces— and the foreign diplomatic corps, Yüan on March 22, 1916, announced his intention to relinquish the throne. The title of his reign, ironically, "Grand

26. Jerome Ch'en, *Yuan Shih-k'ai*, p. 163, describes the ceremony at the Temple of Heaven: "The entire route was covered with yellow sand, as was customary for an imperial drive.... At the southern gate of the temple, the president entered a vermilion coach, which carried him to the temple itself. Then he was carried into the building in a sedan chair and was helped up the marble steps by Generals Yin-ch'ang and Lu Chin. Once inside, he changed out of his field-marshal's uniform into the sacrificial robe and headgear. The robe was royal purple, adorned with 12 circular dragon designs, and the headgear was an oblong board on a tight-fitting cap, an ancient imperial design."

27. Ibid., p. 163.

28. Sung Chiao-jen was one of the most important leaders of the Kuomintang in 1912–13, and the first Minister of Agriculture and Forestry of the Republic. Considering Sung's popular campaign for a parliamentary system a great threat to his power, Yüan had him assassinated in Shanghai on March 20, 1913. See Li Chien-nung, *Chung-kuo chin-pai-nien cheng-chih shih* (Shanghai, 1947), pp. 383–91.

29. Chou Hsia-shou (Chou Tso-jen), *Lu Hsün ti ku-chia* (Hong Kong, 1962), p. 216.

Constitution Era'' (*Hung-hsien*), was formally discarded and this farcical movement came to an end two and a half months before Yüan's death in June, 1916.[30]

Recent studies have tended to explain Yüan's behavior in terms of the existing sociopolitical situation rather than his own character.[31] No doubt this is a timely corrective for the views held by earlier historians like Li Chien-nung, who, writing shortly after the events, overemphasized Yüan's unscrupulousness in explaining what had happened to China between 1912 and 1916. But in giving due weight to the influence of the social and political environment upon his policies we should not overlook the enormous effect of his manipulations upon the Chinese social and intellectual situation in these crucial years.

Anything written about Yüan Shih-k'ai is almost bound to be controversial, but my purpose in discussing him here is not polemical. Against a background of heightened nationalism—resulting, among other factors, from the Twenty-one Demands—and profound exasperation at the failure of the 1911 revolution, Yüan's period of power is doubly relevant to my thesis. First, leaving aside scholarly arguments over the "traditional" nature of his unscrupulous tactics in his quest for power, such tactics were, in the eyes of radical iconoclasts, stark manifestations of traditional evils. And that the demoralization of Chinese society was intensified under the impact of his tactics made it plain to the iconoclasts how deeply rooted and widespread were these evils in China. Secondly, Yüan's appropriation of Confucian symbols served only further to alienate radical intellectuals from the central value system of Chinese tradition.[32] Their animosity toward Yüan's monarchical movement led them strongly to repudiate the symbols of Confucianism that Yüan had used for his own political purposes. Confucianism had been inextricably intertwined with the traditional imperial system, thus facilitating the iconoclasts' contention that it was inherently predisposed to despotism. However, neither the original Confucian texts nor the complex evolution of Con-

30. Li Chien-nung, pp. 412–53.

31. Ernest P. Young, ''The Hung-hsien Emperor as a Modernizing Conservative,'' in Furth, ed., *The Limits of Change*, pp. 171–90, and his *The Presidency of Yuan Shih-k'ai: Liberalism and Dictatorship in Early Republican China* (Ann Arbor, 1977), pp. 138–240.

32. The central value system of Chinese tradition here refers to Confucianism, which had inextricably been interwoven with the idea and the institution of universal kingship since the time of Han Wu-ti (141–87 B.C.) and therefore, following Edward Shils's formulation of the concept of center and periphery, was ultimate and irreducible before 1911 because it was perceived to partake of the nature of the sacred. See note 24 above.

fucianism as a whole necessarily bear out their condemnation. But commitments to logical coherence and empirical truths are often undermined by
immediate realities and emotional involvement.

Before closing this section, we must take note of another episode in the
immediate political background against which the May Fourth radical icono-
clasm arose—the melodramatic twelve-day restoration of the Ch'ing by
Chang Hsün, a warlord formerly serving under Yüan Shih-k'ai. Emerging
from intricate maneuvers among various political and militarist cliques,
Chang Hsün occupied Peking with his queue-wearing troops in June, 1917.
Not to be outdone by the folly of Yüan Shih-k'ai's monarchical movement,
Chang restored the last Ch'ing emperor, Henry Pu-yi, to the throne on July 1.
Meanwhile, K'ang Yu-wei, the erstwhile leader of the reform movement of
1895–98, had secretly reached Peking, where he stayed at Chang Hsün's
home, busying himself in drafting imperial decrees for the occasion. But
Chang adopted none of them.[33] Although K'ang's obstinate wish to restore the
Ch'ing had made him a laughingstock to many, he was still too much a
reformist for Chang Hsün. In any case, in less than two weeks Chang's troops
were crushed by the joint forces of other warlords. The restoration was at its
end.

This episode, only a year after the collapse of Yüan Shih-k'ai's
monarchical movement, brought home more emphatically than ever to radical
intellectuals how firmly entrenched the old elements of Chinese society and
culture were and how little change had been achieved. It reinforced their
long-held notion (to be discussed in the next chapter) that intellectual and
cultural change was a necessary precondition for sociopolitical and economic
changes. And it stirred in many of them a sense of urgency that led to their
direct involvement in the intellectual revolution based on totalistic rejection of
China's past.[34]

33. For instance, K'ang Yu-wei sought to abolish the kowtow ceremony and drafted a decree
to this effect. But Chang Hsün, who liked people knocking their heads on the floor, refused to
adopt it. For a more detailed account of Chang Hsün's restoration of the Ch'ing, see Li Chien-
nung, pp. 493–99.
34. See Hu Shih, "Kuei-kuo tsa-kan," *HCN*, 4.1:20 (January 15, 1918). Lu Hsün, *"Tzu-
hsüan-chi* tzu-hsü," *Nan-ch'iang pei-tiao chi, LHCC*, 4:347.

3

THE ORIGINS OF
TOTALISTIC ANTITRADITIONALISM
IN THE MAY FOURTH ERA—II

THE CULTURAL-INTELLECTUALISTIC APPROACH

Despite the many differences that set the first generation of the Chinese intelligentsia, that of the 1890s, apart from the second generation, that of the 1910s, most members of these two groups were preoccupied with one distinctive concern: that the task of rejuvenating a corrupt and atrophied China involved nothing less than complete transformation of the traditional Chinese world view and total reconstruction of the traditional Chinese mentality. Without a new world view and a new mentality adaptable to modernization, all changes previously implemented would eventually be futile.

In contrast to those theories of change that emphasize political power, social conditions, or modes of economic production, this notion stressed the necessary priority of intellectual and cultural change over political, social, and economic changes. For want of a better term, I shall describe this approach as cultural-intellectualistic. It implied a fundamental belief that cultural change was the foundation for all other necessary changes. It assumed, further, that cultural change—a change in the system of symbols, values, and beliefs—could best be achieved through changing man's ideas concerning his total conception of, and relationship to, both cosmic and human reality; that is, changing his world view.

I use the word ''intellectualistic'' with reluctance because of its association with a rationalistic approach to epistemology, ontology, or ethics in Western philosophical discourse. Yet it is difficult to find a better word to indicate the belief in the power of ideas characteristic of the first two generations of the Chinese intelligentsia. ''Cultural'' alone is inadequate: members of the intelligentsia either implicitly or explicitly assumed that a change of basic ideas *qua* ideas was the most fundamental change, the source of other changes. In other words, two levels of change characterized their approach: first, change of world view, which would then bring about a second basic level, change of the system of symbols, values, and beliefs—this cultural change, in turn, would precipitate other political, social, and economic changes.

Their belief in the power of ideas implied another assumption: the close relationship, almost identification, between understanding and action. These intellectuals tacitly—perhaps unconsciously—assumed that their prime need was to express fully to the people, through the most effective medium, what they believed and to advocate the best programs for implementing those beliefs; then the people, being also endowed with the faculty of understanding, would grasp the meaning and perceive the benefits of those truths and those programs, and act accordingly.

What I am delineating above can best be termed a presupposed mode of thinking (or category of analysis), to be distinguished from presupposed ideas or concepts, such as the axiomatic idea of the inherent liberty and equality of man in Lockeian liberalism or the innate goodness of man in Confucianism. The cultural-intellectualistic approach is a presupposition about the *way to approach* problems of social and political change that stresses the necessary priority of intellectual and cultural change.[1]

The cultural-intellectualistic approach was simplistic, but by virtue of its simplicity it provided an ideological basis for Chinese intellectuals to map out their future paths in the midst of China's unprecedented sociopolitical and

---

1. In a sense, this mode of thinking (or category of analysis) is itself an idea, about the correct way to approach problems of social and political change. But this idea is used dynamically, in a way different from the static usage of, say, such an idea as the natural equality among men—all as children of God—in Lockeian liberalism. Hence, it is better to refer to it as a mode of thinking.

cultural crisis.[2] It was a common presupposition that molded the outlooks of various members of the first two generations—one of the few defining traits that gave them their characteristic identity—but the specific positions of divergent groups among the Chinese intelligentsia were, of course, by no means solely a consequence of this approach.

In this chapter, I shall elucidate two points of major importance to the themes of this book. In the first place, the cultural-intellectualistic approach was influenced by a deep-seated traditional Chinese cultural predisposition, in the form of a monistic and intellectualistic mode of thinking.[3] It was not directly influenced by any Western sources; nor was it decisively shaped by sociopolitical conditions, which were auxiliary factors. Under the Western impact, the ideas and values of the intelligentsia had undergone fundamental change; yet, amid change in content of thought and the metamorphosis of values, this traditional mode of thinking was still so powerful, so pervasive, that it provided the source for the cultural-intellectualistic approach of the first two generations of the Chinese intellgentsia without their necessarily being conscious that their views were so derived. The cultural atmosphere during the formative years of the first two generations was permeated with this monistic and intellectualistic emphasis on the function of the mind. The classical education that members of the second generation undertook was still rigorous enough for their minds to be decisively molded by this traditional mode of thinking, in spite of the vehement totalistic attack against Chinese tradition that many of them later launched.[4] Members of the first generation were given an even more rigorous classical education, and in many ways were

2. Cf. the observation made by Clifford Geertz that ideology is most needed when social and political crisis is compounded by a loss of cultural orientation ("Ideology as a Cultural System," in his *The Interpretation of Cultures* [New York, 1973], pp. 193–233, esp. 215–20). The extreme ideological nature of the cultural-intellectualistic approach revealed itself as a weapon for iconoclastic totalism, as will be noted later, when it evolved into a holistic mode of thinking.

3. To say that a monistic and intellectualistic mode of thinking was a deep-seated traditional Chinese cultural predisposition does not imply that there were no other dominant and yet contradictory trends in traditional Chinese thought. Yü Ying-shih has written perceptively about the anti-intellectualistic tradition in Taoism, Legalism, and the legalized aspects of Confucianism; see his "Fan-chih-lun yü Chung-kuo cheng-chih ch'uan-t'ung," in Yü Ying-shih, *Li-shih yü ssu-hsiang* (Taipei, 1976), pp. 1–46. Nor do I mean that the belief of the Chinese in the power of ideas would necessarily render their ideas intellectually more powerful and persuasive; the belief in the effective role of ideas and the actual content of ideas are clearly separate issues.

4. Ch'en Tu-hsiu passed the civil service examination at the first (or district) level and earned his *hsiu-ts'ai* degree in 1896; he took the examination at the second level in 1897. Ch'en Tu-hsiu, "Shih-an tzu-chuan," reprinted in *Chuan-chi wen-hsüeh*, 5.3:55–58 (September, 1964). For an English translation of this piece, see Richard C. Kagan "Ch'en Tu-hsiu's Unfinished Autobiog-

more thoroughly steeped in traditional Chinese culture. One can demonstrate a line of continuity stretching back to the traditional culture through the first two generations of the Chinese intelligentsia and determining the nature of their approach.

Secondly, the cultural-intellectualistic approach had the potential to evolve into an intellectualistic-holistic mode of thinking, that is, a way of perceiving traditional Chinese society and culture as an organismic entity whose form and nature were effected by its fundamental ideas. (This mode of thinking can be described as holistic because it assumed that the determining role of fundamental ideas is analogous to that of genes in a living organism, which can be viewed as the [potential] whole effecting the nature and form of its parts.)

Before the framework of the Chinese tradition collapsed in 1911–12, the cultural-intellectualistic approach of members of the first generation, while stressing the priority of intellectual and cultural change, did not go so far as to assume that all aspects of the Chinese tradition were parts of an organismic whole effected by its fundamental ideas. Members of this generation still moved within the traditional sociopolitical and cultural-moral orders; their own perspectives took for granted some traditional elements but saw Chinese tradition as a composite of many distinct elements not all compatible with one another. Their iconoclasm was, therefore, not totalistic.

After 1911, the cultural-intellectualistic approach did, indeed, evolve into a holistic mode of thinking and thereby became a weapon for iconoclastic totalism: the Chinese tradition was attacked as an organismic whole whose nature was infected by the disease of the traditional Chinese mind. This holistic potential of the cultural-intellectualistic approach was realized under the pressure of the interaction of various factors: the discrediting of all aspects of traditional Chinese society, culture, and morality for the May Fourth iconoclasts; their exasperation with the failure of the 1911 revolution; their intense nationalist sentiment, with its demand for fundamental sociopolitical

---

raphy," *China Quarterly*, 50:295–314 (April–June, 1972). Lu Hsün took the examination at the first level in 1898 but did not finish it because of the sudden death of his youngest brother, which so grieved him that he could not continue. See Chou Hsia-shou (Chou Tso-jen), *Lu Hsün hsiao-shuo li-ti jen-wu* (Shanghai, 1954), pp. 247–50. Even Hu Shih, the youngest among the three, who did not take the examination, had studied and memorized, according to his own testimony, the *Book of Filial Piety*, the *Analects*, the *Mencius*, the *Great Learning*, the *Doctrine of the Mean*, the *Book of Odes*, the *Book of Documents*, the *Book of Change*, the *Book of Rites*, and other texts during his years in village school. Hu Shih, *Ssu-shih tzu-shu* (Taipei, 1954), pp. 20–21, and "My Credo and Its Evolution," in *Living Philosophies* (New York, 1931), pp. 241–42.

and cultural change, that is, their yearning for a new China, based on new values of freedom, democracy, and science; their keen awareness of pervasive, deep-rooted old evils, brought home to them by Yüan Shih-k'ai's unscrupulous manipulations and abortive monarchical movement and by Chang Hsün's restoration of the Ch'ing, both of which intensified their sense of urgency for change; and their profound alienation from the central value system of traditional China. In short, social and cultural forces in the aftermath of the collapse of the universal kingship were all pushing the traditionally derived, monistic mode of thinking assumed by the May Fourth iconoclasts toward a holistic category of analysis, by which they reached their iconoclastic totalism.

Theoretically, there are various ways for iconoclastic totalism to express itself. A tradition may be conceived of as an organismic entity holistically shaped by its political structure or by its economic system. If the political structure or the economic system is rotten, all aspects of the tradition are infected, and a totalistic rejection of that tradition involves an attack on its roots in the political structure or in the economic system.

The iconoclastic totalism of the May Fourth era did not take either of those directions. Rather, it moved toward cultural iconoclasm, on the assumption that the organismic whole of the traditional Chinese society and culture was effected primarily by its fundamental ideas. In retrospect, the collapse of the universal kingship was crucial for the rise of iconoclastic totalism in that it led to the disintegration of the cultural-moral order and the concomitant loss of the credibility of all aspects of traditional Chinese culture and morality, and it unconsciously helped to generate a perception of the traditional Chinese society and culture as an organismic whole to be rejected in toto. The persistence of the cultural-intellectualistic approach—when it evolved into a holistic mode of thinking—was, however, a most significant factor in shaping the particular form of May Fourth totalistic cultural iconoclasm.

In the next sections, I shall first examine the ideas of four leading figures of the first generation of the Chinese intelligentsia, with reference to their cultural-intellectualistic approach. Secondly, I shall trace the traditional origins of the cultural-intellectualistic approach by examining the main trends in the history of Confucian thought.

THE FIRST GENERATION OF THE CHINESE INTELLIGENTSIA

In the wake of China's defeat in the Sino-Japanese War of 1894–95, Yen Fu (1853–1921) wrote a series of essays articulating his opinions about the causes of the current crisis and suggesting the means of its solution. At the root of these essays lay a fundamental thesis: the power of ideas in human history. Benjamin Schwartz's study of Yen Fu indicates that his great concern for the plight of the Chinese state and society and his search for the secret of the wealth and power of the West led him to regard Herbert Spencer's social Darwinism as the source of Western civilization's dynamic Faustian-Promethean character. Yen's thesis was couched in Spencerian terms, yet his intellectualistic preoccupation had twisted the highly deterministic scheme of Spencer into a voluntaristic world view. He was not entirely unaware of the problematic relationship between the impersonal forces of evolution described by Spencer and Darwin and his voluntaristic assertion of the function of consciousness. But precisely because he took the power of ideas as his point of departure, he maintained that the achievement of progressive evolution in the West was due to Western intellectual leaders' understanding of the process and mechanisms of evolution. This had made possible "the unrestricted operation of the forces of evolution as determinants of modern social development."[5] Conversely, the failure of Chinese sages to grasp the mechanisms of evolution led directly to the lack of progress in China.

Yen Fu's concrete suggestions for reform were put forth mainly in his famous "Ten Thousand Word Memorial" of 1898, which was consistent with his concern for intellectual change. He proposed two kinds of reform: the "fundamental" and the "external." External reforms were military, financial, and diplomatic. Fundamental reforms involved the cultivation of men of ability, change in customs, and, above all, the transformation of "men's minds" *(jen hsin)*.[6] The traditional Chinese world view, according to Yen Fu, prized harmony, passivity, quietude, and social equilibrium. His proposal for its reform implied a total intellectual change: the Chinese mind was to be transformed and directed toward the exaltation of human energy in all its manifestations—intellectual, moral, and physical—with special emphasis on the value of struggle. While not neglecting the need for external reforms, he nevertheless maintained that they would be useless without such a thorough transformation of the traditional mentality.

The way to accomplish this task, Yen argued, was through education. "The gospel of education itself," as Professor Schwartz points out, "does not derive from Spencer. Spencer had not assigned to education or to ideas any

---

5. Benjamin Schwartz, *In Search of Wealth and Power: Yen Fu and the West* (Cambridge, Mass., 1964), p. 45. This brief description of Yen Fu's thought is based especially upon pp. 42–90 and 237–47.

6. Ibid., p. 85.

particular role as a dynamic principle pushing forward the evolutionary process. It is, rather, 'evolution' as a total process which pushes forward all the
separate aspects of human culture.'"[7] On the basis of his belief in the power of
ideas, Yen Fu hoped, however, that the idea of evolution would inspire a new
educational system geared toward inculcating into men's minds the spirit of
dynamism and the value of struggle, which would lead China to involve
herself in the process of evolution.

K'ang Yu-wei (1858–1927) shared Yen Fu's assumptions about the power
of ideas and the priority of intellectual change. In the *K'ang-tzu nei-wai p'ien*
(The inner and outer books of the philosopher K'ang) written in 1886–87[8]—
probably the earliest of his surviving writings—he stated that social customs
and institutions in China had originated from the perceptions of Confucius,
and for that matter, those in India, from the Buddha, in Europe, from Jesus,
and in Moslem areas, from Mohammed.[9] Since K'ang took for granted the
power of ideas, he did not feel any need to explain or justify this statement.
On the basis of his deep-seated intellectualistic assumption, he believed that
new ideas would lead to new action. In the same year (1886) in which he
started to write *K'ang-tzu nei-wai p'ien,* he also began work on *K'ung-tzu
kai-chih k'ao* (Confucius as a reformer), which was completed in 1896 and
published the following year.[10] In this work K'ang elaborated his "new text"
interpretation of Confucianism, intended to provide an intellectual foundation
for institutional change. Ou Chü-chia, a follower of K'ang Yu-wei, explicated
K'ang's cultural-intellectualistic approach in 1897 with great clarity: "The
decadence of China must be traced to the decadence of men's minds. Men's
ignorance is due to the perversion of learning, and learning is perverted

7. Ibid., pp. 89–90.

8. K'ang Yu-wei, "Chronological Autobiography of K'ang Yu-wei" ("Nan-hai K'ang
hsien-sheng tzu-pien nien-p'u"), tr. Lo Jung-pang, in Lo Jung-pang, ed., *K'ang Yu-wei: A
Biography and a Symposium* (Tucson, 1967), pp. 43–44.

9. K'ang Yu-wei, *K'ang-tzu nei-wai p'ien* (microfilm copy of K'ang's manuscript in the East
Asian Collection, the Hoover Library), pp. 8a–9a. See also Richard C. Howard, "K'ang Yu-wei
(1858–1927): His Intellectual Background and Early Thought," in A. F. Wright and D. Twitchett, eds., *Confucian Personalities* (Stanford, 1962), pp. 307–10, for discussion of this work.

10. K'ang Yu-wei, "Chronological Autobiography," p. 55: "I first began writing it [*K'ung-
tzu kai-chih k'ao*] in *ping-hsü* [1886] after a discussion with Mr. Ch'en Shu-yung on the revision
of the *General Inquiry of the Five Rites (Wu-li t'ung-k'ao)."* See also pp. 76 and 83 for dates of
completion and publication. Before K'ang completed *K'ung-tzu kai-chih k'ao,* he published in
1891 his *Hsin-hsüeh wei-ching k'ao,* which was intended to discredit in textual terms the authenticity of the "ancient text" version of the Confucian classics and to prepare the grounds for the
acceptance of his "new text" interpretation of Confucianism.

because the true meanings of the Six Classics are obscured. There is no way to effect reform, if the light of the Six Classics is not made to shine again."[11]

Underlying K'ang's change from a radical advocacy of complete institutional change, in 1898, to a staunchly conservative call for restoration of the monarchical system in the republican period lay a constant preoccupation with the idea of establishing Confucianism as the state religion. Confucianism had been for centuries the dominant and most widely accepted system of values and beliefs in China; but it had failed to respond creatively to the impact of the West, and it had inhibited changes necessary for the preservation of the state. For K'ang the most important task, therefore, was to reorient and reformulate Confucianism in such a way that it would not only justify but also encourage and promote change. K'ang discarded the traditional cyclical view of history in order to build this foundation. He set forth his theory of progress in terms of the concept of three ages—the "age of disorder" (chü-luan shih), the "age of approaching peace" (sheng-p'ing shih), and the "age of universal peace" (t'ai-p'ing shih)—derived from the Kung-yang Commentary on the Spring and Autumn Annals. K'ang argued that progress is the ultimate meaning and reality of history as viewed by the Sage. Those who consider themselves true Confucians should prove their worth by striving for the realization of this view.

K'ang was greatly disturbed by the disintegration of the traditional political community after 1911; the immediate task then became not change but the restoration of order. The way to a restored political solidarity, he thought, lay again in the role to be played by ideas. The world view that, he hoped, the worship of Confucius and the establishment of Confucianism as the state religion would foster was, at this time, not so much directed toward modernization as intended to consolidate the political community.

K'ang Yu-wei's reformulation and reinterpretation of Confucian tenets had already put the traditionally accepted Confucian system out of balance; his disciple T'an Ssu-t'ung went even further. T'an, the scintillating "comet," as Liang Ch'i-ch'ao called him, strongly criticized the li-chiao (the Confucian teachings of the standards and norms of social conduct) and challenged the long-held belief in the sacrosanct Three Bonds and Five Ethical Relationships.

The great significance of T'an's Jen-hsüeh (On humanity), written in 1896,

---

11. Ou Chü-chia, "Lun Chung-kuo pien-fa pi tzu fa-ming ching-hsüeh shih," Chih-hsin pao, no. 38 (November 1, 1897), quoted in Hsiao Kung-ch'üan, A Modern China and a New World: K'ang Yu-wei, Reformer and Utopian, 1858–1927 (Seattle, 1975), p. 103.

lies in his efforts to seek a new universal to replace the broken image of traditional Confucianism. In undertaking a reinterpretation of the Confucian concept of *jen* ("humanity" or "the innate goodness of man"), T'an sagaciously came to discern the tension between *jen* and *li* (the norms of social and ritual conduct) in the Confucian tradition. Drawing freely from many diverse sources, such as Mahayana Buddhism, the philosophies of Mo-tzu (ca. 479–38 B.C.), Chang Tsai (1020–77), Wang Yang-ming (1472–1529), Huang Tsung-hsi (1610–95), Wang Fu-chih (1619–92), and K'ang Yu-wei, and some knowledge of Christianity and Western science, he constructed a syncretic system in which he reinterpreted *jen*. *Jen*, T'an argued, is universal love, which connects everything in the cosmic and human world and gives vitality and meaning to human existence. By implication, *jen* values equality and moral independence. In order to achieve *jen*, one must break through the suffocating networks of the Three Bonds and reform the Five Ethical Relationships. The Three Bonds have for the last two thousand years deprived Chinese people of their very foundation of humanity and brought them untold misery. Among the Five Ethical Relationships, all need to be changed except the relationship between friends and, to a lesser degree, the relationship between brothers (which resembles that of friends). Friendship is founded upon equality, freedom, and mutual feeling; it involves no loss of the right to be one's own master and does not hinder the autonomous development of the individual as a moral being. Indeed, the philosophy of Confucius and Mencius, which expounded moral autonomy based on the doctrine of *jen*, had, in T'an Ssu-t'ung's view, long before been betrayed by Hsün-tzu and his followers, whose ideas were a stark distortion and misunderstanding of Confucius' true teaching.[12]

T'an's iconoclasm is not only an attack on *li-chiao* itself; it consists essentially of the conviction that institutional change must be based on change in the traditional system of belief. Before complete dissociation from *li* and reorientation toward *jen* is achieved, it is futile to ponder institutional change. "Nowadays people everywhere are fond of discussing change of institutions," remarks T'an, "however, there is no starting point for any good way [to adopt institutional change] . . . if our belief in the Five Ethical Relationships, let alone the Three Bonds, is not transformed."[13] It is plain that the

---

12. T'an Ssu-t'ung, *T'an Ssu-t'ung ch'üan-chi* (Peking, 1954), pp. 53–55, 66.
13. Ibid., p. 68. Also cf. Ch'ien Mu, *Chung-kuo chin san-pai-nien hsüeh-shu shih* (Shanghai, 1937), p. 671.

method he proposed for change was also cultural-intellectualistic. Like Yen Fu and K'ang Yu-wei, he argued that a change in the system of belief, based on a change of Confucian ideas as conventionally understood, must constitute the foundation of change in sociopolitical and economic institutions.

T'an stated in 1894, "How can one blame Confucianism for being useless? What is used today is by no means Confucianism."[14] This suggests that he was basically oriented toward a creative transformation of Confucianism even before he began to work on *Jen-hsüeh,* where his negative attack on *li* was directed toward a positive reconstruction of the traditional Confucian vision of morality. He said at the end of the first part of the book that he prayed for the birth of a Martin Luther in China to "revive" the true meaning of Confucianism. T'an's martyrdom at the age of thirty-two in 1898 cut short the life of one of the most brilliant and perceptive minds in modern Chinese history.

The cultural-intellectualistic approach was also deeply embedded in the mind of Liang Ch'i-ch'ao and had served as a point of departure for his social thought since before 1898. In a letter written in 1894 Liang said that "the first principle of our activity is to seek comrades for the change of the climate of opinion."[15] His general ideas about reform were first set forth in his famous serial "Pien-fa t'ung-i" (General discussion on reform) published in *Shih-wu pao* (*Chinese Progress*) in 1896. In these writings Liang shows that he was not unaware of the difficulty of intellectual and cultural change in China, where the educational apparatus was geared toward the civil service examination system controlled by the bureaucracy. While he argued that political renovation of China relied ultimately on the education of the people, he noted that change of the educational system depended on change in sociopolitical institutions. Awareness of the complexity of the problem, however, did not lead him to forsake his premise. Instead, he asserted that the intellectual enlightenment of the Chinese people was not merely important but was "the first principle of self-strengthening."[16]

The failure of political reform in 1898 intensified his conviction that it was necessary to build a cultural foundation for political reform. In the first issue of *Hsin-min ts'ung-pao* (*New Citizen Journal*), published in Japan in 1902,

---

14. T'an Ssu-t'ung, "Ssu-wei yin-yün tai tuan-shu—pao Pei Yüan-cheng," in Shih Chün, ed., *Chung-kuo chin-tai ssu-hsiang-shih tsan-k'ao tzu-liao chien-pien* (Peking, 1957), p. 536.

15. Ting Wen-chiang, ed., *Liang Jen-kung hsien-sheng nien-p'u ch'ang-pien ch'u-kao* (Taipei, 1958), p. 21.

16. Liang Ch'i-ch'ao, "Pien-fa t'ung-i," in his *Yin-ping-shih ho-chi* (Shanghai, 1936), *Wen-chi*, 1:14.

Liang proclaimed that the function of his journal was educational and its aim the renovation of the people. "There is nothing more urgent than using new ideas to change our people's thought for saving present-day China," wrote Liang to his teacher, K'ang Yu-wei, in 1902 after he began to publish the journal. (Immediately following this statement he inserted a parenthesis in which he said that "the rise of Europe has been totally due to this [i.e., new ideas].") "Therefore," he continued, "I desire to break through the net [of the old ethos] and I consider the construction of a system of new thought my primary responsibility."[17]

To construct a new conception of political community with entirely new characteristics was for Liang the ultimate purpose of the new thought. That new conception he called *ch'ün*, which literally means group or grouping. Here it denotes essentially a modern political community in the form of the nation-state and connotes the grouping process in such a community. Liang first outlined this idea in an essay entitled "Shuo-ch'ün hsü" (The preface to a treatise on grouping) written in 1897, and he later spelled it out in detail in his celebrated serial "Hsin-min shuo" (On the renovation of the people, or, On new citizenship) published in 1902–4. The meaning of the nation-state is expressed in social Darwinian terms. Since in the international sphere there is nothing but the struggle for existence among nations, China's survival makes absolutely necessary her evolution from empire to nation. If China cannot bring herself into the "evolution of history," she will be unfit for the struggle and will eventually perish.

Liang's theory of the construction of *ch'ün* is very comprehensive and complicated. Since it has been studied in detail by Chang Hao, I need present only a brief summary here.[18] There are two levels of change: the sociopolitical change and the personality change. On the sociopolitical level, democratic institutions must be established so that every member of society has the opportunity and also the duty to participate in public life. The individual's energy is released to society, and the nation's strength is thereby enriched. Democracy was valued by Liang primarily for building a modern nation-state, which was for him a "terminal community."[19] The justification of democracy

17. Ting Wen-chiang, ed., *Liang Jen-kung hsien-sheng nien-p'u ch'ang-pien ch'u-kao*, pp. 152–53.

18. The following summary draws on Hao Chang, *Liang Ch'i-ch'ao and Intellectual Transition in China, 1890–1907* (Cambridge, Mass., 1971), pp. 95–111, 149–219.

19. Rupert Emerson, *From Empire to Nation* (Boston, 1962), p. 96: "...the nation can be called a 'terminal community' with the implication that it is for present purposes the effective end of the road for man as a social animal, the end point of working solidarity between men."

as a safeguard for individual liberty is pushed into the background. Liang, like Yen Fu, was preoccupied with the overwhelming problem of how to transform the old China into a modern nation-state—a concern that focused his attention on the role of democracy in releasing individual energy for this public enterprise. He was opposed to the traditional monarchical system within which individual energy cannot be released for the public good, and he also criticized traditional parochialism as an obstacle to national integration.

On the level of the personality, the idea of public spirit and public obligation, the notion of human rights and freedom, the ideals of self-respect and mutual aid, must all be instilled in the minds of the people so that they can be constructive members of society and participate actively in a democracy. A spirit of adventure and virility must also be encouraged in order to make the people give up their traditional passivity and quietude, and to lead them to acquire the dynamism needed in this world of struggle.

In short, Liang believed that when the people have understood and adopted the concept of *ch'ün*, they will launch a struggle for its realization. It must be noted that in emphasizing the power of ideas Liang did not deny the importance of institutional changes. However, only after a transformed world view has become implanted in the minds of the Chinese people can the institutional changes envisaged by such a world view be sustained.

This summary of the ideas of some of the most important members of the first generation of the Chinese intelligentsia should make clear one common preoccupation: their stressing of the need to establish a cultural foundation, based on a changed world view, for sociopolitical change. Whether their basic awareness of the new world view's vital force is expressed in Yen Fu's social Darwinian concept of energy and struggle, K'ang Yu-wei's vision of history in terms of progress, T'an Ssu-t'ung's idea of dissociation from *li* and reorientation toward *jen*, or Liang Ch'i-ch'ao's notion of *ch'ün*, their approach essentially rested upon the assumption that new ideas are the fundamental source of change.[20]

---

20. I describe the cultural-intellectualistic approach used by the first generation of the Chinese intelligentsia in full knowledge of their "mystic" propensities. Yen Fu was fascinated by the philosophy of the "inconceivable" and the "void"; he felt a personal need to view the process of Darwinian evolution in the perspective of a Taoist eternity. K'ang Yu-wei's "new text" interpretation of Confucianism was based on the chiliastic *Kung-yang Commentary*, which was characterized as "abounding in unusually bizarre and eccentric ideas." Inspired by this *Commentary*, he thought that he had found the "great principles hidden in esoteric language" of the Confucian classics. (Ho Hsiu, "Kung-yang chuan-chu tzu[*sic*]hsü," quoted in Liang Ch'i-ch'ao, *Intellectual Trends in the Ch'ing Period*, tr. Immanuel C. Y. Hsü [Cambridge, Mass., 1959], pp.

THE ORIGINS OF THE CULTURAL-INTELLECTUALISTIC APPROACH

The cultural-intellectualistic mode of thinking continued to be taken for granted by most members of the second generation. This continuity will be exemplified by the ideas of the three major figures of the May Fourth period to be treated in chapters 4, 5, and 6. The reasons for the formation of this approach lie in the interaction between the demands of the actual sociopolitical situations in which members of the first and second generations of the Chinese intelligentsia found themselves and a deep-rooted cultural predisposition that they inherited from China's past. But the following analysis will indicate that sociopolitical conditions were auxiliary factors, whereas the Chinese cultural predisposition was the main determinant.

As is well known, the first generation of the intelligentsia, as a social group, arose from the reform movement brought on by the traumatic experience of China's defeat in the Sino-Japanese War of 1894–95. This defeat revealed with palpable clarity the complete futility of the "self-strengthening" programs. Members of the emerging intelligentsia came to realize that China's failure to build a strong navy and army did not result from a lack of Western arms; actually, China had a bigger navy than Japan, measured in terms of tonnage. The shocking defeat was traced to deficiencies in the institutional apparatus and to the lack of a vigorous spirit. Furthermore, these men also realized that the creation and efficient use of Western science and technology were closely related to the efficiency of Western social and political institutions and the vital spirit of Western peoples. All of these reflections led them to conclude that science and technology could not be mechanically transplanted from the West with the results they desired, unless there was a corresponding change in the structure of Chinese institutions and in the spirit of the Chinese people. The whole constellation of factors emerging from China's defeat in the Sino-Japanese War suggested change in institu-

---

88, 94.) Both T'an Ssu-t'ung and Liang Ch'i-ch'ao were greatly attracted to Buddhism, especially the Mahayana appeal for universal salvation.

The world views these men held were not altogether unchanging, and were more complicated than I have just summarized, but their "mystic" propensities are not incompatible with my contention that one of the peculiarities of their approach was cultural-intellectualistic. The word "intellectualistic" in this study should not, as already noted, be confused with a rationalistic belief in reason as the ultimate arbiter of order and meaning in the cosmic and human world. It is used strictly to denote a belief that the most fundamental change is a change of the most basic ideas. The new world view may contain a "mystic" element in its origin or content, but this in no way contradicts the belief that it is the fundamental source of other needed changes.

tions, ideas, and spirit as opposed to the mere adoption of Western technology proposed by the "self-strengtheners."

However, our knowledge of the differences between the "self-strengtheners" and the first generation of the intelligentsia should not lead us to fail to notice an underlying similarity of outlook concerning the primacy and power of ideas. Although the immediate purposes in stressing ideas and the content of ideas were different—the "self-strengtheners" reaffirmed the traditional orthodox Chinese world view, for the purpose of maintaining traditional institutions while at the same time adopting Western technology, whereas the intelligentsia advocated a new world view as the necessary first step toward political and technological change—they took for granted the same assumption: that ideas are the foundation for polity and society.

To be sure, actual historical circumstances played a role in leading members of the first generation to urge institutional and cultural changes. But there was nothing inherent in these circumstances to dictate that intellectual and cultural change must take priority in men's minds over sociopolitical change. Nor could awareness of the close relationship among Western science, the vigor of Western spirit, and the efficiency of Western social and political institutions itself inspire the conception of such a priority. On the contrary, ideological inclination toward economic or political determinism would stress the change of economic modes of production or the structure of political power rather than ideas as the prime force for fundamental sociopolitical and cultural change. (For that matter, the vigor of Western spirit is primarily effected by nonintellectual factors.) Or, a pluralist interpretation of history might lead one to see ideas and institutions as mutually influential, maintaining that it is by no means easy, or perhaps not even possible, to ascertain exactly the historical function of ideas and of institutions—much less the hierarchical relationship (if one exists) between them.[21]

One particular sociopolitical argument that is likely to arise in opposition to my view that this advocacy of the priority of intellectual and cultural change had originated primarily from a traditional Chinese mode of thinking might see the cultural-intellectualistic approach of the first and second generations as caused mainly by the failure of political reform in 1898 and of the political revolution of 1911. This argument is particularly appealing with

21. The evidence does not reveal any trace of possible influence by certain strands of Western idealism or intellectualism on the formation of the cultural-intellectualistic approach at this time (see also pp. 49–50, below).

reference to the second generation, when, as we shall come to see, bleak social and political realities made political change all but impossible. The lack of any real opportunity for political change might have forced most members of the second generation to fall back upon the only resource left to them— their ideas. It may be argued that they advocated the priority of intellectual change because this was the only thing they could do, or that they were so affected by the profound crisis of social and political disintegration that they demanded an overall solution of contemporary problems through the construction of a new intellectual and cultural foundation for social and political change.

It was certainly true that the post-1911 social and political realities had, as indicated earlier, impelled the holistic potential of the cultural-intellectualistic approach to reveal itself. But the influence of these external realities cannot explain the urge of many members of the second generation to proclaim the priority of intellectual change *before* 1911, when there was real hope for political revolution;[22] nor can it account for the notion of the priority of intellectual change in the first generation *before* 1898, when they were hope-

---

22. Both Hu Shih and Lu Hsün advocated the priority of intellectual change before 1911 (see chaps. 5 and 6). After an extensive search of all major libraries in the United States, Japan, Taiwan, and Hong Kong, I have not found any pre-1911 essays by Ch'en Tu-hsiu except the record of a speech ("Anhwei ai-kuo-hui yen-shuo," *Su-pao* [May 26, 1903], pp. 2–3) that he gave in the organizing meeting of the Anhwei Patriotic Society on May 17, 1903, and an unsigned announcement for the convening of this meeting (cited in "Anhwei ai-kuo-hui chih ch'eng-chiu," *Su-pao* [May 25, 1903], pp. 1–2), which was most likely written by him. There must be some essays by Ch'en in the pages of the *China National Gazette (Kuo-min jih-jih pao)*, 1903, since he was involved in that enterprise after the *Su-pao* was closed down. But all of the essays except contributions by non-staff members in the *China National Gazette* were unsigned and thus are not identifiable. We also know the titles of two articles written by Ch'en prior to 1911: "K'ai-pan *Anhwei su-hua pao* ti yüan-ku" and "Kua-fen Chung-kuo" both published in *Anhwei su-hua pao* in 1904 (see Ho Chih-yü, comp., "Tu-hsiu chu-tso nien-piao," p. 2, in the galley copy of the first volume of *Tu-hsiu ts'ung-chu* presented to the Library of Congress by Hu Shih); but they are probably not available anywhere outside China. Many of Ch'en's classical poems of the pre-1911 period, such as the elegies for his elder brother, are readily available. But they were not concerned with intellectual or social issues. In the aforementioned speech Ch'en made a passionate plea for national resistance against Russian imperialism, more specifically, for organizing the Anhwei Patriotic Society in the wake of knowledge that had come to light concerning a secret treaty signed between the Chinese and Russian governments, allowing the Russians to control the bureaucracy, to "protect" the railways, to exploit the mines, etc., in Manchuria. One of the measures that Ch'en advocated that his audience take in confronting this grave situation was to employ as a weapon the power of ideas: by using their own ability to speak, they should awaken the masses so that the potential for patriotic spirit that lay within the masses would be developed and realized. This stress on the power of ideas was foreshadowed by the announcement for the convening of this meeting, which concluded that "thought and discussion are the mother

ful that the reform movement would be successful in every respect.[23] External factors, then, can account for the changing intensity of the cultural-intellectualistic approach (in realization of its holistic potential) but cannot explain its origin. To do this it is necessary to understand the powerful and persistent Chinese cultural predisposition toward a monistic and intellectualistic mode of thinking, and, to this end, I shall briefly review the major trends in the history of Confucian thought, in which it continuously manifested itself.

One of the most important characteristics of Confucian modes of thinking or categories of analysis is the stress placed on the function of the inward moral and/or intellectual experience of the mind. This emphasis can be traced all the way back to Mencius and Hsün-tzu, who both shared it, despite the fact that their ideas about the nature and the mind of man were very different. When Mencius talked about *hsin* (mind), he referred primarily to its moral rather than its intellectual faculty. Indeed, a cardinal point in the *Mencius* is the demonstration of the innate goodness of the mind. This is evident in the following celebrated passage:

> When I say that all men have a *hsin* which cannot bear to see the suffering of others, my meaning may be illustrated thus: if a man suddenly sees a child about to fall into a well, a feeling of alarm and distress will inevitably arise in his *hsin* . . . From such a case, we see that a man without the *hsin* of commiseration is not a man; a man without the *hsin* of shame and dislike is not a man; a man without the *hsin* of deference and compliance is not a man; a man without the

---

of reality." The above evidence does not, of course, demonstrate conclusively that Ch'en maintained the priority of intellectual change at this time because, given the meager nature of the source, one can argue that the stress on the power of ideas was put forth in an ad hoc manner and hence did not necessarily lead to the notion of the priority of intellectual change. It does, however, add weight to the suggestion that Ch'en shared the cultural-intellectualistic approach generally held by his contemporaries, or at least does not deny the probability of his employing such a mode of thinking. But in view of the scarcity of relevant source materials for Ch'en in this period, my reading of his views should be regarded as provisional.

23. To be sure, men such as K'ang Yu-wei, Liang Ch'i-ch'ao, and T'an Ssu-t'ung of the first generation, and Ch'en Tu-hsiu and Lu Hsün of the second generation, did not in their social and political activities adhere consistently to their belief in the priority of intellectual change. The discrepancy between their intellectualistic pronouncements and their social and political involvement does not invalidate this analysis of their cultural-intellectualistic approach, but does indicate a contradiction between word and deed. It further reveals an inadequacy and a dilemma inherent in the monistic nature of the cultural-intellectualistic approach: belief in the necessary priority of establishing an intellectual and cultural foundation for sociopolitical change, for instance, did not itself provide an adequate means for building such a foundation; for intellectual and cultural change were dependent upon change in the educational apparatus and programs, and that in turn was dependent upon certain political changes.

hsin of right and wrong is not a man. The *hsin* of commiseration is the beginning of *jen*; the *hsin* of shame and dislike is the beginning of righteousness; the *hsin* of deference and compliance is the beginning of propriety; and the *hsin* of right and wrong is the beginning of *chih* [intelligence, or wisdom]. [*Mencius,* IIA.6; see also VIA.6.]

But, the usage of *"hsin"* in the *Mencius* is not without its ambiguity. The moral faculty and the intellectual faculty are not clearly differentiated here, because *chih,* which comes from the *hsin* of right and wrong, can be understood in terms of intelligence *or* in terms of wisdom. In another part of the work Mencius said:

He who exerts his mind to the utmost knows his nature. He who knows his nature knows Heaven. To preserve one's mind and to nourish one's nature is the way to serve Heaven. [*Mencius,* VIIA.1; tr. Wing-tsit Chan.]

Here, the mind is regarded as a faculty that will enable a person to know his nature, if he exerts it to the utmost. From the syntax of this statement, one can assume that Mencius is probably referring to the intellect when he uses the word "mind" here. (The mind is a subject; nature is an object of the mental faculty of knowing.) If we adopt the view that Mencius has on this occasion made slight but subtle changes in his philosophy in order to clarify the ambiguity of his concept of mind expressed in the previous statement, then this statement can be regarded as indicating a shift from a simple emphasis on the moral faculty of the mind to a position in which the intellectual faculty of the mind was given precedence over the moral faculty. But if one maintains that no change can possibly be found between the passage quoted earlier and this part of the *Mencius* and that various parts of it are manifestations of different elements of an organic philosophical system, the Mencian concept of mind is either left unclarified in one's reading of the passage quoted just above or understood in accordance with the stress on the moral faculty of the mind. One has to argue, then, that an exertion of the moral faculty of man's mind to the utmost will naturally give rise to a certain state which is recognized by his intellect as the innate goodness of his nature. (Here, "mind" must denote both the subject [of knowing] and the object [of being known], which is "nature.")

It is not, however, of the greatest importance for our present purpose to gain a definitive understanding of the above passage in the *Mencius.* It should be remembered that Chu Hsi and large numbers of the Confucian literati throughout the centuries since the Sung—under the influence of Chu's authoritative annotation in his *Meng-tzu chi-chu* (Collected annotations of the *Mencius*)—interpreted the *"hsin"* in this statement in terms of the intellect of the mind.[24]

According to Hsün-tzu, the source within man which corrects his basic "evil" tendency and leads him to live a moral life is the intellectual faculty of his mind.[25] No philosopher can argue deductively that man can do no wrong. But the peculiarity of Hsün-tzu's philosophy is that it starts from a fundamentally pessimistic view of human nature. The tension between his understanding of human "evil" and his desire to follow Confucius' call for propagation of the message of moral life he hoped would be resolved by his faith in the intellect of the human mind. The early sage-kings realized the need for social life among men; they therefore established *li* (norms of social and ritual conduct) and *i* (righteousness) so that cooperation and mutual support could be ensured (*Hsün-tzu,* chap. XIX). A common man, though not so charismatically creative, can know the Way by his mind and follow it in terms of utilitarian considerations. Insofar as man can break away from his inherent "evil" tendency, he can do so only through the intellectual-moral function of the mind. (To hyphenate "intellectual" with "moral" here is to designate a belief that the particular intellectual function of the mind in question will bring about desired moral effects.)

It should be noted that the stress placed on the intellectual-moral function of the mind crops up in various forms in all strands of Neo-Confucianism. It is unlikely that this is a direct consequence of the ideas of Hsün-tzu, which were an important influence in the Han, but thereafter faded into the background until the nineteenth century. As is commonly known, Neo-Confucianism was inspired to a great extent by Mencius. The Neo-Confucians perhaps understood the Mencian concept of mind according to the notion Mencius may possibly have held of the priority of the intellectual faculty of the mind; or they might have been able to "clarify" the ambiguity of Mencius' concept of mind on the basis of some new understanding unrelated to the possible clarification in Book VIIA, chapter 1 of the *Mencius.*

24. Chu Hsi, *Meng-tzu chi-chu,* SPPY ed., 7:1a.
25. "Evil" is used here in a technical sense, not in the ordinary sense of being wicked or malicious. According to Hsün-tzu, human desire will, if unchecked, necessarily lead to social strife and disorder because of its inherent aggressiveness and the scarcity of goods in society. Thus Hsün-tzu regards human nature as being originally "evil." For an incisive elucidation of Hsün-tzu's theory of human nature in contrast to that of Mencius, see D. C. Lau, "Theories of Human Nature in *Mencius* and *Shyuntzyy,*" *Bulletin of the School of Oriental and African Studies,* 15:541–65 (1953).

But how did this change, this emphasis among the Neo-Confucians on the intellectual-moral function of the mind, occur? The precise historical reasons for it await further study. The formation of the Neo-Confucian presupposition of the intellectual-moral function of the mind might have been affected by sociopolitical factors as much as by intellectual factors. One probable intellectual source of influence was Buddhism, whose introduction to China was crucial in the rise of Neo-Confucian speculations. Among all the different strands of Buddhism, the concept of *karma* is a common assumption. According to this concept, "all phenomena of the universe of an individual sentient being are the manifestations of his mind." [26] The retribution of *karma* is a direct result of thinking. Mencius' ambiguous concept of mind might well have been "clarified" by Neo-Confucians under the influence of this Buddhist category of analysis.

In the philosophy of Chu Hsi (1130–1200) the mind (*hsin*) is described as an "enclosure of the nature (*hsing*)," [27] nature being the principle (*li*) in *ch'i* (matter or material force). Because of the purity of the mind's *ch'i*, the mind has consciousness and intellectual faculty, which perform a dynamic role in leading man to realize the principle. Chu Hsi said:

> The mind is that with which man rules his body. It is one and not a duality, is subject and not object, and controls the external world instead of being controlled by it. Therefore, if we examine external objects *with the mind,* their principles will be apprehended. [Italics mine.] [28]

Thus Chu Hsi regards the mind as a master of man's nature and feelings:

> The mind means master. It is master whether in the state of activity or in the state of tranquility. It is not true that in the state of tranquility there is no need of a master and there is a master only when the state becomes one of activity. By master is meant an all-pervading control and command existing in the mind by itself. The mind unites and apprehends nature and feelings, but it is not united with them as a vague entity without any distinction. [29]

> Chang Tsai said, ". . . The mind commands man's nature and feelings." . . . Chu Hsi said, "The nature is substance, while feelings are function. Both come

26. Fung Yu-lan, *A Short History of Chinese Philosophy* (New York, 1960), p. 243. See also L. de la Vallée Poussin, "Karma," in James Hastings, ed., *Encyclopedia of Religion and Ethics,* 7:674.

27. Chu Hsi, *Chu-tzu ch'üan-shu,* Ku-hsiang-chai ed., 42:7a. This was originally said by Shao Yung and was quoted by Chu Hsi.

28. Chu Hsi, *Chu-tzu wen-chi,* SPPY ed. entitled *Chu-tzu ta-ch'üan,* 67:18b–19a, tr. Wing-tsit Chan, in his *Source Book in Chinese Philosophy* (Princeton, 1963), pp. 602–3.

29. Chu Hsi, *Chu-tzu ch'üan-shu,* 45:4a–b, tr. Wing-tsit Chan in his *Source Book,* p. 631.

from the mind, and therefore the mind can command them. To command them is like commanding troops, that is, being their master.''[30]

To be sure, the inner logic of Chu Hsi's "dualistic" philosophy finally leads him to assert that the mind is not its own master; rather, it needs a master itself—a point on which the Lu-Wang school of Neo-Confucianism differs sharply. There must be a principle governing the mind, Chu Hsi says: "The mind is the will of a master . . . but what is called master is precisely principle itself.''[31] This principle is identified with and contained in the Great Ultimate (*t'ai chi*).[32] The confusion resulted from assigning the status of "master" to both mind and principle is actually due to Chu Hsi's language rather than his thinking.

The assumption of the priority of principle upon which the Ch'eng-Chu school of Neo-Confucianism is founded necessarily entails an assertion of the ultimate "mastership" of principle, while the status of "master" for the mind can be understood in terms of the twofold intellectual-moral function of the mind—that is, first, through a persistent effort in the "investigation of things," the principle of reality can be brought to light by the intellectual faculty of the mind; and, second, the understanding of the principle of reality, a certain conceptualization in consciousness (formulation of ideas in the mind), will become the foundation of moral self-cultivation.

In contrast to Chu Hsi's doctrine that identifies nature with principle, Wang Yang-ming (1472–1529) held that "the mind is principle.''[33] According to Yang-ming, the reality of multiple things exists only insofar as the human mind knows that it exists, and the principles of multiple things are organically related to the mind in that they are, in fact, extensions of the principle in the mind.

The original nature of the mind is goodness (*jen*), whose dynamic manifestation is love—a quality that embraces everything in the world.[34] The natural ability of the mind is knowing.[35] It knows *liang-chih* (the innate knowledge of

30. Chiang Yung, ed., *Chin-ssu-lu chi chu,* comp. Chu Hsi and Lü Tsu-ch'ien (1844 ed.), 1:31a–b; or Chu Hsi and Lü Tsu-ch'ien, comps., *Reflections on Things at Hand,* tr. Wing-tsit Chan (New York, 1967), p. 34.

31. Chu Hsi, *Chu-tzu ch'üan-shu,* 49:23a.

32. Ibid., 44:1b: "The Principle of the Mind is the Great Ultimate."

33. Wang Yang-ming, *Ch'uan-hsi lu,* pt. 1, in *Wang Wen-ch'eng-kung ch'üan-shu,* SPTK ed., 1:3a: "The mind is principle. Is there any affair in the world outside of the mind? Is there any principle outside of the mind?"

34. Wang Yang-ming, *Ta-hsüeh wen,* in *Ch'üan-shu,* 26:2a–3a.

35. Wang Yang-ming, *Ch'uan-hsi lu,* pt. 1, in *Ch'üan-shu,* 1:10b: "The mind is naturally able to know."

the good). When Yang-ming discusses *liang-chih*, he refers to at least three different categories of things: knowing that, the referent of knowing that, and knowing how.[36] "Knowing that" refers to the innate knowledge in the human mind of right and wrong and an awareness of the moral quality of the mind.[37] *Liang-chih* sometimes also designates the moral quality itself; this I call the referent of "knowing that."[38] Furthermore, it refers to the Way or the Principle of Nature (*t'ien-li*), implying that the mind inherently knows *how* one conducts himself morally according to the Way or the Principle of Nature.[39]

Hence, *liang-chih* entails *chih liang-chih* (extending the innate knowledge of the good) in the following manner. First, man, on account of his inborn moral nature, is called to an actualization and development of the moral quality into an ever larger realm and onto an ever higher level according to the Principle of Nature that is known by the mind. For Yang-ming, as for other Confucians, "is" implies "ought." The cognitive and normative aspects of his philosophy are integrated in the symbols of moral discourse. Secondly,

---

36. Concerning the differentiation between "knowing that" and "knowing how," see Gilbert Ryle, *The Concept of Mind* (New York, 1949), pp. 25–61. The following explication of Yang-ming's key concepts—*liang-chih, chih liang-chih,* and *chih-hsing ho-i*—differs considerably from those expounded in the standard texts, such as Fung Yu-lan's *A History of Chinese Philosophy* (Princeton, 1953), vol. 2, chap. 14, and Wing-tsit Chan's introduction to his translation of *Instructions for Practical Living and Other Neo-Confucian Writings* by Wang Yang-ming (New York, 1963). I think both Fung and Chan have overlooked the various denotations of each of these three concepts in Yang-ming's ambiguous language. Here is not the place to elucidate his philosophy in detail; however, I believe I can defend my explication on the basis of Yang-ming's writings.

37. Wang Yang-ming, *Ta-hsüeh wen*, in *Ch'üan-shu*, 26:8a–b: "This innate knowledge of the good is what Mencius meant when he said, 'The sense of right and wrong is common to all men.' The sense of right and wrong requires no deliberation to know, nor does it depend on learning to function. This is why it is called innate knowledge. It is my nature endowed by Heaven, the original substance of my mind, naturally intelligent, shining, clear, and understanding." Tr. Wing-tsit Chan, *Source Book*, p. 665. See also Wang Yang-ming, *Ch'uan-hsi lu*, pt. 3, in *Ch'üan-shu*, 3:45b: "The *liang-chih* is to know good and evil."

38. Wang Yang-ming, *Ta-hsüeh wen*, in *Ch'üan-shu*, 26:4a–b: "The highest good is the ultimate principle of manifesting character and loving people. The nature endowed in us by Heaven is pure and perfect. The fact that it is intelligent, clear, and not beclouded is evidence of the emanation and revelation of the highest good. It is the original substance of the clear character which is called innate knowledge of the good." Tr. Wing-tsit Chan, *Source Book*, p. 661.

39. Wang Yang-ming, *Ch'uan-hsi lu*, pt. 2, in *Ch'üan-shu*, 2:48b: "Innate knowledge is identical with the Way. That it is present in the mind is true not only in the cases of the sages and worthies but even in that of the common man. When one is free from the driving force and obscurations of material desires, and just follows innate knowledge and leaves it to continue to function and operate, everything will be in accord with the Way." Tr. Wing-tsit Chan, *Instructions*, sec. 165, p. 146.

since *liang-chih* sometimes refers to the Principle of Nature, the extension of *liang-chih* can be taken as a description of the process of giving multiple things their principles by the mind which knows the Principle of Nature.[40]

Yang-ming's philosophy culminates in the doctrine of *chih-hsing ho-i* (the unity of knowledge and action), by which he meant, primarily, that when a person can so extend his innate knowledge of right and wrong that his mind is totally and intensely occupied by such knowledge, there inevitably arises a will and thereupon an action to do right and not to do wrong.[41] In the innate knowledge of the good lies the initial impulse to do good, and doing good results from the complete extension of (or occupation by) that knowledge.

In Yang-ming's doctrine of the priority of the mind, the importance and vitality of the mind's function are also plain, as they are in the philosophy of Chu Hsi. His three key concepts are, in fact, bridged by the intellectual function of the mind. The mind contains a moral quality which tends to radiate toward the outside world. But this "extension" is precarious because it is often obstructed by selfish desire (*ssu-yü*). Until the mind becomes conscious of its own goodness, it cannot sustain its effort of moral practice. The mind's consciousness of its innate goodness is the vital aspect of *liang-chih*. *Chih liang-chih* depends upon *liang-chih*, in that the very consciousness of the

40. Wang Yang-ming, *Ch'uan-hsi lu*, pt. 2, in *Ch'üan-shu*, 2:9b: "The innate knowledge of my mind is the same as the Principle of Nature. When the Principle of Nature in the innate knowledge of my mind is extended to all things, all things will attain their principles." The translation is taken with a revision from Wing-tsit Chan, *Instructions*, sec. 135, p. 99.

41. According to Ch'ien Te-hung's *Nien-p'u*, in *Ch'üan-shu*, 32:15a–17a, 33:35b–37b, Yang-ming first propounded the idea of the "unity of knowledge and action" when he was 38 *sui* (1509) and he did not explicitly advocate the "extension of the innate knowledge" until he was 50 *sui* (1521). The historical sequence of Yang-ming's discussions of the three key concepts of his philosophy appears to be inconsistent with the logical sequence of these concepts as expounded here. However, Yang-ming came to grasp the true meaning of the Confucian doctrine of the "investigation of things" and the "extension of knowledge" through his "enlightenment" in 1508—one year before he put forth the idea of the "unity of knowledge and action." *Ch'üan-shu*, 32:13b–14a. Although the *Nien-p'u* does not provide a detailed account of Yang-ming's "enlightenment"—hence we do not know the precise content of his idea of the "extension of knowledge" in 1508—it might be that he had already implicitly come to the idea of the "extension of the innate knowledge" at that time. In any case, if we follow the *Nien-p'u* we know that when Yang-ming first set forth the idea of the "unity of knowledge and action" in 1509 he stated that knowledge is substance and action the function of substance; thus knowledge necessarily implies action. In his later years he was more concerned with the actual dynamic moral process than with ramifications of his formal definition of the innate knowledge; he therefore reached the point of stressing explicitly the "extension of the innate knowledge." The logical sequence of his three key concepts presented here is more in line with his later views of the actual dynamic moral process.

existence of innate goodness in the human mind constantly demands actualization of this goodness. Moreover, as we said earlier, *chih-hsing ho-i* depends upon the extension of the self-consciousness of innate goodness to the utmost. In brief, according to the monistic idealism of Wang Yang-ming, the idea of innate goodness rather than innate goodness itself occupies a pivotal position and plays a dynamic role in leading man to realize Confucian moral ideals in the world.

From this analysis we know that an emphasis on the intellectual-moral function of the mind is a common postulate of the two major schools of Neo-Confucianism, although the channels through which the mind functions are conceived of differently. (Chu Hsi's ideas of the principle of reality are conceptualized by the mind through an "investigation of things" in the external world; whereas Wang Yang-ming's idea of the innate goodness of man is gained through internal reflections within one's own mind.) One cannot assert that the cultural style of a people is completely reducible to the common category of analysis used by different philosophers of that people or vice versa. But one can say that this common category of analysis of the different schools of postclassical Confucian philosophers through time indicates a distinctive predisposition of postclassical Confucian culture: a monistic and intellectualistic mode of thinking, which approaches moral and political problems by stressing the power and priority of fundamental ideas, however they are defined and gained. On the philosophical level, the intellectual faculty of the mind as a means of grasping fundamental ideas and the function of these apprehensions in facilitating the solution of moral and political problems are common emphases across the boundaries of different schools of postclassical Confucianism. On a pervasive, cultural level, a Chinese tends to stress the power and priority of fundamental ideas, as he understands them, when he is confronted with moral and political problems.

The new school of "evidential investigation"[42] (*k'ao-cheng hsüeh-p'ai*), or the "Han Learning," which emerged after the downfall of the Ming, appeared to be anti-intellectualistic. But a close examination of its content

42. This is Hu Shih's translation (Hu Shih, "The Scientific Spirit and Method in Chinese Philosophy," in Charles A. Moore, ed., *Philosophy and Culture—East and West* [Honolulu, 1962], pp. 211, 218). I think it is more accurate than the generally used term, "school of empirical research," which covers a far broader scope than the school is entitled to claim, for it is primarily engaged in textual criticism and the like. For a justification for using "school of empirical research," see Immanuel C. Y. Hsü's introduction to his translation of Liang Ch'i-ch'ao's *Intellectual Trends in the Ch'ing Period*, p. 3.

reveals that it actually presupposed a conventional intellectualistic mode of thinking. The famous accusation by Ku Yen-wu (1613–82), a founder of the Han Learning, that Wang Yang-ming's idea of *liang-chih* had sowed the seeds of collapse for the Ming,[43] seemed not only to represent a general aversion to metaphysical speculation at this time but also to reflect a postclassical Confucian mode of thinking in stressing the power and priority of ideas.[44] The Han Learning reached its apogee in the eighteenth century with the great contributions of Tai Chen (1723–77). Apart from his many important philological works, he was also concerned with the elucidation of certain major concepts of Confucian philosophy. While his concept of principle differed sharply from that of Chu Hsi—principle being immanent in *ch'i* for him but prior to *ch'i* for Chu Hsi—his concept of mind was similar to Chu Hsi's. The faculty of knowing, he believed, enables man to grasp moral principles of human conduct. He prided himself on his *Meng-tzu tzu-i shu-cheng* (Elucidation of the meaning of words in the *Mencius*) because he believed that this work contained "the essential ideas of rectifying men's minds."[45] His stress on the intellectual-moral function of the mind and the power and priority of ideas was clearly in line with an attitude toward which postclassical Confucian culture was particularly predisposed.

It seems clear, then, that the cultural-intellectualistic approach of the first two generations of the Chinese intelligentsia was primarily molded by a deep-seated Chinese cultural predisposition as embodied in a monistic and intellectualistic mode of postclassical Confucian thinking. But, there are at least two major possible objections to this argument.

The first and most obvious lies in the question of Western intellectual

---

43. Ku Yen-wu, *Jih-chih lu* (Taipei, 1962), 18:439.

44. It must be also remembered that the Ch'eng-Chu school was an orthodox doctrine in the Ch'ing court. Partly because of the encouragement of the court and partly because of the prevailing hostility to Wang Yang-ming's philosophical doctrine, a group of literati set out with great vehemence to revive the Ch'eng-Chu school. Although their originality and sophistication might not match their desire for purging the "heresy" and maintaining the "orthodox" Confucian tradition, their writings nevertheless reveal a predisposition common in Confucian culture, stressing the function of the mind. Lu Lung-chi (1630–93) said: "Of the ways of the Holy Kings to govern the world, none is better than to correct people's minds. When people's minds are corrected, the political institutions can work; when the political institutions work, the government of the world can be achieved" (cited in Hellmut Wilhelm, "Chinese Confucianism on the Eve of the Great Encounter," in M. B. Jansen, ed., *Changing Japanese Attitudes Toward Modernization* [Princeton, 1965], p. 295).

45. Tai Chen, "Letter to Tuan Yü-ts'ai," dated May 30, 1777; reprinted in Hu Shih, *Tai Tung-yüan ti che-hsüeh* (Taipei, 1967), p. 8.

influence. Of course, many foreign ideas influenced Chinese intellectuals; indeed, their avid absorption of Western ideas had caused a drastic change in their intellectual outlook. But although there are strands of thought in the West that stress the power of ideas, none of these strands of Western intellectualism or idealism is a common denominator of Western culture. Different members of the Chinese intelligentsia were subject to the influence of varieties of Western thought which were by no means compatible with one another. The notion of Western influence cannot explain why almost all members of the first two generations of the Chinese intelligentsia commonly followed the cultural-intellectualistic approach, since many of them were subject to the influence of strands of Western thought that would themselves reject the validity of Western intellectualism or idealism. Further, the notion of Western influence cannot explain why many intellectuals tenaciously clung to the cultural-intellectualistic approach although their ideas fluctuated in accordance with different waves of foreign ideas that reached China.

It seems that the intellectualistic climate of opinion of Confucian culture was so pervasive and deeply embedded that a category of analysis of the Chinese intelligentsia was decisively molded by it without their being aware of the fact. In spite of the drastic change of content in the thought of the modern Chinese intelligentsia, a traditional Chinese monistic and intellectualistic mode of thinking had infiltrated into the minds of members of the first two generations of intelligentsia and led them to maintain their belief in the power and priority of ideas.

The second objection is more theoretical. It may be argued that the postclassical Confucian emphasis on the function of the mind theoretically does not preclude the possible exercise of "further functions." Conceptualization in human consciousness may well be conceived of not as self-generating but as decisively influenced by nonintellectual factors, such as political power, economic conditions, and social organization. The functions of these nonintellectual factors are therefore the "further functions" in question. This argument can of course proceed ad infinitum. Moreover, it should be noted that human thinking is capable of logical contradiction and intellectual tension. The postclassical Confucian literati might stress the function of the mind and the power and priority of fundamental ideas, but they might also stress nonintellectual factors in determining human action. Rather than being hierarchically structured, these two kinds of emphasis might be maintained on an equal footing, without their relative causal weights being clearly decided. Had postclassical Confucian thought failed to give the mind's function a position of precedence, the Chinese intelligentsia's placing priority on intellectual change could not have been the result of a Chinese cultural predisposition as embodied in the postclassical Confucian monistic and intellectualistic mode of thinking.

This second objection is theoretically legitimate but historically groundless. It is a matter of historical fact that a monistic and intellectualistic mode of postclassical Confucian thinking takes the power and priority of fundamental ideas obtained by the intellectual function of the mind as a terminal or ultimate point of analysis. Such a mode of thinking is coterminous with the cultural-intellectualistic approach of the Chinese intelligentsia, which also assumes the power and priority of ideas as a terminal point of analysis. Hence it can be said that the cultural-intellectualistic approach of the Chinese intelligentsia was primarily influenced by this traditional mode of thinking.

But why did this intellectualistic assumption become a terminal point of analysis in a postclassical Confucian mode of thinking? I cannot provide any definitive answer, but I suggest that it might be closely related to the anthropogenic constructivism that abounds in the literature of Confucianism, from the *Mencius* and the *Hsün-tzu* to the writings of K'ang Yu-wei. Anthropogenic constructivism here refers to a belief that the social, political, and moral orders of the world are intentional constructions by sage-kings and sages of antiquity. The theme of the purposeful creation of social and moral orders by ancient sage-kings and sages is among the most frequently occurring themes in Confucian literature; it is not necessary to give a detailed documentation here, but I shall cite a few examples:

In the *Mencius,* Book IIIA, chapter 4:

> But men possess a moral nature; and if they are well fed, warmly clad, and comfortably lodged, without being taught at the same time, they become almost like the beasts. This was a subject of anxious solicitude to the sage Shun, and he appointed Ch'i to be the Minister of Instruction, to teach the relations of humanity:—how, between father and son, there should be affection; between sovereign and minister, righteousness; between husband and wife, attention to their separate functions; between old and young, a proper order; and between friends, fidelity. [Tr. James Legge.]

In the *Hsün-tzu,* chapter 23:

> The sages gathered together their thoughts and became skilled by their acquired training, and thus produced social norms and righteousness and instituted laws and institutions.[46]

---

46. Wang Hsien-ch'ien, ed., *Hsün-tzu chi-chieh* (Taipei, 1962), p. 291.

In K'ang Yu-wei's writings, this anthropogenic constructivism was stretched to the point of absurdity when K'ang was intent on making it relevant to the modern situation. K'ang interpreted Mencius' saying that "[In a state] the people are the most important" (*Mencius*, VIIB.14) as a deliberate design for modern democracy.[47]

There are, of course, sources suggesting that the original power of creating social, political, and moral orders was not self-generated by the sage-kings and sages themselves, but came to them through their contact with divinity. It is characteristic of Confucianism, however, to push the divine origins of culture, morals, and institutions into the background and assume the self-generating powers of sage-kings and sages—sometimes at the expense of logical consistency.

It is also true that certain passages in the *Analects* attribute a deterministic role to *ming* ([heaven's] ordering or "fate"), while some statements in the *Doctrine of the Mean* regard *Ch'eng* (Sincerity) or *t'ien-tao* (the way of heaven or cosmos) as possessing self-generating power:

> Confucius said, "If the *Tao* is to advance, it is so ordered by *ming*. If it is to perish, it is so ordered by *ming*. What can Kung-po Liao do where such ordering is concerned?" [*Analects*, XIV.38.]

> *Ch'eng* (Sincerity) is the *tao* of *t'ien* (heaven or cosmos) . . . *Ch'eng* means the completion of the self, and the *tao* is self-directing. *Ch'eng* is the beginning and end of things. Without *Ch'eng*, there would be nothing. [*The Doctrine of the Mean*, XX.18, XXV.1–2.]

According to these passages, the *ultimate* origins of social and moral orders might well be attributed to the mythical role of *Ch'eng* or *t'ien-tao*. One can argue that the rise of social and moral orders might not have been so clear a concept in classical Confucianism as my exposition of its anthropogenic constructivism suggests. This is not the place to elucidate the difficult and involved problem of the nature and function of *Ch'eng* or *t'ien-tao* in Confucianism, nor do I wish to "systematize" the composite philosophy of classical Confucianism by glossing over its intellectual tensions (or logical contradictions). It seems to me, however, that the above notion of *Ch'eng* or *t'ien-tao* does not alter the relationship between the anthropogenic constructivism of Confucianism and the postclassical Confucian stress on the intellectual-moral function of the mind. Metaphysically speaking, the ultimate source of social and moral orders can be traced to *Ch'eng* or *t'ien-tao*. But the

47. Hsiao Kung-ch'üan, *Chung-kuo cheng-chih ssu-hsiang shih* (Taipei, 1954), 5:688–89.

sage-kings and sages had already embodied *Ch'eng* (*The Doctrine of the Mean*, XX.18). When they wanted to create social and moral orders for mankind, they did not, empirically speaking, rely on any external source. However, they had to have an internal operational source from which they derived their power of construction. It is a natural corollary of this position to think of the mind as the empirical (but not metaphysical) source of Confucian constructivism. When the "work" of sage-kings and sages came to be unequivocally revered and appreciated in postclassical times, belief in the power of their minds seemed to become deeply embedded in postclassical Confucian culture. Thus, the intellectualistic assumption became a terminal point of analysis.

Even if Confucians wanted to look beyond their own framework of ideas and assumptions, they were hardly provided with any alternative of thinking within the range of Chinese culture. Taoism asserts that everything in the universe originates from nothingness. The question of the origin of social and moral orders is left unanswered by this radical philosophy of negativism. Legalism and Moism did not offer any new theory. In fact, they had a similar anthropogenic constructivism for interpreting the emergence of human institutions and morals, despite the differences from Confucianism in the content of their ideas. There seems never to have emerged on the intellectual scene a clear conception of various spontaneous orders in society and a sustained effort to understand the evolution of social and moral orders in terms of Adam Ferguson's statement, in 1767, that they were "the result of human action, but not the execution of any human design."[48]

Within the polarity in Confucian thought between moral self-cultivation (*hsiu-shen*) and the ordering of the world (*chih-kuo p'ing t'ien-hsia*),[49] it is always possible to lean toward the latter pole, from which a more realistic comprehension of the importance of institutions is possible. The importance of institutions was stressed from time to time by some who were more concerned with objective conditions of state and society than with moral self-cultivation. The thoughts of Wang An-shih (1021–80) of the Northern Sung (960–1127) and of the school of "Practical Statesmanship" of the Ch'ing are cases in point. In the history of Chinese thought, some original figures even reached toward ideas of the natural evolution of a sociopolitical order (such as

48. Adam Ferguson, *An Essay on the History of Civil Society* (London, 1767), p. 187. Cited by F. A. Hayek, *Studies in Philosophy, Politics and Economics* (Chicago, 1967), p. 96.

49. Benjamin I. Schwartz, "Some Polarities in Confucian Thought," in D. S. Nivison and A. F. Wright, eds., *Confucianism in Action* (Stanford, 1959), pp. 50–62.

Liu Tsung-yüan's [773–819] explanation of the origins of the ancient Chinese "feudalism" [*feng-chien*])[50] and conceptions of differentiated and independent roles of institutions (such as the notion of Yeh Shih [1150–1223] of the inherent weakness of the imperial autocracy caused by excessive concentration of power).[51] These fresh ideas might have offered possibilities of breaking through the confines of the Confucian framework of analysis. However, the ideas of Liu, for which he was described as a "heretic,"[52] and those of Yeh had little consequence. Liu was remembered for his prose style, but hardly at all for his remarkably perceptive view of the origins of the "feudalism" of antiquity, and Yeh for his "utilitarian" concern for the state and society, but not for his subtle analysis of the nature of the imperial system. That these new departures of thought did not take root in the minds of the Chinese literati bears witness to the powerful dominance of anthropogenic constructivism. Indeed, the constructivist mode of thinking is one of the most important characteristics of traditional Chinese culture.

According to Confucianism, neither a sage-king nor a sage is generically different from a common man, inasmuch as they are all endowed with the same human nature, although the Mandate of Heaven bestowed upon a sage-king has made him a unique man with tremendous ability and great responsibilities. After all, Mencius said that "every man can become a Yao and a Shun" (*Mencius,* VIB.2). Charisma sets a sage-king or a sage apart from his fellow men, but a common man must look to the model of thought and action established by the sage-king or the sage as his own norm. If a common man wants to cultivate and develop his nature, he must use the same method so successfully employed by the sage-king or the sage. A common man may not have the power to create social and moral orders as does the sage-king or the sage, but he must rely on his mind to understand these orders, and conduct his life accordingly.

Change in the most basic ideas in the human mind is, therefore, the most basic kind of change, according to the monistic and intellectualistic mode of thinking that I have analyzed. Only intellectual persuasion can bring about this intellectual change. It can hardly be induced by imposing extraintellectual forces upon the mind, for a fundamental change of ideas must be based on an

---

50. Hou Wai-lu et al., eds., *Liu Tsung-yüan che-hsüeh hsüan-chi* (Peking, 1964), pp. 7–10. Also cf. E. G. Pulleyblank, "Neo-Confucianism and Neo-Legalism in T'ang Intellectual Life, 755–805," in A. F. Wright, ed., *The Confucian Persuasion* (Stanford, 1960), pp. 103–4.

51. Hsiao Kung-ch'üan, 4:465–69.

52. Hsiao Kung-ch'üan, 3:408.

understanding of the ultimate validity of this change. To be sure, the human mind can be influenced by extraintellectual forces, such as the thrust of social and economic changes; a fundamental change of ideas can be directed by a change in external stimuli to which the mind always responds. But this argument is certainly contrary to the traditional Chinese mode of thinking. Because there are many possible ways for the mind to respond, no change of external stimuli can assure a desired intellectual change. Intellectual persuasion, on the other hand, is justified by a traditional Chinese belief in the natural ability of the human mind to grasp truths—however defined—when they are fully explicated.

The above analysis has shown that the cultural-intellectualistic approach of the first and second generations of the Chinese intelligentsia was decisively molded by a deep-seated, traditional Chinese predisposition, a monistic and intellectualistic mode of thinking. When the cultural-intellectualistic approach, with its monistic character, was pushed to its extreme by the pressure of sociopolitical realities in China after 1911, it evolved into an intellectualistic-holistic mode of thinking, by which the May Fourth iconoclasts perceived the Chinese tradition as an organismic totality to be rejected in toto. Since this totality was regarded as being organismically shaped by its fundamental ideas, the form that the May Fourth iconoclasm took was totalistic cultural iconoclasm.

The cultural-intellectualistic approach, in its areas of application and in its evolution into a holistic mode of thinking, cannot be said to be exactly identical with the traditional mode of thinking discussed here. As our analysis has shown, however, it retained a generic identity as a distinctive mode of thinking whose monistic and intellectualistic nature was traditionally derived. Paradoxical as it may seem, the Chinese iconoclasts in the May Fourth era were so much influenced by their tradition—in the sense that I have defined—that they became totalistic antitraditionalists.

4

THE ICONOCLASTIC TOTALISM
OF CH'EN TU-HSIU

SOCIAL DARWINISM AND NATIONALISM

In the early phase of the May Fourth era, most members of the Chinese intelligentsia took the Darwinian concept of change to be a universal law of nature and society. One is particularly struck by the pervasiveness of this concept in the pages of *New Youth (Hsin ch'ing-nien), New Tide (Hsin ch'ao)*, and other popular magazines of the time. No matter what the topic of discussion, the stylish Darwinian catchwords, such as "struggle for existence," "survival of the fittest," and "natural selection," appear almost invariably in every article. Almost all prominent leaders of the Chinese intelligentsia, men such as Ts'ai Yüan-p'ei, Ch'en Tu-hsiu, Lu Hsün, and Hu Shih, explicitly expressed their belief in Darwinism at one time or another. The manner in which they used Darwinian expressions reflects a general belief that Darwinism is a universal law of the cosmological and the human as well as the biological world. The authors do not state why only the fittest can survive through the process of natural selection; they accept it as axiomatic, needing no elaboration.

The great attraction of the Darwinian concept of change is evident well before the May Fourth era, of course. With the publication of Yen Fu's translation of T. H. Huxley's *Evolution and Ethics* in 1898, Darwinian ideas and images became increasingly popular among the first generation of the Chinese intelligentsia, and the second generation, in their fascination with the Darwinian concept of change, simply continued that same intellectual trend. But the persistence of this concept across different generations of the Chinese intelligentsia presents an interesting and curious phenomenon. In effect, the concept of change in terms of struggle is incompatible with the dominant traditional Chinese world view, which assumed the cosmos to be benevolent in its essential nature, and the rapid acceptance of this concept by the modern Chinese intelligentsia seems contrary to certain anthropological notions of acculturation that the more closely akin an element of foreign culture is to the indigenous culture, the more easily it will be assimilated. How, then, does one account for this prevalence of social Darwinism on the Chinese scene? Here one has to consider the factor of cognitive understanding of the world and the factor of ideological commitment to change. From a purely cognitive point of view, the Darwinian concept of change served as a vehicle for comprehending and explaining the unprecedented experience of humiliation and consternation resulting from the Western intrusion. It provided an intellectual framework that helped Chinese intellectuals to cope with the intolerable anxiety about failing to understand China's crisis.[1] Considering the intelligentsia's ideological commitment to change, the attraction of social Darwinism can be illustrated by examining Ch'en Tu-hsiu's ideas. In the course of this exploration I shall locate the proper place of Ch'en's idea of social Darwinism in his thought and see what role it played in his revolt against Chinese tradition.

For Ch'en, the governing law of the universe is the principle of natural selection, according to which "it is impossible [for anything] to avoid the struggle for survival."[2] This law of nature applies to human society as well as

1. Susanne K. Langer has perceptively written: "[Man] can adapt himself somehow to anything his imagination can cope with; but he cannot deal with Chaos. Because his characteristic function and highest asset is conception, his greatest fright is to meet what he cannot construe—the 'uncanny,' as it is popularly called." *Philosophy in a New Key,* 4th ed. (Cambridge, Mass., 1960), p. 287.

2. Ch'en Tu-hsiu, "Ching-kao ch'ing-nien," *THWT,* 1:5. This essay is translated in Ssu-yü Teng and John K. Fairbank, *China's Response to the West* (Cambridge, Mass., 1954), pp. 240–45.

to biological organisms. The old and new cells of an organism are engaged in a constant struggle for existence; so are old and new members of a society. Just as the health of a person depends upon the proper functioning in his body of the forces of natural selection, by which "the old and rotten [cells] are incessantly eliminated to be replaced by the fresh and living [cells],"[3] so, it is argued, the well-being of a society relies on whether or not vigorous persons can gain ascendancy over the old and the corrupt. Moreover, the Darwinian natural law applies with equal force in the international arena of struggle among nations. The weak nation will be eliminated by the strong, whose power is derived from its ability to make progress in the process of evolution.

The social Darwinian world view thus made explicit by Ch'en was, of course, used not merely to conceive and explain the working principle of the universe. It was also applied with poignancy to the plight of the Chinese state and society. Since the process of natural selection is a process in which the unchanged is eliminated, every person or nation must change and progress in order to survive. The argument for change is founded on Darwinism because of its scientific (therefore universal) claim as a law of nature. It is used here as an impetus to and a justification for change. For Ch'en, the necessary condition for the existence of biological and societal entities as well as for the existence of the individual is change; thus the Chinese people must change themselves for the sake of their self-preservation and self-advancement.

The appeal for change in terms of natural law is quite understandable. However, a natural law, such as Ch'en considers social Darwinism to be, does not necessarily entail either a desire or a decision for change. A natural law describes a strict, unchanging regularity in nature. It is a given and unalterable fact. A decision is related to facts; it cannot be deduced from facts.[4] It is always possible for men to adopt different attitudes and make different decisions concerning the same fact or law of nature. For instance, the climate of opinion in the United States at the end of the nineteenth and the beginning of the twentieth centuries erected the Darwinian concept of change into a conser-

3. Ch'en Tu-hsiu, "Ching-kao ch'ing-nien," *THWT*, 1:1.

4. This understanding of the relationship between facts and decisions—a critical dualism of facts and decisions—can best be explained by an illustration given by Sir Karl Popper: "The decision, for instance, to oppose slavery does not depend upon the fact that all men are born free and equal, and that no man is born in chains. For even if all were born free, some men might perhaps try to put others in chains, and they may even believe that they ought to put them in chains. And conversely, even if men were born in chains, many of us might demand the removal of these chains." K. R. Popper, *The Open Society and Its Enemies*, 4th ed., rev. (New York, 1963), 1:62.

vative ideology in defense of the status quo—in opposition to conscious, directed change.[5] Chinese nationalism at about the same time saw in the same concept a radical ideology supporting change. Facts or natural laws—however one interprets them—are basically neutral.

While Ch'en himself took his ideas of social Darwinism as if they had been necessary derivatives from a law of nature, he nevertheless vacillated between two interpretations of the Darwinian concept of change. According to Darwin's law of evolution, change is a process in which the unfit cannot survive in the struggle for existence. Nature "red in tooth and claw" eliminates the unfit without mercy. Considering the physical weakness, moral feebleness, and intellectual languor of the Chinese people, as well as the social disintegration, economic insufficiency, and political corruption in Chinese society, Ch'en could not find anything that would bolster his hope for the preservation and advancement of the Chinese nation. From every conceivable point of view, that nation was totally unfit for struggle. Facing these hard and bleak realities, Ch'en succumbed at times to pessimism. To his friend Pi Yün-ch'eng he wrote:

> My pessimism is not caused by having no quick success in our undertaking. It has developed from an awareness of the hopelessness of our catching up with European and American civilizations. They are progressing a thousand *li* a day, while we are left far behind. The majority of our people are lethargic and do not know that not only our morality, politics, and technology but even common commodities for daily use are all unfit for struggle and are going to be eliminated in the process of natural selection. Although there are a few awakened people in the country, who can save us from the fate of perishing?[6]

Here social Darwinism, instead of being used as an impetus to change, becomes an argument for utter hopelessness and fatalistic pessimism. Ch'en's use of the same doctrine to support two opposing positions perhaps reflects an uncritical approach; it also reveals that his acceptance of the Darwinian concept of change did not itself automatically lead him to commit himself to change.

What, then, was the fundamental source of that desire for change in Ch'en? Part of the answer, as already suggested, lies in the role nationalism played in his thinking.

In the early phase of the May Fourth era Ch'en examined nationalism almost exclusively from an individualistic perspective. There exists what

5. Richard Hofstadter, *Social Darwinism in American Thought,* 2nd ed., rev. (Boston, 1955).
6. *HCN,* 2.3 (November 1, 1916), correspondence sec., p. 3.

appears to be, but in fact is not, a tension between his nationalism and this individualism. Thus we need to make clear the relationship between the two. In order to do so, we may consider Ch'en's strongly worded statement of his misgivings about patriotism in his famous essay, "Patriotism and Self-consciousness" ("Ai-kuo-hsin yü tzu-chüeh-hsin"). This essay, published in November, 1914, is a useful source for elucidating Ch'en's ideas of nationalism and individualism in the periods immediately before and after the launching of *New Youth* in September, 1915. Ch'en maintained in this essay that there are two different elements—emotion and reason—that contend for control of men's minds. Patriotism arises from emotional commitment to one's *kuo-chia* (abbrev. *kuo,* country). Although patriotism is important, the *kuo-chia* should not be extolled blindly, because, however important patriotism may be, it must be channeled by a consciousness of the end of *kuo-chia,* which can be understood only through exercise of the faculty of reason.

What is the end of *kuo-chia*? It is "to protect individual rights and to enrich individual happiness."[7] *Kuo-chia* exists for the sake of the individual, but the reverse does not hold true; if a *kuo-chia* cannot protect individual rights and enrich individual happiness, it does not deserve to be loved. If the people love their *kuo-chia* without awareness of its end, they are likely to be deluded and abused by an opportunistic and self-seeking ruler. Both patriotism and consciousness of the end of *kuo-chia* are prerequisites for building a *kuo-chia.* But the use of patriotism must be regulated by reason.

In the China of his day, Ch'en said, two things were clear. First, externally, the Western powers and Japan were waiting for the best opportunity to assault China; internally, the economy was crushed by the burden of indemnity, politics were corrupt, and the people ignorant and slothful, lacking both a rational awareness of the end of *kuo-chia* and a true emotional commitment to it. China in all fairness was not to be regarded as a true *kuo-chia.* Secondly, instead of protecting individual rights and enriching individual happiness, the *kuo-chia* was actually oppressing the people. "It is quite proper to love one's own *kuo-chia,* if the *kuo-chia* can protect its people; but why," asks Ch'en, "should the people love their *kuo-chia,* when it is actually oppressing them?"[8]

It is clear that what Ch'en meant by *kuo-chia* was actually "state," not

7. Ch'en Tu-hsiu, "Ai-kuo-hsin yü tzu-chüeh-hsin," *Chia-yin tsa-chih,* 1.4:2 (November, 1914). For a discussion of this essay in the context of Li Ta-chao's disagreement, see Maurice Meisner, *Li Ta-chao and the Origins of Chinese Marxism* (Cambridge, Mass., 1967), pp. 21–26.
8. Ch'en Tu-hsiu, "Ai-kuo-hsin yü tzu-chüeh-hsin," p. 6.

"nation," although he did not make this distinction himself when talking about love of one's own country. That which he opposed is a blind love of, or an unconditional commitment to, one's own government and its authority, that is, the state; he did not say that he opposed commitment to one's own political community, if by political community is meant a group of people who feel they belong together because they share a common heritage and have a common destiny; that is, the nation.[9] When Ch'en accused the *kuo-chia* of not being able to resist the encroachment of foreign powers from without and failing to protect the rights and enrich the happiness of the people from within, he was referring to the state, not the nation.

Moreover, Ch'en made a startling final assertion. Believing that it would be only a matter of time before China was cut up like a melon, he stated that it would not be unfortunate to be under colonial rule if the ruling power could govern China by law. This statement is quite understandable in light of Ch'en's personality and his profound pessimism at the time he wrote the essay. Bitterly pained by the plight of his country and the misery of his people, Ch'en, a man with strong moral passions, seemed to be little inclined to ponder the implications and ramifications of his statements or assertions. Nor was he subject to any deep psychological disturbance when he shifted positions or held two contradictory notions at the same time.[10] Ch'en wrote this essay while exiled in Japan. Watching helplessly while Yüan Shih-k'ai trod the republic underfoot, reflecting upon the deplorable character of his people, and holding on to his belief in the social Darwinian concept of the survival of the fittest in the struggle for existence, Ch'en in despair gave up hope for China and for himself. Since there was no hope for change, only further suffering could lie in store for the people, and colonial rule under a democratic foreign power (which would presumably dominate through the rule of law) could hardly be conceived of as worse than the regime of Yüan Shih-k'ai.

This essay, in short, showed Ch'en's alienation from the Chinese state as embodied in Yüan's regime, but it revealed a great deal more: his individualistic suspicion of the state as such, his distrust of a blind emotional commitment to it, and his belief that such a commitment might be detrimental not only to the welfare of the people in general but to that of its adherents. Although the state cannot be abolished, it is not the highest good nor the ultimate end, and

9. Rupert Emerson, *From Empire to Nation* (Boston, 1962), p. 95.
10. Cf. Benjamin I. Schwartz, "Ch'en Tu-hsiu and the Acceptance of the Modern West," *Journal of the History of Ideas*, 12.1:61–74 (January, 1951).

its existence can be justified only in terms of its function of "protecting individual rights and enriching individual happiness."

Any tension that one perceives in this aspect of Ch'en's thought, then, was in fact a tension between his individualism and his conception of the state.[11] If nationalism is understood as a "commitment to the preservation and advancement of the societal entity known as the nation," no tension existed between Ch'en's individualism and his nationalism. On the contrary, almost all facets of his thought in the May Fourth era, including his totalistic iconoclasm, should be understood against the background of his commitment to this nationalistic goal.[12]

However, "nationalism" is an ambiguous and extremely ill-defined concept. Ch'en's nationalism—and that of his fellow iconoclasts—needs to be clarified in light of his sense of the identity of the Chinese nation. This identity can be said to have been given to—or imposed upon—the Chinese intelligentsia by the intrusion of the Western powers. It emerged naturally from the confrontation between China and the West. It would not, however, have been so easily conceptualized if China had experienced no previous history of homogeneous political community.

It has been frequently observed that the growth of national consciousness in Europe was fostered by interaction between the expansion of the secular state and the emergence of national culture (history, vernacular literature, folkways, etc.). A sense of national identity was brought forth by the gradual emergence of a consciousness of the particular quality of national life. In contrast, the Chinese national consciousness did not emerge from internal historical evolution but came instead through a traumatic blow struck from the outside.

After the sudden change in China's position in the world, traditional Chinese culture and polity no longer was viewed as the universal model for the world, but as the source of that particular Chinese national life which had failed to cope with the Western challenge. Because of the close integration of traditional Chinese culture and polity (in which the persistent dominance of

11. In terms of the classic distinction made by Alexis de Tocqueville, it can be said that Ch'en Tu-hsiu was opposing "instinctive patriotism" but not the "patriotism of reflection": *Democracy in America,* ed. P. Bradley (New York, 1954), 1:250–53.

12. Ch'en and many other May Fourth intellectuals did not regard their individualistic values as subversive of their nationalistic commitment. On the contrary, they thought these values performed effective functions for the realization of nationalistic goals. See Yü-sheng Lin, "Radical Iconoclasm in the May Fourth Period and the Future of Chinese Liberalism," in Benjamin I. Schwartz, ed., *Reflections on the May Fourth Movement* (Cambridge, Mass., 1972), pp. 23–26.

the universal kingship over centuries was a major factor), there was lacking any potentially viable and powerful alternative system or symbol that could be resurrected in the name of national identity. (Certain variants of neo-traditionalism did emerge. But, owing at least partly to the lack of any such alternative system or symbol from Chinese tradition, they were hardly capable of taking root in twentieth-century China.) Against this background the iconoclastic nationalism of many May Fourth intellectuals arose: although regarding their traditional culture and polity as the source of Chinese national life, they were estranged from them and felt obliged to attack them for the sake of the Chinese nation.

This iconoclastic nationalism urgently demanded change; it thus transformed the prevailing social Darwinian theory *of* change into an ideology *for* change.[13]

THE CONTEXT OF TOTALISTIC ANTITRADITIONALISM

If we measure a person's greatness in terms of his ability to harness potent and hitherto undefined forces in society and channel them into an explosive social and intellectual movement, thereby bringing about a major historical change, Ch'en Tu-hsiu can be regarded as one of the greatest men in Chinese history. Not only was he the cofounder of the Chinese Communist Party, but also it was he who first struck the spark of the totalistic iconoclasm of the May Fourth era. That Ch'en lacked a highly subtle and sophisticated mind contributed, by default, to the directness of his thought.[14] In a cultural anomie in which most people were confused and bewildered, Ch'en's combination of intellectual straightforwardness with moral passion and dogged persistence became highly charismatic. Ch'en emerged as a natural leader of the May

13. This gave rise to the notion of the complete incompatibility of the old and the new, an example of which can be found in Wang Shu-ch'ien, "Hsin-chiu wen-ti," *HCN*, 1.1, article 4, pp. 1–4. As an ideology, change as such became a value and possessed the minds of the iconoclastic intellectuals to the extent that they scorned the past ideas and values not only of Chinese tradition but of any tradition. Under its influence, the iconoclastic intelligentsia's zeal for learning from the West was directed toward the most up-to-date ideas and things, which were presumably the fittest ideas and things.

14. A. O. Lovejoy made a useful distinction between two kinds of mind in his *Great Chain of Being* (Harper Torchbook ed., New York, 1960), p. 7: "There is, for example, a practically very important difference between (we have no English term for them) *esprits simplistes*— minds which habitually tend to assume that simple solutions can be found for the problems they deal with—and those habitually sensible of the general complexity of things, or, in the extreme case, the Hamlet-like natures who are oppressed and terrified by the multiplicity of considerations probably pertinent to any situation with which they are confronted, and the probable intricacy of their interrelations."

Fourth intelligentsia not because his mind was highly original but because he had the ability to give form and precision to the potent forces of iconoclasm in Chinese society in the early years of the May Fourth era. In the following pages I shall describe Ch'en Tu-hsiu's cultural-intellectualistic approach, examine the immediate context of his attack on the Chinese tradition, and, by scrutinizing his arguments, justify the factors of his iconoclastic totalism analyzed above and in chapters 2 and 3.

In the opening issue of *New Youth*, published on September 15, 1915, Ch'en proclaimed that the purpose of his magazine was to try to help the youth of the country reconstruct their thinking and cultivate their personalities. "If our countrymen have not reached a fundamental awakening in their ideas, there are no grounds for blaming the political administrators [for not having achieved much]."[15] The magazine must, he believed, be viewed as apolitical in aim; it was not to become involved with criticizing current political issues. Its basic purpose was to promote a cultural change (specifically, a change of morals) through the change of fundamental ideas. Ch'en firmly believed that social and political reforms could not be achieved and sustained without a solid cultural foundation.

One may argue that Ch'en Tu-hsiu's proclamation that his purpose was apolitical was due to his realization of the danger and, indeed, the impossibility of criticizing political issues under the tyrannical regime of Yüan Shih-k'ai. However, while Yüan's tyranny might have reinforced Ch'en's belief in the necessary priority of intellectual and cultural change, such a belief sprang from a deep-rooted presupposition rather than simply from an awareness of the current dangers, for after the collapse of Yüan's regime, Ch'en still continuously and vigorously advocated the cultural-intellectualistic approach. In an article published on November 1, 1916, Ch'en reconfirmed his conviction of the necessary priority of intellectual and cultural change. He maintained that the most urgent and basic change was a change of "fundamental ideas," and defined fundamental ideas in terms of a new conception of morality "without which people were still in a state of confusion." Then, all change in politics and scholarship would be futile. "Even if, for the time being, the old is discarded and the new is sought, without a change of fundamental ideas the old pattern of behavior will naturally and definitely re-emerge."[16]

---

15. Ch'en Tu-hsiu's reply to Wang Yung-kung, *HCN*, 1.1 (September 15, 1915), correspondence sec., p. 2. *New Youth* was, to be exact, then titled *Youth Magazine (Ch'ing-nien tsa-chih)*. The title was changed to *New Youth* beginning with vol. 2, no. 1 (September 1, 1916).

16. Ch'en Tu-hsiu, "Hsien-fa yü K'ung-chiao," *THWT*, 1:103.

Ch'en Tu-hsiu called upon the youth of China to carry out the intellectual revolution that he envisioned. On the first page of the opening issue of *New Youth,* he made the following formal announcement:

> The strength of our country is weakening, the morals [of our people] are degenerating, and the learning [of our scholars] is distressing. Our youth must take up the task [of rejuvenating China]. The purpose in publishing this magazine is to provide a forum for discussing the ways of *hsiu-shen* (self-cultivation) and *chih-kuo* (the methods of governing the state).[17]

Amidst old Confucian terms such as *hsiu-shen* and *chih-kuo,* Ch'en's anxiety about the weakness of his country and the deterioration of the quality of life of the Chinese people, and his hope of effecting change through the young, are clearly evident in this announcement, still written in classical Chinese.

Following this, Ch'en immediately addressed his young compatriots in his first article, "Call to Youth," demanding independence, dynamism, and even aggressiveness, and urging a radical revolt against various aspects of the Chinese tradition. The vitality of Western people, their spirit of independence, the power that Western nations had derived from science and technology, and the benefit their peoples had received from utilitarian concerns were sharply contrasted with the passivity, servility, superstition, and empty formalism of the Chinese people. In the name of national survival, Ch'en passionately called for a change in the Chinese way of life to bring it in accord with the Western model.

While this article did not radically depart from the general exaltation of the Faustian-Promethean dynamism of the West that had been initiated by Yen Fu and Liang Ch'i-ch'ao more than a decade before, it nevertheless contained two features we should especially note. First, Ch'en cited Confucius and Mo-tzu as models for Chinese youth when he exhorted them to be dynamic and not retiring—a fact that suggests that his totalistic antitraditionalism was not yet full-fledged.[18] One can argue that the singling out of Confucius and

---

17. Ch'en Tu-hsiu, "She-kao," *HCN,* 1.1 (September 15, 1915), unnumbered opening page. This announcement by Ch'en of his editorial policy was omitted by later Chinese (Ch'ün-i shu-she) and Japanese (Daian) reprintings of *HCN.* But the latest reprinting of *HCN* in Japan in 1970 by Kyūko Shoin was happily based on the original issues of *HCN,* and hence contains this piece.

18. Ch'en Tu-hsiu, "Ching-kao ch'ing-nien," *THWT,* 1:6: "I wish that our youth would become Confucius and Mo-tzu and not [the hermits] Ts'ao-fu and Hsü Yu." I am inclined to date the beginning of the attack on Confucianism later than Tse-tsung Chow, who says: "The all-out attack on Confucianism began when Yüan Shih-k'ai was preparing to set himself up as emperor. From the first issue (September 1915) onward, Ch'en Tu-hsiu's monthly "New Youth" or "La Jeunesse" *(Hsin ch'ing-nien)* published articles attacking the whole framework of the Chinese

Mo-tzu was meant only to illustrate the "dynamism" that they formally exemplified, and did not imply approval of the substance of that "dynamism," but it seems strange that anyone should choose to illustrate his point with a historical personage to whose ideas he is wholly opposed. Although in this article he was already taking a dichotomous stance, praising the West and condemning China, Ch'en probably had not thought through the implications of the totalistic tone he adopted, and had not explicitly conceived of the Chinese tradition as an organismic or holistic totality to be rejected altogether.

Secondly, the keynote of Ch'en's nationalistic iconoclasm, dressed in social Darwinian terms, was resolutely sounded when he proclaimed:

> All our traditional ethics, law, scholarship, rites and customs are survivals of feudalism. When compared with the achievement of the white race, there is a difference of a thousand years in thought, although we live in the same period. Revering only the history of the twenty-four dynasties and making no plans for progress and improvement, our people will be turned out of this twentieth-century world, and be lodged in the dark ditches fit only for slaves, cattle, and horses. What more need be said? I really do not know what sort of institutions and culture are adequate for our survival in the present world if in such circumstances conservatism is still advocated. *I would much rather see the past culture of our nation disappear than see our nation die out now because of its unfitness for living in the modern world.* Alas, the days of the Babylonians are past. Of what use is their civilization now? "When the skin has vanished, what can the hair adhere to?" The progress of the world is like that of a fleet horse, galloping and galloping onward. Whatever cannot skillfully change itself and progress along with the world will find itself eliminated by natural selection because of failure to adapt to the environment.[19]

In successive issues of *New Youth,* Ch'en criticized many aspects of Chinese traditional culture and institutions (such as certain aspects of Confucianism, Taoism, Legalism, Buddhism, the political system, the family system, etc.), and published Yi Pai-sha's "An Appraisal of Confucius" ("K'ung-tzu p'ing-i")[20]; but he did not attack Confucianism in toto until

---

traditional ethics, customs, and institutions; he based his arguments on science, human rights, and democracy." Tse-tsung Chow, "The Anti-Confucian Movement in Early Republican China," in A. F. Wright, ed., *The Confucian Persuasion* (Stanford, 1960), p. 293.

19. Ch'en Tu-hsiu, "Ching-kao ch'ing-nien," *THWT,* 1:4–5. The translation is taken with a minor change from Teng and Fairbank, *China's Response to the West,* p. 242. Italics mine.

20. Some scholars regard this piece, published in two parts in the February and September, 1916, issues of *HCN,* as a major tract of anti-Confucianism at this time. As a matter of fact, the

November 1, 1916, when he published "Constitution and Confucianism" ("Hsien-fa yü K'ung-chiao") in *New Youth*. Before explicating Ch'en's arguments for and the implications of his totalistic anti-Confucianism, I shall note the reasons for the iconoclasm he expressed *before* November, 1916, because they form a general tendency leading to his totalistic denunciation of Confucianism.

In the first place, Ch'en's attack on Chinese tradition resulted in part from the interplay between his individualism and his nationalism. Although he never took the nation as the highest good or ultimate end, he was profoundly concerned for the survival of the Chinese nation. His individualism, which was mainly concerned with the emancipation of the individual from the shackles of traditional Chinese culture and society, was functionally related to his nationalism. The emancipated individual, he believed, can contribute to both his own good and the good of his nation. "The nation consists of many persons. When the stature of these persons is elevated," said Ch'en, "then the stature of the nation is elevated. When the rights of these persons are consolidated, then the rights of the nation are consolidated."[21] The emancipation of the individual, then, has a twofold justification: it is necessary for national survival as well as for personal moral fulfillment.

It should be noted, parenthetically, that the stress placed on the importance

author vacillates between two incompatible opinions about Confucius and Confucianism. On the one hand, he argues, on the basis of some dubious sources, that the reason for Chinese emperors' manipulations of Confucius' ideas in suppressing the Chinese people lies in the inherent nature of Confucian ideas. Confucius advocated the indispensability of universal kingship, unlimited authority for the king, and government by men instead of by law. These ideas could be, and were, used by Chinese emperors to enhance their autocracy. Moreover, Confucius was "a sage of timeliness" *(sheng-chih-shih-che yeh)* who did not hold any idea firmly. This attitude of Confucius set a model of opportunism for latter-day Confucians. (Here, the author is contradicting his earlier statement about the absoluteness of Confucian ideas.) On the other hand, Yi Pai-sha asserts in the latter part of his article that Confucius and many of his followers were revolutionaries both in words and in deeds, who wanted to make "the *Tao* prevail in the world and to save the common people from the oppression of despotic rulers." Influenced by the "new text" interpretation of Confucianism, he said that the purpose of his article was to reveal the "esoteric message and true meaning" *(wei-yen ta-i)* of Confucianism and to show that "the manipulations of Confucianism by traditional despotic rulers were contrary to the true spirit of Confucius." Yi Pai-sha, "K'ung-tzu p'ing-i," *HCN*, 1.6 (February 1, 1916), article 3, pp. 1–6, and *HCN*, 2.1 (September 1, 1916), article 4, pp. 1–6. In short, the whole piece discloses a state of uncertainty and confusion in the author's mind rather than a clear criticism of Confucius and his philosophy. The author committed suicide in 1921 and did not leave any other writing to clarify his article, which also revealed a confusion symptomatic of the cultural anomie in which he wrote.

21. Ch'en Tu-hsiu, "I-chiu i-liu nien," *THWT*, 1:44–45.

of the individual by Ch'en Tu-hsiu and by iconoclastic intellectuals in general at this time cannot, from our historical perspective, be identified with the Western concept of individual liberty based on an ethical conviction of the worth of the individual, which evolved mainly through a secularization of religious faith, but rather represented an aspect of the revolt on the part of these intellectuals against the traditional suppression of the individual in Chinese society. In their attempt to break the fetters of moral precepts and social norms (the Three Bonds and the Five Ethical Relationships) by an attack on Chinese tradition, the status of the individual loomed large.

To be sure, the revolt against traditional Chinese culture and society was in part justified, in an immediate sense, by the iconoclasts' appreciation of certain individual rights and of individualistic ideas and values enjoyed and entertained by the people in democratic societies of the West, but this appreciation did not take deep root in their consciousness. When the high tide of iconoclasm ebbed, the May Fourth individualism waned.

Secondly, Ch'en Tu-hsiu further developed his social Darwinism into a cosmological foundation for his iconoclasm. In an article which bears the title "The Power of Resistance" ("Ti-k'ang li"), Ch'en exalted energy and vitality in cosmological terms. The "way of heaven (or nature)" (*t'ien-tao*) is brutal and harsh. Everything must resist nature in order to survive; the evolution and existence of each thing depend upon whether or not it has this power of resistance. If there is no such power, there is no life, nor even motion. The deepest cosmological reason for China's humiliation under Western powers lies in the absence of the power of resistance among the Chinese people. "The most regrettable fact is the feebleness of the moral leaders of our society. . . . Whenever they confronted obstacles, they let themselves become frustrated. Some would commit suicide, others would flee to a life of contemplation, still others would drown themselves in wine. Such men—so passive, feeble, and decrepit—are our great moral heroes."[22] A chief reason for such a lamentable lack of the power of resistance among Chinese people is the baneful effect of Chinese culture: "Taoism favors [the attitude of] withdrawal, Confucianism venerates rites and [trains people] to yield (*jang*), and Buddhism advocates [a theory] of vacuity. . . . The spirit of our people is not filled with a single aggressive and energetic thought; hence the power of resistance cannot take root in our people."[23] It is significant to note that even in Ch'en's harsh

22. Ch'en Tu-hsiu, "Ti-k'ang li," *THWT*, 1:31–32.
23. Ibid., p. 33.

cosmos the ultimate agent that determines a people's survival or extinction is not the cosmos itself but the kind of ideas they have.

Thirdly, Ch'en Tu-hsiu felt that traditional Chinese culture and society had led the Chinese people to become addicted to empty formalism and impracticality:

> Our present social system and thought are inherited from the Chou and Han dynasties. Empty formalism was emphasized by the social norms and religious ritual of the Chou dynasty, and under the Han dynasty Confucianism and the Taoism of Lao-tzu were elevated to high positions, while all other schools of thought were interdicted. The long-revered precepts of ethical convention, the hopes and purposes of the people, all run counter to the practical life of society. If we do not restring our bow and renew our effort, there will be no way to revive the strength of our nation, and our society will never see a peaceful day. As for praying to gods to relieve flood and famine, or reciting the *Book of Filial Piety* to ward off the Yellow Turbans [a group of rebels of the Later Han dynasty], all people today, as long as they are not infants and morons, can see through these absurdities. Though a thing be of gold or of jade, if it has no practical use, then it is of less value than coarse cloth, grain, manure, or dirt. That which brings no benefit to the practical life of an individual or of society is all empty formalism and the stuff of cheats. And even though it were bequeathed to us by our ancestors, taught by the sages, advocated by the government, and worshiped by society, the stuff of cheats is still not worth one cent.[24]

Ch'en suggested that science should be used as a remedy for this loss of practicality. He did not know very much about the nature of science, but he saw the benefits that science had brought to the modern powers of the West. Science he understood in a scientistic sense; it was a weapon against the empty formalism of Chinese tradition.

THE ARGUMENT

We know that antitraditionalism was a dominant theme of Ch'en Tu-hsiu's thought from the beginning of the publication of *New Youth*. But for all his militant attacks on many aspects of traditional Chinese culture and society, he did not single out the enemy as Confucianism in toto until November, 1916. There were several factors behind the specific timing of this attack. First, as noted earlier, *New Youth* began its publication one month after Yüan Shih-k'ai's monarchical movement was formally launched, and the animosity of radical intellectuals toward this movement led them to increasingly resent the

---

24. Ch'en Tu-hsiu, "Ching-kao ch'ing-nien," *THWT*, 1:8. The translation is taken with revisions from Teng and Fairbank, *China's Response to the West*, p. 244.

symbols of Confucianism that were manipulated by Yüan for his own purposes. That Confucianism was once again being used to promote the establishment of a monarchy confirmed Ch'en's belief that "Confucianism and the
Chinese monarchical system had an inextricable relationship."[25] The unfold-
ing of Yüan's monarchical movement undoubtedly drove Ch'en's feeling
against Confucianism in a more radical direction and soon dispelled the early,
short-lived state of uncertainty exemplified by his use of Confucius as a model
for dynamism while criticizing Confucian moral teachings. But probably
through fear of being prohibited by Yüan's regime from publishing or circulat-
ing New Youth, Ch'en restrained himself from openly attacking Confucianism
in a totalistic fashion even though he might already have reached the point
where he felt the need to do so.

Secondly, Ch'en's totalistic attack on Confucianism in a series of articles
beginning with the November, 1916, issue of New Youth was a direct reaction
against the renewal of K'ang Yu-wei's obstinate effort to establish Confucianism as a state religion—an effort that can be traced back to the Reform
Movement of 1898. Inspired on the one hand by his observation of the
function of Christianity in integrating Western democratic societies, while on
the other ignorant of the controversy over separation of church and state in the
West, and under the influence of the Chinese tradition that identified the
cultural center with the political center, K'ang came to believe that establishing Confucianism as a state religion was necessary for China's salvation. In
1898, in his memorial to the throne, he had already proposed that Confucianism be proclaimed the state religion and Confucian "churches" be
established throughout the country. In 1912, K'ang's disciple Ch'en Huan-
chang and others founded the Confucian Society (K'ung-chiao hui). K'ang
himself began publishing the magazine Pu-jen (Compassion) in February,
1913, to promote the establishment of a Confucian state religion. When the

25. Ch'en Tu-hsiu, "Po K'ang Yu-wei chih tsung-t'ung tsung-li shu," (October 1, 1916),
THWT, 1:100. On the basis of his cultural-intellectualistic approach, Ch'en predicted in May,
1917—almost a year after the collapse of Yüan Shih-k'ai's monarchical movement—that if
Confucian ideas and values were not wiped out from the minds of Chinese people, the monarchy
could always be restored. Ch'en Tu-hsiu, "Chiu ssu-hsiang yü kuo-t'i wen-t'i," THWT, 1:147–
51. The brief restoration of the last Ch'ing emperor, Henry Pu-yi, by Chang Hsün in July, 1917,
strengthened further Ch'en's cultural-intellectualistic approach and, for that matter, his belief that
Confucianism and monarchy were indissolubly interrelated—see "Fu-p'i yü tsun-K'ung," (published August 1, 1917), which once again argued the inextricable relationship between Confucianism and monarchy and the total incompatibility between Confucianism and republicanism.
THWT, 1:161–68.

Constitutional Commission began to draw up a draft constitution for the Republic of China in July, 1913, Ch'en Huan-chang proposed to the Parliament that a Confucian state religion be formally stipulated in the forthcoming constitution. This proposal was supported by Yüan Shih-k'ai's followers and some members of the Chinputang (Progressive Party) but opposed by members of the Kuomintang. After many debates, Article XIX of the draft constitution of the Republic of China, known as the "Temple of Heaven Draft," contained this provision, made under Yüan Shih-k'ai's influence: "Confucius' principles shall be the basis for the cultivation of character in national education." In the autumn of 1916, when the Parliament was in session in Peking, this article became a center of debate. Yüan Shih-k'ai was dead, and many members of the Parliament felt free to oppose the provision for "Confucius' principles." In protest against this trend, K'ang Yu-wei wrote a public letter to President Li Yüan-hung and Premier Tuan Ch'i-jui, proposing again the establishment of a Confucian state religion.[26]

The anachronistic activities of K'ang's group after the collapse of Yüan Shih-k'ai's monarchical movement reminded Ch'en how deeply the theory and practice of Confucianism (as Ch'en understood them) were rooted in the minds and behavior of the Chinese people. It was against this immediate background that Ch'en Tu-hsiu poured his fully fermented anti-Confucianism into a series of attacks on Confucianism as a whole; these attacks, based on a holistic way of thinking, soon embraced the totality of the Chinese tradition. From November, 1916, to November, 1919 (when the last issue of volume 6 was published), this was the focus of concern in *New Youth*.[27] Not even the call for a literary revolution and, later, the introduction of Marxism occupied as prominent a place in this most influential review of the May Fourth era.

In Ch'en's anti-Confucianism the most striking feature was the discrepancy between his persistent attacks on Confucianism as a whole and his specific arguments against Confucianism. Ch'en claimed that he was attacking Confucianism in toto, but his arguments do not support this claim. He did not

26. The above summary of the movement for establishing a Confucian state religion led by K'ang Yu-wei draws mainly on Chow Tse-tsung, *The May Fourth Movement* (Cambridge, Mass., 1960), pp. 291–93, and his "The Anti-Confucian Movement in Early Republican China," in Wright, ed., *The Confucian Persuasion*, pp. 290–93.

27. In "Po K'ang Yu-wei chih tsung-t'ung tsung-li shu"—the first article (published on October 1, 1916) of this series of writings—Ch'en criticized K'ang's absurd arguments for making Confucianism a state religion but did not make a detailed criticism of Confucianism. His full-scale assault began with the second article, "Hsien-fa yü K'ung-chiao," published on November 1, 1916.

examine exhaustively all aspects of the theory and practice of Confucianism
over the centuries, and he was not bothered by the problems of authorship and
dating of the various Confucian classics he used, nor did he face the important
problem of changes in the history of Confucianism or the problem of the
interplay of Confucian ideas and nonintellectual factors in traditional China.
What he resented was the *li-chiao* (Confucianist teachings of proper norms of
ritual and social conduct). But he felt that he had not only to argue against the
li-chiao itself but, more important, to strike at its roots, which, according to
Ch'en, were the ideas of Confucius.

In the aftermath of sociopolitical and cultural disintegration, it became
possible to discredit all aspects of the tradition, and Ch'en could, as it were,
look at it, as a totality, from outside. From the perspective of his cultural-
intellectualistic approach, which had, as shown in chapter 3, already evolved
into a holistic mode of thinking, Ch'en conceived of the Confucian tradition
as a holistic entity in that all later developments of Confucian theory and
practice were organismic derivatives of the original whole, consisting of the
ideas of Confucius. He did not consider the problems of historical change and
the interplay of ideas and nonintellectual factors as such: whatever changes
occurred through time were assumed to be variations and ramifications of the
essential nature of the tradition, and the possible role of nonintellectual factors
in history had also to be ignored if the intellectualistic and holistic mode of
thinking was valid. The assumption that all social, political, and economic
aspects of the Confucian tradition, and, for that matter, all its cultural aspects,
including the ideas and dicta contained in different Confucian classics and the
later developments in that tradition, were organismic derivatives of the ideas
of Confucius eliminated the necessity of basing an iconoclastic attack upon
exhaustive research on all those aspects of the Confucian tradition and on
textual problems—those kinds of research could, indeed, be dismissed as
pedantic.

Furthermore, if the Confucian tradition was assumed to be a holistic entity
that determined the essential nature of the Chinese tradition, the necessity for
examining and attacking non-Confucian aspects of the Chinese tradition became minimal. While Ch'en did occasionally criticize Taoism, Buddhism,
and Legalism, and so on, he considered them relatively insignificant, because
they could not have changed the essential nature of the tradition once it was
conceived of as generically shaped by a holistic Confucianism. We should
therefore consider Ch'en's totalistic attack on Confucianism as representing
the main thrust of his totalistic antitraditionalism.

In short, what Ch'en offered, without fully being aware of what it was, was a formalistic argument against the Confucian tradition as a whole. Our inquiry into the formalistic nature of his arguments—the result of the discrepancy between what he claimed and what he actually offered, and his lack of awareness of, or of concern with, his formalistic fallacy—will lay bare the dominance of the cultural-intellectualistic approach in his iconoclastic totalism.

Following the antitraditionalist orientation of his early writings in *New Youth,* Ch'en's arguments against Confucianism are built around the central notion that Confucianism is not compatible with the modern way of life, whose defining characteristic, according to Ch'en, is the independence of the individual in the spheres of ethics, politics, economics, law, and social relations. Here Confucian teachings of social ethics and social norms run counter to the modern way of life on all counts. The essence of the modern spirit is equality and independence, whereas the epitome of Confucian ethics is the Three Bonds and the Five Ethical Relationships, which can only be defined as the morality of inequality.[28] Specifically, Ch'en's arguments can be seen in the following passages of his celebrated essay, "The Way of Confucius and Modern Life" ("K'ung-tzu chih-tao yü hsien-tai sheng-huo"):

> The pulse of modern life is economic and the fundamental principle of economic production is individual independence. Its effect has penetrated ethics. Consequently the independence of the individual in the ethical field and the independence of property in the economic field bear witness to each other, thus reaffirming the theory [of such interaction]. Because of this [interaction], social mores and material culture have taken a great step forward.
>   In China, the Confucianists have based their teachings on their ethical norms. Sons and wives possess neither personal individuality nor personal property. Fathers and elder brothers bring up their sons and younger brothers and are in turn supported by them. It is said in chapter thirty of the *Book of Rites* that "While parents are living, the son dares not regard his person or property as his own." This is absolutely not the way to personal independence.[29]

Ch'en goes on to cite extensively from the *Book of Rites,* a basic canon for the traditional *li-chiao,* to show that the wife and the son cannot make independent political judgments because they have to obey the husband and the father,

28. Ch'en Tu-hsiu, "Hsien-fa yü K'ung-chiao,'*THWT,* 1:108–9.
29. Ch'en Tu-hsiu, "K'ung-tzu chih-tao yü hsien-tai sheng-huo," *THWT,* 1:117–21. The quotation is from p. 117. The translation is taken from Wm. T. de Bary et al., comps., *Sources of Chinese Tradition* (New York, 1964), 2:153–54. Almost all bibliographical references to chapter numbers in the *Book of Rites* supplied in this translation are incorrect, although in the original Chinese text, Ch'en's references to chapter titles of his citations are correct.

whereas such judgments by everyone are essential to a modern constitutional state, and that social intercourse between men and women is not allowed either, whereas it is a common and necessary practice in a modern society. Women and young people received the greater share of sympathy and attention in this piece, since they were more deprived of their individuality and were forced by their subjugation to men and adults to become less independent and productive members of the society; the essay is, however, a general statement of Ch'en's view of the incompatibility between the way of Confucius and modern life.

Although Ch'en noted here the role of economics in modern life, he did not take heed of this notion to qualify the intellectualistic and holistic argument for his iconoclasm. The distinctive feature of his anti-Confucianism revealed in this essay—as its title indicates—is his insistence that all the impractical and immoral practices of social etiquette and precepts of morality must be defined as the way of Confucius because they are derived from the original ideas of Confucius. If Confucianism is defined as a holistic entity, Ch'en has no recourse but to advocate its total rejection.

In Ch'en's arguments against Confucianism, we find no criticism of Confucian tradition on its own philosophical plane. He never touched upon the central concept of classical Confucian philosophy, *jen,* nor did he refute the classical Confucian conception of the relationship between *jen* and *li.* Since Ch'en had had an early training in Confucian classics, he was undoubtedly familiar with the *Four Books* and the *Five Classics*—one can even safely assume that he knew many of them by heart because that was the way of his early education. That his arguments against Confucianism showed little concern for it as a moral philosophy was certainly not due to ignorance of its literature.

Ch'en's conception of Confucian tradition as a holistic entity led him to assume that the original ideas of Confucius, whatever they were, were unfit for modern life on the ground that their derivatives, the orthodox Confucianist norms of social conduct, were unfit. There was, then, no need to criticize Confucianism as a philosophy. When Ch'ang Nai-te urged Ch'en to make a distinction between the original ideas of Confucius and latter-day Confucianism, Ch'en's haughty reply exhibited clearly his holistic conception of the Confucian tradition, and for that matter, of any tradition:

> In my opinion, although the theories of later masters of Buddhism or Christianity may not be completely the same as the doctrine of the original founder

and may be more complex and elaborate, their basic ideas are identical with those of the founder. The merit or demerit of each religion should therefore be attributed to the original founder.... This is also true of Confucianism. You want to distinguish the original teachings of Confucius from the Confucianism of the Han and the Sung and the Confucianism of today's Confucian Societies. You also said that the original Confucianism was distorted by latter-day Confucianists. I should like to ask: Why did Confucianists since the Han and the T'ang rely on and derive [their doctrines] from the ideas of Confucius rather than Taoism, Legalism, Moism, and the ideas of Yang Chu? Why were the doctrines of latter-day Confucianists inextricably connected with the ideas of Confucius? If you can ponder [these problems], you will know the reason.... You said that Confucianism was distorted by Li Ssu, Shu Sun-t'ung, Liu Hsin, and Han Yü. I do not know to what you refer. If you use only muddle-headed language, you will not convince the ancients [that they did distort the original teaching of Confucius]. Can you single out one or two items that were not originated by Confucius and Mencius but created by Li Ssu, Shu Sun-t'ung, Liu Hsin, and Han Yü?[30]

This conception of the holistic nature of Confucian tradition makes it impossible to reform Confucianism either by introducing foreign cultural elements into China or by self-effort. If one maintains, as Ch'en did, that everything in a cultural tradition is organismically related and generically peculiar to that culture, there is no room to absorb a generically different element from a foreign culture; for there is no place where such a foreign element can be integrated into the indigenous system. On the other hand, the neotraditionalist formula of promoting democracy by claiming, as K'ang Yu-wei did, that democratic principles are contained in the original Confucianism can lead, at best, only to a revival of the original Confucianism, not to a realization of democracy. Hence, K'ang Yu-wei's involvement as an adviser to Chang Hsün's restoration of the Ch'ing—as Ch'en took pains to remind his readers—was quite consistent with his neotraditionalism.[31] It is simply impossible to synthesize the traditional culture of China and the modern culture of the West. If one wants a basic change, the only alternative is to destroy the traditional culture of China completely and to replace it with the modern culture of the West. (From Ch'en's perspective, the modern culture of the

30. Ch'en Tu-hsiu, "Ta Ch'ang Nai-te," dated December 1, 1916, THWT, 3:25. Li Ssu was a disciple of Hsün-tzu but was generally regarded as a Legalist, not a Confucianist. In his letter to Ch'en, Ch'ang Nai-te mentioned Li Ssu as one of the figures who distorted the original Confucianism; Li Ssu is also mentioned thus in Ch'en's reply.

31. Ch'en Tu-hsiu, "Fu-p'i yü tsun-K'ung," THWT, 1:161-62.

West was likewise assumed to be a monolithic entity, one that was capable of being brought to China.) Ch'en said on November 1, 1916:

> If we want to build a new state and organize a new society according to the Western model in order to survive in this world, the basic task is to import the *foundation* of the Western society, that is, the new belief in equality and human rights. We must be thoroughly aware of the incompatibility between Confucianism and the new belief, the new society, and the new state. We must courageously decide to throw away that which is incompatible with the new belief, the new society, and the new state!''[32]

Ch'en repeatedly made similar remarks during this high tide of iconoclasm. On March 1, 1917, he said in *New Youth*:

> If someone thinks the old Confucianism is right, he must regard the newly imported culture of Europe wrong. There is absolutely no place where the new [European culture] and the old [Confucian culture] can coexist and be blended together. We can only choose one of these two.[33]

Ch'en Tu-hsiu's ideas concerning the impossibility of reforming Confucianism from within can be illustrated by his correspondence with Yü Sung-hua, who, after arguing that Confucianism should be defined as a special kind of religion, stated:

> There are of course elements of Confucianism that do not fit modern life. But this is true of other religions, too. Most other religions underwent many changes, whereas Confucianism changed little. This difference results from the later history [of other religions and of Confucianism] but is not related to the original doctrines. The doctrine of Confucianism contains many things that should not be slighted. [We must] select good elements [of Confucianism] to which we should adhere, and single out bad elements in order to change them. The task of enlightening Confucianism is in making it change with the pace of time. We cannot say that the literary styles of the Chou, Ch'in, Han, and T'ang were without beauty; but because they cannot accommodate the changes in ideas and other things, my friend Hu Shih advocated reforming Chinese literature. To reform Chinese literature is a good thing. Is it not rather absurd to substitute a foreign language for classical Chinese because it is not adequate for our present use? The culture of every country has its identity. If Chinese literature can be reformed but should not be discarded, then Confucianism likewise can be reformed but should not be discarded.

32. Ch'en Tu-hsiu, "Hsien-fa yü K'ung-chiao," *THWT*, 1:111–12.
33. Ch'en Tu-hsiu, "Ta p'ei chien ch'ing-nien," *THWT*, 3:48.

Ch'en replied:

> You said that Confucianism can be reformed in the way in which Chinese
> literature is reformed. I cannot agree. The doctrine of Confucianism is formless,
> whereas Chinese literature consists of both a formless part [i.e., thought] and a
> part having form [i.e., the script]. Is it not right that your opinion concerning
> literary reform is to discard the formless part and to retain the part with form?
> Accordingly, it is incorrect to say that both Confucianism and literature can be
> reformed and neither of them should be discarded.[34]

Confucian tradition, according to Ch'en Tu-hsiu, does not have the capacity for reformation (or transformation). Gradual change within its structure, he
believed, would always entail derivations from or ramifications of its basic
nature; it did not occur to him that reformation could involve dialectical
change through which the basic nature of Confucianism is transformed without a total break. The only alternative to the continuity of the holistic Chinese
tradition is revolution—a total discarding of the tradition. Since Ch'en did not
think Confucianism and Chinese literature were analogous, he opposed the
argument by analogy that Confucianism can be reformed. Chinese literature
could be reformed because the script—the part with form—was not organismically related to the thought in the old literature. Ch'en believed he could use
the old script to express new thought; hence he recognized the possibility of
reforming the Chinese language. But he could not hold this opinion for long in
the swift current of totalistic iconoclasm. When Ch'ien Hsüan-t'ung, a professor of linguistics at National Peking University and an associate of the *New
Youth* magazine, argued in March, 1918, for a total rejection of Confucianism
and all other aspects of the Chinese tradition by first discarding the Chinese
script, Ch'en Tu-hsiu concurred on April 15, 1918: "The Chinese script
cannot communicate new things and new principles. It is, furthermore, the
home of rotten and poisonous thought. I have no regret in abandoning it. . . .
In this transitional period, we should first get rid of the Chinese script, but
retain temporarily Chinese speech and use alphabets of romanized Chinese
speech in writing."[35]

The dominant role of Ch'en's cultural-intellectualistic approach in shaping

---

34. Yü Sung-hua's letter to Ch'en Tu-hsiu, *HCN*, 3.1 (March 1, 1917), correspondence sec.,
p. 21 (*THWT*, 3:63–64); and Ch'en Tu-hsiu's reply, ibid., 3.1, correspondence sec., p. 23
(*THWT*, 3:66–67).

35. Ch'ien Hsüan-t'ung's letter to Ch'en Tu-hsiu, dated March 14, 1918, *HCN*, 4.4:350–56
(April 15, 1918) (*THWT*, 3:150–59); Ch'en Tu-hsiu's reply, ibid., p. 356 (*THWT*, 3:159–60).

his totalistic anti-Confucianism can be further examined by noticing the ambiguities in his use of that approach. In his reply to Yü Sung-hua, Ch'en continued:

> I recognize without the slightest doubt that Confucianism is a powerful doctrine in the history of our country and a formless instrument that unifies and controls our spirit. Confucius has been unifying and controlling the minds of Chinese people since the Ch'in Fire (in which the theories of one hundred schools were annihilated) and Han Wu-ti's elevation of the Confucian School. Because of this, what we see today is the consequence of the influence of Confucius over the last two thousand years on the political, social, and intellectual life of our country.[36]

The references to the Ch'in Fire and Han Wu-ti's elevation of the Confucian school might be read as an indication that Ch'en recognized the bearing of a complex interplay of factors, some of them nonintellectual, upon the dominance of Confucianism in traditional Chinese society. Perhaps if Ch'en had probed further into the implications of this recognition, he might not have clung to his cultural-intellectualistic approach in such a doctrinaire fashion.

But why did Ch'en still maintain the cultural-intellectualistic approach in spite of his recognition of multiple reasons for the prevalence of Confucianism in traditional China? Here I would suggest that it was owing not so much to the poverty of his imagination as to the dominance of his deeply ingrained mental category of analysis (or mode of thinking). As his reply to Ch'ang Nai-te made plain, his mind was so occupied by the cultural-intellectualistic approach that he wanted to dissolve all contradictory notions by marshaling them into alignment with it. He was too much dominated by this category of analysis which he took for granted to break out of it and consider on its own merit each possible contradiction that he sensed or that others brought to his attention. If my understanding of his category of analysis is correct, I suspect that Ch'en would have "clarified" the ambiguity of the above statement by saying that it was because the original ideas of Confucius contained sources capable of inspiring imperial autocracy that the early Han emperors were led to search for the remaining Confucian classics after the Ch'in Fire and that Han Wu-ti was induced to elevate the Confucian school.

There are two other statements of Ch'en's in this period that may raise questions about the validity of my elucidation of Ch'en's cultural-

---

36. Ch'en Tu-hsiu's reply to the letter of Yü Sung-hua, *HCN*, 3.1 (March 1, 1917), correspondence sec., p. 24 (*THWT*, 3:68).

intellectualistic approach. First, in the September, 1916, issue of *New Youth*, he expressed a vague notion concerning the effects of population increase and economic institutions upon morals, and the need of social and economic changes for an improvement of morals.[37] Secondly, in the July, 1917, issue of *New Youth*, Ch'en noted that a certain level of political development was a prerequisite for making social progress through educational and industrial developments.[38]

These statements, it is quite true, contradict his cultural-intellectualistic approach. But to say that Ch'en took this approach as his basic category of analysis does not preclude his making contradictory statements about it. As already indicated, it is well known that Ch'en was anything but a consistent thinker.[39] The point at issue here, however, is what Ch'en did about these statements. Was he aware of making statements contradictory to this approach? Did he probe the implication of the tensions created by holding two opposing views? A reading of all of Ch'en's writings in this period shows that he was hardly aware of, or not at all bothered by, his own contradiction. He was so convinced of the validity of his cultural-intellectualistic approach that

37. In his letter in reply to Ch'eng Shih-ko, Ch'en addressed himself to the question of whether or not the morals of today are inferior to those of yesterday: "I dare not say whether or not the morals of today are really inferior to those of yesterday. There are two ways to explain why people think the morals of today are inferior to those of yesterday. First, the population has increased but economic institutions have not been improved. Consequently, the wealth of society is not equally distributed and money itself produces many evils that cannot be eliminated by those who only talk about ethics. Secondly, the conventional moral code can no longer confine the minds of people. Ideas and norms are changing rapidly in modern society, while morals, religions, customs, and habits of the feudal age are still trying to dominate the thought and behavior of the people. Under these circumstances, it is difficult to make distinctions between the good and the bad and between right and wrong. Thus, that which is good or right according to public opinion may not be really good or right; that which is bad or wrong according to public opinion may not be really bad or wrong. In order to change this situation, the following twofold measures must be adopted: First, we must change the social and economic institutions, not allowing immoral money to produce many evils in society. Second, we must obey truth and reject the conventional morals accordingly, not allowing the immoral "moral" code to produce many tragedies in society." Ch'en Tu-hsiu's reply to Ch'eng Shih-ko in *HCN*, 2.1 (September 1, 1916), correspondence sec., p. 9. This piece is not included in *THWT*.

38. When Ch'en was urged by Ku K'e-kang not to become involved with criticism of current political issues but to keep his original promise of fashioning intellectual change through discussions of intellectual issues, he replied: "Politics cannot help being an important part of human life. If we disregard it, we become a great obstacle to the progress of our social group. The progress of a social group consists essentially in education and industry but not in politics. However, education and industry can be developed only if politics can be advanced beyond a certain level." *HCN*, 3.5 (July 1, 1917), correspondence sec., p. 6 (*THWT*, 3:126).

39. Cf. Schwartz, "Ch'en Tu-hsiu and the Acceptance of the Modern West," p. 63.

he scarcely took heed of his vague notion of the effect of social and economic institutions on morals and education. Ch'en's cultural-intellectualistic approach permeated almost every article; it was an operational tool with which he argued his case and approached his problems, whereas his occasional mentions of social and economic factors, which can be seen to pose a difficulty for his position, were peripheral and isolated. Instead of weakening my elucidation of Ch'en's cultural-intellectualistic approach, these isolated, exceptional cases—while potentially providing a ground for his later shift to a Marxist economic determinism—actually reinforce my point. That Ch'en was not interested in drawing, or was unable to draw, implications from his awareness of the roles of nonintellectual factors shows how deeply this approach was embedded in his mind. It seems plain that Ch'en's mind was so shaped by the holistic and intellectualistic category of this approach that he was unable to do anything about his commonsense awareness of the roles of nonintellectual factors. To bring that awareness to bear upon his general outlook requires an analysis of the interplay between intellectual and nonintellectual factors in history and society. This Ch'en could not do because of the lack of a differentiating apparatus in his mind.

Before closing this chapter, we have yet to deal with an important problem in Ch'en Tu-hsiu's anti-Confucianism. His totalistic rejection of Confucianism did not preclude his recognition at the level of common sense of some positive values in the Confucian tradition. This recognition might have raised a number of pertinent questions, such as: What were the sources of these positive values? Since the values were found in the Confucian tradition, how were they related to its holistic nature as he had perceived it? But instead of probing the implications of his commonsense recognition of positive values and dealing with the above questions rigorously if he was aware of them, Ch'en argued that they were universal moral values common to all traditions. In so doing, he implied that they could not indicate or explain the peculiar nature of Confucianism, and therefore were irrelevant to that peculiar nature:

> My anti-Confucianism does not imply that the [Confucian] virtues of cordiality, uprightness, courtesy, temperance, deference, faithfulness, righteousness, honesty, sense of shame, and the [Confucian] way of conscientiousness and reciprocity (*chung-shu chih tao*) are worthless. However, these virtues are common to all practical moral systems of the world. Therefore, we should not take pride in the fact that Confucianism has them.[40]

40. Ch'en Tu-hsiu's reply to "a certain reader," *HCN*, 3.5 (July 1, 1917), correspondence sec., p. 3 (*THWT*, 3:119). This is, almost verbatim, the statement that was first uttered in his

In his later writings, Ch'en's iconoclasm became even more radical, as evinced by his agreement with Ch'ien Hsüan-t'ung about the necessity of wiping out all Chinese traditions, including Chinese script and speech. Clearly, the "qualifications" Ch'en occasionally expressed did not change his general approach of totalistic anti-Confucianism.

However, by asserting that positive values in Confucianism were a part of the common denominator of all moral systems, Ch'en admitted implicitly that there were elements in Confucianism not partaking of its holistic nature. Although this contradiction breaks up, logically, the entire holistic argument for totalistic anti-Confucianism, Ch'en Tu-hsiu never seemed clearly conscious of it. Even if he was, the dominance of his cultural-intellectualistic approach made him unable to face it squarely. In the final analysis, his common sense had not proved itself equal to the force of the deep-seated traditional Chinese cultural predisposition that molded him and by virtue of which he kept insisting on the necessity and validity of rejecting the Chinese tradition in toto. For all Ch'en's ardent call for liberation from the Chinese tradition, his totalistic antitraditionalism was itself, in a sense, a victim of that tradition.

"Hsien-fa yü K'ung-chiao," November 1, 1916 (*THWT*, 1:110). Contrary to Ch'en's assertion that these virtues are "common to all practical moral systems of the world," a strong argument can be made that, while containing universal moral elements, they are distinctively Confucian morals.

5

THE PSEUDOREFORMISM OF HU SHIH

HU SHIH'S MODE OF THINKING

In the most general terms, Hu Shih's thought seems to be marked by contradictory strains.[1] While he sometimes denounced Chinese tradition totalistically, he often argued for a gradual and "organic assimilation"[2] of Western culture. He was famous for his advocacy of wholesale Westernization in 1929.[3] Yet, without offering any intellectual justification, he proclaimed, as a cultural nationalist in his last years, that the purpose of his cultural doctrine

---

1. I am grateful to Professor Wang Hao, who has saved me from a logical error in my earlier draft on Hu's iconoclastic thought. For a different interpretation of Hu Shih's iconoclastic thought and ideas of Westernization, see Jerome B. Grieder, *Hu Shih and the Chinese Renaissance* (Cambridge, Mass., 1970), pp. 284–89, 317–21.

2. Hu Shih, *The Development of the Logical Method in Ancient China* (Shanghai, 1922), p. 7.

3. Hu Shih first used "wholesale acceptance" and "whole-hearted acceptance" interchangeably in an article entitled "Conflicts of Cultures," *China Christian Year Book, 1929* (Shanghai, 1930), pp. 112–21. In an address delivered at the fourth conference of the Institute of Pacific Relations (of which he was the president) in Hangchow and Shanghai, 1931, he argued that China should "adopt" Western civilization "whole-heartedly" and "unreservedly accept this modern

was to "vitalize the older culture."[4] Hu changed his opinions about a number of things in his life, but the confusion in his thought about Chinese tradition and Westernization is not due to that fact. Indeed, it is characteristic of Hu that throughout his later life he steadfastly clung to each of the major ideas concerning Chinese tradition and Westernization that he expressed in the May Fourth period.

The best way to grapple with the elusive nature of Hu's iconoclasm is through an analysis of the implications of the lifelong contradiction—of which he appeared to be not clearly aware—between his commitment to both the evolutionary reform of Chinese tradition and the totalistic rejection of that tradition. In order to ascertain what this contradiction implies and why he was not clearly conscious of it, we should first of all be aware of the difference between Hu Shih's formally stated claims and their substance. This analysis

---

civilization of the West," but did not use the term "wholesale acceptance" (Bruno Lasker, ed., *Problems of the Pacific, 1931* [Chicago, 1932], p. 477). The revision of terms was probably due to the review by P'an Kuang-tan (Quentin Pan) of Hu's article in *China Christian Year Book*. P'an pointed out that there is some discrepancy in meaning between "wholesale acceptance" and "whole-hearted acceptance." *China Critic*, 3.9:210–11 (February 27, 1930).

In 1935, less than three months after Hu rightly criticized the famous ten professors' "Declaration for Cultural Construction on a Chinese Base" ("Chung-kuo pen-wei ti wen-hua chien-she hsüan-yen") as neotraditionalism in a new garb, he wrote "Sufficient Cosmopolitanization and Wholesale Westernization" ("Ch'ung-fen shih-chieh-hua yü ch'üan-p'an hsi-hua"), in which he acknowledged P'an Kuang-tan's review and proposed to substitute the awkward term "sufficient cosmopolitanization" for his earlier expression "wholesale Westernization," which has provoked "many trivial debates." He admitted that "wholesale Westernization" could not be easily achieved from a "quantitative point of view" and that "civilizations are by nature conservative" (Hu Shih, *Hu Shih lun-hsüeh chin-chu* [Shanghai, 1935], pp. 552–61). However, despite these later qualifications, largely polemic in intent, Hu's attitude toward Westernization was not changed in any basic sense. By "sufficient cosmopolitanization" he did not mean a conscious effort toward a creative synthesis or integration of all civilizations in the world. Rather, his usage of the term betrayed his assumption of the universal validity and viability of modern Western civilization, which Hu had long believed "is fast becoming the world civilization" (Hu Shih, "The Civilizations of the East and the West," in C. A. Beard, ed., *Whither Mankind* [New York, 1928], p. 25). For Hu, a champion of the idea of progress, the content of modern Western civilization was by no means ambiguous. The pragmatic American civilization epitomized by John Dewey's instrumentalism is *the* modern civilization of the West. To be sure, the factual result of "sufficient cosmopolitanization" would hardly be identical with the modern civilization of the West, as Hu readily admitted. But, the program that the Chinese people should adopt, whether it was to be called "wholesale Westernization," "whole-hearted modernization," or "sufficient cosmopolitanization" should be, according to Hu, acceptance of the modern civilization of the West to the greatest possible extent. Insofar as Hu's positive attitude was concerned, he was oriented toward an all-out or totalistic Westernization.

4. Hu Shih, "The Chinese Tradition and the Future," *Sino-American Conference on Intellectual Cooperation: Reports and Proceedings* (Seattle, 1962), p. 21.

will show that the contradiction in question was merely a formal (or logical) one. Hu Shih's reformism cannot, in fact, be accepted at its face value. It must, instead, be understood as a pseudoreformism—a means for implementing his program of the totalistic Westernization of China, not an end as such. The scientific (or protoscientific) method that Hu found in Chinese tradition, while useful in his reformist (or gradualist) program of Westernization, was irrelevant to his iconoclastic evaluation of Chinese tradition. His recognition of the existence of such a positive element in Chinese tradition provided no bar against an attack on that tradition and the advocacy of Westernization in totalistic terms. Substantively, then, there was dominant in Hu's consciousness an iconoclastic totalism on the basis of which his demand for totalistic Westernization arose.

In the following I shall first trace the origins of Hu's cultural-intellectualistic approach, which shaped his impulse to revolt against Chinese tradition into a totalistic cultural iconoclasm, and then distinguish between his formal claim of scientific reformism and the actually iconoclastic nature of his thought.

Hu Shih's cultural-intellectualistic approach was evident in his earliest writings. While a student at the China National Institute (Chung-kuo kung-hsüeh) in Shanghai he began in the autumn of 1906 to contribute articles to a newly established magazine, *The Struggle* (*Ching-yeh hsün-pao*), which, according to Hu Shih's own account, was "primarily interested in instilling new ideas into"[5] the masses. He became its editor in 1908 at the age of seventeen.[6] Hu's lifelong emphasis on the power and primacy of ideas was already unmistakably manifest in these writings. In one article deploring the state of superstition in China he remarked, "the prevalence of theories that deceive has made Chinese people fall into the darkest abyss."[7] This assigning to ideas of a decisive role in shaping human affairs revealed an intellectualistic mode of thinking so deeply embedded as to require no further elaboration or defense. In his short story, "The Island of Unchanging Reality" ("Chen-ju tao"), in which he set out "to destroy superstition and enlighten the people's intellect,"[8] Hu lamented the Chinese people's mental laziness: their stupidity was owing "totally to their unwillingness to think."[9] His youthful stress on

5. Hu Shih, "My Credo and Its Evolution," in *Living Philosophies* (New York, 1931), p. 249.

6. Hu Shih, *Ssu-shih tzu-shu* (Taipei, 1954), p. 63.

7. Ibid., p. 65.

8. Ibid., p. 62.

9. Ibid., p. 66.

the power of ideas in shaping the life and history of the Chinese people was, therefore, twofold: first, it assigned a decisive role to the quality of ideas; second, it placed a strong emphasis on the role of intelligent thinking.

Hu reread these early writings on the occasion of preparing for his *Autobiography at Forty (Ssu-shih tzu-shu)*. He was pleasantly surprised that his early tendency to emphasize the importance of thinking actually presaged his later adoption of John Dewey's experimentalist philosophy. It is true that his later discovery of Dewey's experimentalism served to confirm, reinforce, and sophisticate rather than change an intellectualistic stance already held before Hu went to study in the United States. It should be noted, however, that Dewey emphasized the efficacy of thought in terms of the efficacy of the "scientific method" as he defined it. The "scientific method" will give rise to "creative intelligence," which can deal effectively with problems in social life. Hu Shih's youthful emphasis on the role of intelligent thinking provided a point of departure for his later assimilation of the Deweyan conception of "scientific method," but, to Dewey, the reasons for the shape of the life and history of a people are very complex; he never assigned a decisive role to the quality of ideas as such in molding them, although in stressing rationality he did talk about the quality of the mind. This, in Hu Shih, was a manifestation of a cultural-intellectualistic approach that would evolve into an intellectualistic-holistic mode of thinking after the breakdown of the traditional Chinese cultural-moral order. Hu Shih talked a great deal about the Deweyan conception of "scientific method" and "creative intelligence" in his writings, but his stress on the holistic role of the traditional Chinese mind in shaping the nature of the Chinese tradition (to be delineated later) was clearly derived from his youthful monistic notion described above—a notion that reflected a deep-seated Chinese cultural predisposition.

Hu Shih's cultural-intellectualistic approach manifested itself on many occasions throughout his life. When he wrote to the *Chinese Students' Monthly* in 1914 from Cornell University as an undergraduate, he regarded the political revolution of 1911–12 as a natural result of the "revolution of thought."[10] After he returned to China in 1917 he came to support the developing intellectual revolution with great vigor. Like Ch'en Tu-hsiu, Hu was deeply dismayed by the Chinese people's apathy, effeteness, and ignorance, which persisted in spite of political changes. "The China I saw when I returned from a foreign sojourn was the same old China with which I had been well ac-

10. Suh Hu (Hu Shih) "The Confucianist Movement in China," *Chinese Students' Monthly,* 9.7:534 (May 1914).

quainted before I departed,'' said Hu in the first article he published after returning.[11] No wonder, he thought, that Chang Hsün's farcical coup for restoration of the Ch'ing (news of which reached Hu at Yokohama on his way home) occurred just one year after the anachronistic fantasy of Yüan Shih-k'ai's monarchical movement had ended. The bleak political and social realities that emerged from the 1911 revolution confirmed and reinforced his deep-rooted belief that it was pointless to try to fashion political changes without first establishing a solid cultural foundation for the transformation of Chinese society. He determined ''not to talk about politics for twenty years,'' let alone to involve himself with political activities; rather, he would try to build ''a nonpolitical foundation through thought and literature for reforming Chinese politics.''[12]

When Hu was hailed by some readers for his sensible discussions of current political issues in the *Weekly Endeavor* (*Nu-li chou-pao*) in 1922 and criticized by others for his failure to hold fast to his promise of not talking about politics for twenty years, he responded with a ready admission of his failure to keep his promise, blaming the urgency of current events, and with a staunch reassertion of the power and primacy of ideas:

> We still maintain that thought and literature are of first importance. The sickness
> of our country is not rooted in the behavior of warlords and bureaucrats but in
> our mental laziness, superficial ideas, superstition in placing all our reliance on
> Heaven, and lack of public spirit. These evils are our real enemies—they are the
> forebears of corrupt politics. Because their descendant—corrupt politics—is too
> rotten to be left alone, we cannot refrain from striking at it first. However, we

11. Hu Shih, ''Kuei-kuo tsa-kan,'' *HCN*, 4.1:20 (January 15, 1918), or *HSWT*, 1st coll., 4:1.

12. Hu Shih, ''Wo ti ch'i-lu,'' *HSWT*, 2nd coll., 3:96, 108. Hu consistently held this opinion throughout his life and repeatedly expressed it. See Hu Shih, ''Ch'en Tu-hsiu yü wen-hsüeh k'e-ming,'' in Ch'en Tung-hsiao, ed., *Ch'en Tu-hsiu p'ing-lun* (Peiping, 1933), p. 51. Vincent Y. C. Shih, ''A Talk with Hu Shih,'' *China Quarterly*, 10:163 (April–June, 1962). It is curious to note that in the midst of describing Hu Shih's stress on cultural change and of quoting from John Dewey's two articles, which were actually reports about the student revolt and ''the new culture movement'' in China, Chow Tse-tsung asserts that ''after an analysis of the history of Westernization movements in China, Dewey came to the same conclusion that 'China could not be changed without a social transformation based upon a transformation of ideas. The political revolution was a failure, because it was external, formal, touching the mechanism of social action but not affecting conceptions of life, which really control society' '' (Chow Tse-tsung, *The May Fourth Movement* [Cambridge, Mass., 1960], pp. 223–24). This is a misreading of the sources. The statements cited by Chow are not Dewey's own view but his summary of some of the views of the Chinese intellectuals. See John Dewey, ''The Sequel of the Student Revolt,'' *New Republic*, 21.273:380–82 (February 25, 1920) and ''New Culture in China,'' reprinted in his *Characters and Events*, ed. Joseph Ratner (New York, 1929), 1:270–84, esp. 272.

must not forget the evil result of Chinese thought and literature of the last two thousand years. To overthrow the corrupt politics of today needs our common effort; but to destroy the forebears of corrupt politics—the "ghosts" of thought and literature of the last two thousand years—requires more hard work![13]

FROM REFORMISM TO "REFORMISM"

Beginning in his student days in the United States, Hu Shih's attitude toward Chinese tradition was consistently reformist, although the nature of his reformism varied radically through time. Before he committed himself to Dewey's experimentalism (or instrumentalism) his views of Confucianism were by no means negative. Mainly because Hu Shih moved in a foreign environment remote from China, his consciousness, as indicated in chapter 2, was not immediately affected by the breakdown of the traditional cultural-moral order resulting from the collapse of the universal kingship in 1911–12, but by the time he returned to China he was as much influenced by it as other May Fourth intellectuals were. In the early years of his overseas studies, he was groping toward a way of reforming Confucianism. For instance, in "The Confucianist Movement in China," published in 1914, Hu made a number of critical comments on the movement—sponsored by many of the first generation of Chinese intellectuals—that sought to establish Confucianism as a state religion, because it represented, in his eyes, merely an attempt at the revival of Confucianism. In Hu's criticism a desire to reform Confucianism was clearly revealed; he did not question the necessity of its existence but addressed himself to the problem of making it viable in modern China. "A real Confucian Reformation has yet to come. The Confucianists," said Hu, "have to face problems far more important and vital than the mere governmental recognition of an established religion."[14] In order to initiate a possible reform, Hu posed the following four questions:

> I. What does the term "Confucianism" actually imply? Does it simply comprise the doctrines contained in the Confucian Classics? Or shall it also include the State religion of ancient China, which had existed long before the time of Confucius, and which has often been loosely identified with the religious element in Confucianism? Or shall it also include the metaphysical and ethical philosophies which sprang up in the Sung and Ming dynasties?

> II. What shall we recognize as the authentic fundamental scriptures of Confucianism? Shall we accept all the Sacred Books as they are? Or shall we apply

13. Hu Shih, "Wo ti ch'i-lu," *HSWT,* 2nd coll., 3:108.
14. Suh Hu (Hu Shih), "The Confucianist Movement in China," pp. 535–36.

to them the scientific methods of modern historical research and criticism in order to ascertain their authenticity?

III. Shall the new Confucianism be a religion in the Chinese sense (that is, *Kiao* [*chiao*], or education in its fullest meaning), or a religion in the Occidental sense? In other words, shall we content ourselves with reinterpreting the ethical and political doctrines of the Confucian school, or shall we also reconstruct the Confucian conception of God or *Tien* [*t'ien*] and that of life and death, so that Confucianism may become a spiritual and transmundane power as well as a guiding light in every-day life and human relations?

IV. By what means and through what channel are we going to propagate the Confucian teachings? How shall we inculcate and instill the Confucian doctrines into the minds of the people? How can we adapt the Confucian teachings to the modern needs and to the modern changes?[15]

This reformist attitude can be corroborated by a reading of *Hu Shih's Diary While Studying Abroad* (*Hu Shih liu-hsüeh jih-chi*), in which the article just quoted from is summarized under the entry for January 23, 1914.[16] His opinions about the Chinese traditional social norms and ethos were eclectic. In one place, he attacked Chinese family values because they bred mutual dependency among the family's members and put the welfare of family before that of society. In another, Hu, who was to become one of the ardent champions of the emancipation of women from the traditional Chinese family system after he returned to China, wrote that the status of women in Chinese society was higher than that of Western women because the Chinese woman did not need to go out to find a husband herself by means of attracting and pleasing men in social gatherings.[17] One feature clearly emerged: although Hu disliked some aspects of traditional Chinese culture and society, he took a positive attitude toward others and his basic stance was that of a reformist.

Hu's discovery of John Dewey decisively transformed this earlier vague, tentative, but genuinely reformist attitude into a clear and straightforward advocacy of reformist means to Westernize China according to the model of modernity and modernization provided by Dewey's early experimentalism. Hu Shih began to study Dewey's philosophy systematically in the summer of 1915, and completed his Ph.D. dissertation in April, 1917, under the direction of Dewey.[18] During these crucial years he experienced a profound change in

15. Ibid., p. 536.
16. Hu Shih, *Hu Shih liu-hsüeh jih-chi* (Taipei, 1959), pp. 157–60.
17. Ibid., pp. 154, 168–69, 250–52.
18. Hu Shih, "Tzu-hsü," ibid., pp. 5–6. Hu Shih, *The Development of the Logical Method in Ancient China*, "A Note" preceding the introduction (n.p.). According to Hu's own account,

ideas and values, yet persisting amid this change and in some sense preparing for it was the gradualist and intellectualistic approach that he had held before he came into contact with Dewey. This fundamental intellectual change resulted, in part, from his adopting without reservation Dewey's scientistic notion of the universal applicability of the scientific method to every sphere of human endeavor and led him to move from groping toward a program of transforming Confucianism to looking for a way to transplant the Deweyan idea of scientific method to the soil of China.

Actually, if one were to use the scientific procedure defined by Dewey to study the concrete problems of China at that time, one might well reach the conclusion that many social and political reforms should take priority over intellectual change; or to put it another way, through a creative application of the Deweyan method of science, one might well present an argument against the policy of introducing the Deweyan idea of science as a matter of first importance. But the convergence in Hu Shih's mind of a preexisting cultural-intellectualistic approach with the adoption of the Deweyan ideology which stressed the meaning and the role of science in a scientistic sense led him to regard the solution of China's problems as dependent first of all on introducing the Deweyan idea of scientific method to China so that the Chinese people would grasp a key to "creative intelligence," a prerequisite for a successful approach to any problem in China's modernization.

It is ironic that the Deweyan idea of science became, in Hu Shih's interpretation, a precondition for resolving China's social and cultural problems, which arose from wholly different backgrounds and which were very different in nature from those problems with which Dewey was immediately concerned in his philosophy. Whether one is sympathetic to or critical of Dewey's philosophy, it is quintessentially American.[19] It arose from American social and religious backgrounds and took for granted some of their basic assumptions. It was intimately in touch with immediate American social and cultural problems, and pointed to the road of progress in the American future. I do not mean to imply that Dewey's philosophy is an ironclad organic system that

---

the books of Dewey that influenced him most were *How We Think* (Boston, 1910) and *Essays in Experimental Logic* (Chicago, 1916). Hu Shih, "Dr. Hu Shih's Personal Reminiscences," an interview conducted, compiled, and edited by Te-kong Tong, with Hu's corrections in his own handwriting, typescript, 1958 (Department of Special Collections, Butler Library, Columbia University), pp. 95–106.

19. For a perceptive analysis of Dewey's philosophy from a sympathetic point of view, see Paul K. Conkin, *Puritans and Pragmatists* (New York, 1968), pp. 345–402.

cannot provide any suggestions for the solutions of the problems of another society. Nevertheless, Hu Shih's fundamentalist adoption of the early ideas of Dewey proved to be less viable in Chinese society than he had expected. One should not, however, criticize Hu unsympathetically. Some factors of personality, of history, and of the character of Dewey's early ideas were beyond the control of Hu's conscious effort but nevertheless had an important bearing on the manner in which he adopted Dewey's experimentalism. Hu's mind was more notable for urbanity than for profundity. In a sense, his inner intellectual and spiritual resources did not fit him for cultural leadership in confronting the unprecedented difficulty and complexity of the sociopolitical and cultural problems generated in a Chinese society facing deep crisis in every sector of its life. In addition, the cultural disintegration then apparent in China made a simple and all-embracing answer the more attractive because of the very urgency of the need to fill the cultural "vacuum." Moreover, Dewey's ideas in their formal aspect address general problems of man and society as such and claim universal applicability. Their stress on "methodology" gives an added impression of transcending cultural boundaries. Dewey's early ideas possessed such a high degree of simplicity and generality that—by virtue of their great contribution to economy of thought—they reveal themselves almost in the manner of self-evident truths. It is quite difficult for a convinced Deweyan to realize that Dewey's formal ideas were deeply influenced by his substantive concerns, and hence may not be viable for the particular problems of another society and culture, problems with which Dewey was not concerned. And further, Hu Shih believed deeply in the evolutionary idea of progress; he regarded Dewey's philosophy as the latest and most advanced fruit of the evolution of human civilization as a whole.[20] Dewey was not only relevant to American society but also was or would be relevant to all other societies when they evolved to the same stage as American society. Thus, from the standpoint of Hu Shih's cultural-intellectualistic approach, Chinese

---

20. Hu Shih's idea of progress sometimes induced him to hold unwittingly opinions that could well embarrass his admirers. But his belief in the inevitability of progress in almost every sphere of human activity led him to express these opinions as if they were truths. Once he argued with a friend that Shakespeare could not possibly be compared with later European dramatists, who had *progressed* much further than the Elizabethans. According to Hu, *Othello* is a melodrama, and he found little merit in *Hamlet*. Hu Shih's literary criticisms probably were not influenced solely by the idea of progress, but the whole conversation was based on the assumed validity of that idea. See Hu Shih's unpublished diaries (microfilm in the archives of the Oral History Project, Columbia University), entry for June 3, 1921. I am grateful to Professor C. Martin Wilbur for his kind permission to read these materials.

society could catch up with the advanced society of America more quickly by adopting Dewey's ideas.

Dewey argued for gradualist rather than revolutionary social and cultural change. Hu Shih's earlier reformist tendency was confirmed and reinforced by his adoption of Deweyan ideas, despite the radical change of values that came from adoption of the Deweyan idea and valuation of science. It should be clearly noted, however, that the nature of his reformism was categorically changed.

In the introductory chapter to his doctoral dissertation, Hu Shih set forth the style and life work of his intellectual endeavor, advocating an evolutionary and reformist means to realize a very radical end—modernization of China in the image and upon the model of ideas and ideals provided by Dewey. The denotations and connotations of modernization and modernity for Hu were thus not ambiguous, but meant all those things positively affirmed and argued for by Dewey's early experimentalism. (Hu seemed not to have followed the more mature and subtler later development of Dewey's philosophy. For instance, he was not very familiar with Dewey's development of the concept of "quality" in aesthetic and religious dimensions of experience.) The aim of Hu's intellectual endeavor was simple and clear. It consisted of making Chinese culture a scientistic one in which everything—including ethics—was to be arbitrated by science and the Deweyan method of science.[21]

According to Hu, it is through an "organic assimilation" of "the best in modern civilization"[22] by the indigenous civilization of China that this end can be achieved. Hu set out to find a "congenial stock"[23] in Chinese civilization to which the Chinese people could organically link the scientific culture of America as defined and epitomized by Dewey's experimentalism. "In the light and with the aid of modern Western philosophy"[24] Hu made the Confucian doctrine of "rectification of names" a sort of logic in his thesis, but the Confucian "logic" could not satisfy him. He leaned toward the *Mo-tzu* and the *Kung-sun Lung-tzu,* where he found a very important "logical" method that could be taken as a prototype of the Deweyan method. Hence by his "pedagogical"[25] discovery of the logical theories and methods of ancient

21. Hu Shih, "K'e-hsüeh yü jen-sheng-kuan hsü," *HSWT,* 2nd coll., 2:1–29. Concerning the untenability of the Deweyan proposition that ethics be made an empirical science, see Morton White, *Social Thought in America* (Boston, 1957), pp. 203–19.
22. Hu Shih, *The Development of the Logical Method in Ancient China,* p. 7.
23. Ibid.
24. Ibid., p. 9.
25. Ibid.

China he prepared the Chinese people to see "that these methods of the West are not totally alien to the Chinese mind."[26] In short, the Deweyan method of science is not generically different from, even though much more refined than, the traditional Chinese scientific method. Consequently, an "organic assimilation" of the modern civilization of the West is not only desirable but possible. What Hu Shih proposed to do was to reform the traditional Chinese scientific method according to the model of the Deweyan method of science. In so doing, Hu believed that instead of forsaking an element of traditional Chinese culture he had so transformed it as to make it become a part of modernity.

After Hu returned to China he continued to occupy himself with the task of demonstrating the generic similarity between a prototype of scientific method developed in China and the Deweyan method of science. He argued that Chu Hsi's exaltation of the ideal of going to things and conducting investigations into the reasons of things was scientific in spirit and method.[27] Although other ideas in Neo-Confucianism—ideas, according to him, influenced mainly by Buddhism—had impeded the progress of scientific inquiry, they had not been able to inhibit the rise of the School of Evidential Investigation in the last three hundred years, which was a "renaissance" of the indigenous scientific tradition—a tradition "of boldness in doubt and hypotheses coupled with a meticulous care in seeking verification."[28]

Looking at this aspect of Hu's intellectual endeavor, we know that he not only argued for the generic similarity between modern civilization in the West and traditional Chinese civilization but also asserted that scientific spirit and inquiry are distinctive characteristics of the Chinese tradition and closer to those of the modern West than is the Indian tradition. Leaving aside the question of whether or not Hu Shih's interpretation of Chu Hsi's philosophy was a distortion of Chu Hsi's essential ideas, Hu's doctrine of totalistic Westernization cannot, on the basis of the above propositions, be construed as implying a total rejection of Chinese tradition. For, by definition, the totalistic Westernization of China, through an "organic assimilation" of the modern civilization of the West by the distinctive Chinese scientific tradition, means that such an enterprise is founded upon the indigenous scientific tradition even

26. Ibid.

27. Hu Shih, "Ch'ing-tai hsüeh-che ti chih-hsüeh fang-fa," HSWT, 1st coll., 2:208–11.

28. This is Hu's own translation of his well-known statement about the essentials of the scientific method: "Ta-tan chia-she; hsiao-hsin ch'iu-cheng," which he uttered on numerous occasions. Hu Shih, "The Scientific Spirit and Method in Chinese Philosophy," in Charles A. Moore, ed., Philosophy and Culture—East and West (Honolulu, 1962), p. 221.

though those elements of Chinese tradition incompatible with modern Western civilization will be eliminated in this process.

As I said earlier, Hu's doctrine of evolutionary "organic assimilation" of modern Western civilization by Chinese civilization was based upon a notion of generic similarity between the two. This similarity he explained in terms of biological and environmental determinism. A civilization is a way of life in which a people adapt themselves to their given environment according to their biological needs. Particular variations in different civilizations are only the consequences of environment and time. The modern achievement of science and democracy in the West is due to the environmental imperatives in the history of the West during the last three hundred years. Believing as he did in the historical progress of mankind in general, Hu perceived the advent of the challenge of similar environments and problems to the Chinese. He predicted that science and democracy would undoubtedly flourish in China in the future. In short, in pursuit of his argument he denied any possibility of qualitative differences between Chinese and Western civilizations.[29]

As a cosmopolitan intellectual arguing on behalf of the idea of progress, Hu Shih was unabashedly committed to the ideas and values of John Dewey not only as a set of particular Western ideas and values but as the most advanced ideas and values of world civilization, which every civilization should, according to him, sooner or later follow. It is quite plain that Hu Shih's scientistic reformism was primarily a means for the Deweyanization of China, not, so far as his intellectual commitment and reasoning were concerned, an authentic search for a Chinese cultural identity in the process of China's modernization. If Hu's "reformism" did not originate in a search for a Chinese cultural identity, what were the major reasons for it? One we have just noted: he saw it as the route to the Deweyanization of China. Another lay in the cultural nationalism which he retained at an implicit level of his consciousness, despite his misgivings about various kinds of nationalism. He was in search of something in Chinese tradition from which he could derive a sense of self-respect as a Chinese to counteract his genuine sense of the inferiority of Chinese tradition in the face of his adopted Western values. He associated himself with the scientific tradition of China partly as a cultural nationalist who took pride in the existence of a tradition that enabled him to propose an "organic assimilation" of the modern civilization of the West.[30]

29. Hu Shih, "Tu Liang Sou-ming hsien-sheng ti *Tung Hsi wen-hua chi ch'i che-hsüeh*," *HSWT*, 2nd coll., 2:57–85.
30. Hu's ready and frequent admissions of defects in Chinese tradition gave an impression of tough-mindedness that was immune to the psychological need to assuage a sense of inferiority by

Hu Shih sometimes said, it should be pointed out, that the result of a totalistic Westernization of China would be a vitalized Chinese civilization on an indigenous basis and thus gave the impression that his doctrine of totalistic Westernization was merely a means to the end of vitalizing Chinese civilization.[31] But this is a confusion on Hu's part between his notion of what ought to be and his notion of what is or will be, and his "resolution" of the tension between his intellectual reasoning and commitment and his cultural nationalism. Insofar as his intellectual reasoning and commitment were concerned, a totalistic Westernization of Chinese civilization was a process as well as an end. The process was to be an evolutionary "organic assimilation" of the modern civilization of the West. Since his conception of modern Western civilization was not ambiguous but monistic, the end was clearly perceived: to make Chinese civilization become Deweyanized.

However, Hu also realized that the end that China ought to strive for was in practice out of reach: given the conservative nature of civilization, total Westernization was quantitatively impossible. Sometimes he talked as though he rather appreciated this impossibility and would be glad to see Chinese civilization remain on an indigenous basis. But this feeling is an expression of his cultural nationalism, and nowhere can we find in his writings a substantial change of his doctrine of totalistic Westernization.

Hu's failure to discriminate between what ought to be and what is came increasingly to serve as a "resolution" of the tension between his intellectual commitment and his cultural nationalism in his later years. While Hu felt, under internal and external pressures, the strain upon his theory of totalistic Westernization, he was not able to face the problem squarely and to provide a viable theory for a creative transformation of Chinese tradition that would reject undesirable elements in the tradition, strive for modernity, and maintain

---

asserting, as did many of his contemporaries, that China possessed equivalents of many Western achievements. Hu's sense of pride in his hardheaded recognition of many Chinese defects gave additional weight to the notion that he was free from this psychological tension. However, although he had little emotional attachment to China's past, his finding of the scientific tradition in China was his own way of asserting that China had an equivalent (or protoequivalent) to an important development in America, and was a source of psychological stability which at least partly supported his tough-mindedness. This finding of a scientific tradition in China was a result of the interaction between Hu's psychological need to have a Chinese resource for facing the superior culture of America and his intellectual need to construct a reformist means for the drastic purpose of Deweyanizing China.

31. Hu Shih, "Shih-p'ing so-wei 'Chung-kuo pen-wei ti wen-hua chien-she'," in *Hu Shih lun-hsüeh chin-chu*, pp. 552–57.

in this process of modernization an authentic Chinese cultural identity. Instead, he claimed that his doctrine of totalistic Westernization was actually meant as a means to the end of vitalizing the indigenous civilization. In so doing, he could assure himself and others that there were no grounds to fear that the nation might lose its own civilization, while advocating that everyone should still try as hard as possible to become Deweyanized. Hu sometimes said that if there were real treasures in Chinese tradition they would be vitalized through the process of Westernization; but he simply evaded the question of *how* this would happen.

Hu sometimes also asserted that Chinese culture and Western culture should be synthesized. But this again is a rhetorical assertion promoted by his cultural nationalism. If everything in the indigenous tradition except a scientific method that was, at best, less advanced than that of the West was to be rejected, how could this synthesis possibly be justified and conducted? Hu Shih could hardly argue that John Dewey needed to learn the scientific method of the Han Learning for improving his theory and practice of scientific method. Since Hu held that traditional Chinese culture had nothing to offer the modern West, his suggestion of a synthesis between traditional Chinese and modern Western culture was a contradiction in terms.

TOTALISTIC ICONOCLASM

The story of Hu's attitude toward Chinese tradition is not fully told by an exposition of his scientistic reformism. That reformism, based upon a conception of generic similarity between traditional Chinese and modern Western civilization, was, in turn, supported by a theory of biological and environmental determinism which, far from encouraging pessimism and inaction, was used by Hu to support his hope for the success of a totalistic Westernization. As an optimistic reformist, he believed that new circumstances in Chinese society would induce China to become Westernized. History, he thought, was on his side; his role was to make the Chinese people aware of this historical trend and to point to a clear path along which the Westernization of China could be achieved.[32] However, Hu's "reformism" did not temper his iconoclastic urge to attack Chinese tradition in a totalistic fashion. He did not seem aware of the discrepancy between that sort of attack and the theory of biological and environmental determinism as a basis for his "reformism." If everything is determined by biology and environment, the evils in the tradition are

32. Hu Shih, "Tu Liang Sou-ming hsien-sheng ti *Tung Hsi wen-hua chi ch'i che-hsüeh*," *HSWT*, 2nd coll., 2:82–85.

reducible to two externally and historically given factors. Nothing can be legitimately blamed; there is thus no case for iconoclasm. But Hu was so much influenced by the cultural-intellectualistic approach, which in his case had by then already evolved into an intellectualistic-holistic mode of thinking, that he assumed that the evil of Chinese tradition was caused, in the final analysis, by a disease of the traditional Chinese mind. A deep-rooted, cultural predisposition had blocked him from recognizing a contradictory implication of his theory of biological and environmental determinism.

Hu felt that cruelty, laziness, and suppression of the individual are the fundamental and distinctive features of the Chinese tradition. Nothing less than the notion that the traditional Chinese mind is wickedly diseased could account for the nature of that tradition.

In his joint reply, with Ch'en Tu-hsiu, to a reader's letter in the October 15, 1918, issue of *New Youth*, he said "The old literature, old politics, and old ethics have always belonged to one family; we cannot abandon one and preserve the others."[33] In his preface to the *Collected Essays of Wu Yü* (*Wu Yü wen-lu*) he hailed Wu as "the old hero from Szechwan who beat Confucius and Sons single-handedly."[34] Hu praised Wu Yü as the man who, by his assaults on Confucianism as a whole, swept away all the dirt in the street so the young could travel. Hu's ultimate justification for a totalistic attack on Confucianism was similar to Ch'en Tu-hsiu's justification for his anti-Confucianism. Indeed, Hu quoted the key passage of Ch'en's reply to Ch'ang Nai-te (see above, pp. 74–75) to support his approval of Wu Yü's attack on Confucianism, although a certain ambiguity in his language should be noted. Hu said, "Because the cannibalistic *li-chiao*, laws, and institutions for the last two thousand years have all hung out a signboard of Confucius, this signboard of Confucius—whether it is from the old shop or a counterfeit—must be crushed and burned!"[35] The sentence, read out of context, might be taken to imply that all the *li-chiao*, laws, and institutions have been conducted in the name of Confucius, but that it is an open question whether or not the original teachings of Confucius would agree with their form and content. However, in this essay Hu expressed his approval of Ch'en Tu-hsiu's reply to Ch'ang

33. *HCN*, 5.4:433 (October 15, 1918).
34. Wu Yü, *Wu Yü wen-lu* (Shanghai, 1921), p. vii, or *HSWT*, 1st coll., 4:259. Wu Yü appreciated some of the ideas in Taoism, Legalism, and Buddhism but regarded them as inconsequential because they failed to change the Confucian nature of traditional Chinese culture and society. *Wu Yü wen-lu*, 1:23–46; 2:1–10, 15–20.
35. *Wu Yü wen-lu*, pp. vi–vii, or *HSWT*, 1st coll., 4:259.

Nai-te; it is therefore clear that, completely in line with Ch'en's holistic anti-Confucianism, Chinese *li-chiao,* laws, and institutions for the last two thousand years had for Hu also derived from the original teachings of Confucius, and that Confucianism as such should be overthrown.

The two pieces of Hu's writings just cited are the main evidence of his attack on Confucianism in toto. In his later attacks on the Chinese cultural tradition he did not single out any particular strain as his target. Hu would undoubtedly have admitted that the Chinese cultural tradition consisted of many things: Confucianism, Taoism, Legalism, literature, art, and so on. But he was not interested in making differentiations in his attacks on the Chinese tradition. His antitraditionalism can therefore be legitimately described as totalistic.

Hu did not slight Confucius in his scholarly writings. Confucius had grasped some universal human values, such as *chung* (loyalty), *hsiao* (filial piety), *jen* (benevolence), and *ai* (compassion). But Hu argued, as did Ch'en Tu-hsiu, that to defend Chinese tradition in terms of these values is beside the point: they are universal ideals of mankind shared by all civilizations in the world and hence cannot explain the particular nature of Chinese tradition. Moreover, there is no way to realize them in China, and they are, Hu said, "merely empty terms."[36] What has characterized Chinese tradition are China's "unique treasures": "eight-legged essays, bound feet, eunuchs, concubinage, five-generation households, memorial arches for honoring chastity, hellish prisons, and law courts filled with instruments of torture."[37] Hu pointed out that "in the span of seven or eight hundred years of the prevalence of Neo-Confucianism not even one Neo-Confucian sage or worthy had recognized that binding young girls' feet was an inhuman and barbarous act."[38] On the contrary, "everybody believed in the injunction of the cannibalistic *li-*

---

36. Hu Shih, "Tsai lun hsin-hsing yü fan-hsing," in *Hu Shih lun-hsüeh chin-chu,* pp. 488, 490.

37. Hu Shih, "Hsin-hsin yü fan-hsing," ibid., p. 483.

38. Ibid. Hu was so much carried away by ideological ardor that he failed to mention or remember Li Ju-chen's diatribe against the custom of binding women's feet in his novel *Flowers in the Mirror (Ching-hua yüan).* Li Ju-chen may not be regarded as a Neo-Confucian sage or worthy, but his excoriation of the custom of binding women's feet was not influenced by any foreign sources. Li's novel, according to Hu Shih's research, was published about 1825. Another account dates it about 1820. Hu Shih, "Ching-hua yüan ti yin-lun," *HSWT,* 2nd coll., 4:119–68 (written during February–May, 1923). See also Pao Chia-lin, "Li Ju-chen ti nan-nü p'ing-teng ssu-hsiang," *Shih-huo yüeh-k'an,* n. s., 1.12:12–21 (March 1972). It seems that when Hu was engaged in a totalistic attack on Chinese tradition, his mind had no room to accommodate any challenging evidence. He thus, perhaps unconsciously, brushed it aside.

chiao that 'To be starved to death is a petty thing but to lose chastity is a great event.' '''[39] Hu did not reduce these evils or China's "unique treasures" to biological or environmental factors but to the evil nature of the traditional Chinese mind—they were "the evils created by our ancestors.'''[40] Since the traditional Chinese mind is evil, every element of the cultural tradition shares this nature, according to Hu's holistic mode of thinking. An attack on Chinese tradition, if it is to serve any purpose, had to be totalistic.

Hu quite readily admitted that "there are bedbugs in the West, too,''[41] such as chastity belts and *droit du seigneur*. But these Western evils were isolated instances, not comparable to the "unique treasures" of China, which were not isolated or accidental cases but typical products of the traditional Chinese mind.[42]

It should be noted that Hu came to appreciate, "after twenty years of reflection," three valuable things in Chinese tradition: the simple grammar of the Chinese language, the comparatively more equal social structure of traditional Chinese society, and a mentality little inclined to religious superstition.[43] Of these three things, the first two could not affect his totalistic iconoclasm. The first had to do with a formal aspect of the language that could hardly be considered to have any bearing on the moral quality of the tradition. The second Hu explained in terms of historical circumstances, thus detaching its merits from the traditional Chinese mind. The third, however, might have changed or modified his iconoclasm. He recognized a particular naturalistic and secular element in the traditional Chinese mind. ("Naturalistic," "rational," and "scientific [or protoscientific]" were quite synonymous for

39. Hu Shih, "Hsin-hsin yü fan-hsing," p. 483.

40. Hu Shih, "San-lun hsin-hsin yü fan-hsing," in *Hu Shih lun-hsüeh chin-chu,* p. 495.

41. A sarcastic remark by Chou Tso-jen, in his letter to Hu Shih, about those who took pleasure in learning that there were also reprehensible desires, customs, and so on, in the West. Chou Tso-jen, "Hsi-yang yeh-yu ch'ou-ch'ung," *Tu-li p'ing-lun,* 107:12 (July 1, 1934). Hu quoted this remark in *Hu Shih lun-hsüeh chin-chu,* p. 494.

42. Hu Shih, "San-lun hsin-hsin yü fan-hsing," pp. 494–95.

43. Ibid., pp. 496–97. It is not clear how Hu would have reconciled the discrepancy (if he was aware of it) between his assertion that the traditional Chinese mentality was little inclined to religious superstition, presumably because of a strong place accorded to reason, and his frequent condemnations of other kinds of deeply ingrained superstitions of the Chinese, such as the superstitious beliefs in names (or labels). See Hu Shih, "Ming-chiao," *HSWT,* 3rd coll., 1:91– 107. Why were the Chinese susceptible to other kinds of superstitions if they were little inclined to "religious superstition"? Even if he was aware of this question, he never faced it or dealt with it in any substantive or sustained manner. In any case, as I indicate in the text below, Hu's conception of the rational mentality of the Chinese did not modify his iconoclastic perspective.

him.) Such a recognition was implicitly related to his identifying, in his doctrine of evolutionary Westernization, a distinctive Chinese element as a sort of scientific rationality, and it should have implied to him that there was at least one element in Chinese tradition not to be attacked. This could have led him to modify his totalistic iconoclasm. But from examining Hu Shih's iconoclastic thought as a whole, it is clear that he did not draw such an inference. While Hu believed, with Dewey, that scientific rationality was inherently moral, he knew that such a rational element in the traditional Chinese mind, although it was useful for the construction of his doctrine of evolutionary Westernization, did not function in any moral sense. Hence, such a rational element in the traditional Chinese mind is irrelevant to the moral (or immoral) nature of Chinese tradition.

That the notion of the irrelevancy of the traditional rational element was implicit in Hu's evaluation of Chinese tradition can be borne out through an analysis of his conception of the harmful influence of Buddhism upon Chinese civilization. When Hu was more susceptible to his mood of cultural nationalism, he tended to see the cruelty of Chinese people in terms of the influence of Buddhism.[44] But in his iconoclastic writings he did not regard Chinese cruelty as the result of the Buddhist influence, for emancipation from the Buddhist influence by the reassertion of an indigenous rational element in the Chinese mind during the Sung and Ming periods, he realized, had not correspondingly produced a more humane civilization. Thus, there were no grounds for attributing the cruelty of the Chinese to a foreign influence. In short, it seems difficult to escape from the conclusion that Hu regarded the traditional Chinese mind as fundamentally and categorically wicked. The rational element in it was holistically bound or governed by a more fundamental element that was evil.

Since the traditional Chinese mind was so diseased, it could not cure itself through its own resources. Its salvation was possible only after the advent of Western civilization on the Chinese scene. The elimination of eight-legged essays, bound feet, and so on, Hu said, was not at all due to the effort of Ch'eng I, Chu Hsi, Ku Yen-wu, Tai Chen, and others, but to the contact of Chinese people with the modern civilization of the West. But, although the evil custom of binding young girls' feet and the sterile style of eight-legged essays have been destroyed, "the cruel and barbarous psyche of torturing

44. For instance, Hu Shih, "The Indianization of China," *Independence, Convergence and Borrowing in Institution, Thought and Art* (Cambridge, Mass., 1937), pp. 244–46.

people and of binding young girls' feet still is occupying the *minds* of infinite numbers of old and young people [in China]. China today is still a cruel and barbarous nation. That is why [we] have never reached the road to the rule of law, let alone *jen, ai,* and *ho-p'ing* (benevolence, compassion, and peace)."[45] Presumably, then, a complete salvation of the Chinese people depends on whether or not they can be totally Westernized.

It can be seen that it is a logical contradiction on the part of Hu to make a traditional element the basis for his evolutionary reformism while attacking the tradition in a totalistic fashion. From Hu's iconoclastic perspective, however, the traditional Chinese scientific element, useful though it was as a means to get China Westernized and thus not to be attacked, was in Chinese tradition an irrelevant element. It is therefore understandable that this logical contradiction was not acutely felt by Hu, who always thought his primary duty, as a true Deweyan, was to think clearly.[46]

In Hu's later years he made a number of qualifications of his doctrine of totalistic iconoclasm and totalistic Westernization. If they are read in isolation without having their implications weighed in the context of Hu's thought, they might seem to contradict my analysis. But carefully considered, these qualifications emerge as a rhetorical patchwork—resulting from a need to relieve the strain of the earlier doctrine—rather than as a tenable defense or genuine revision of that doctrine. For instance, during an interview in 1958 Hu Shih said: "Many people consider me an anti-Confucianist, and I have been critical of many aspects of this long history of Confucianism. But on the whole, I've shown in all of my writings a fairly high respect for Confucius and his early followers such as Mencius. And I have great respect for one of the founders of Neo-Confucianism in the twelfth century, Chu Hsi. I do not call myself essentially an anti-Confucianist."[47] But, what did he mean when he said that he had shown respect for Confucius, Mencius, and Chu Hsi? Can we take his statement at face value? As indicated earlier, in his scholarly writings Hu Shih did not slight Confucius. And Chu Hsi had demonstrated the Chinese rational mentality through his scientific methodology in his scholarly research.

45. Hu Shih, "Tsai-lun hsin-hsin yü fan-hsing," p. 491. Italics mine.
46. Hu Shih used to say that "it is from Professor Dewey that I have learned that the most sacred responsibility of a man's life is to endeavor to think well. To think sluggishly, to think without strict regard to the antecedents and consequences of thought, to accept ready-made and unanalyzed concepts as premises of thinking, to allow personal factors unconsciously to influence one's thinking, or to fail to test one's ideas by working out their results is to be intellectually irresponsible." Hu Shih, "My Credo and Its Evolution," p. 255.
47. Hu Shih, "Dr. Hu Shih's Personal Reminiscences," p. 263.

Sometimes—usually before a foreign audience—Hu even said that Confucius and Mencius had planted seeds for democracy through the Confucian idea of equality in education and the Mencian advocacy of "the right of rebellion against tyrannical government."[48] But what did his statements imply? Even granting that all these ideas were not afterthoughts but implicitly grasped by Hu during the flood-tide of his antitraditionalism, they did not prevent him from remorselessly attacking Chinese tradition in totalistic terms. As I have shown, they were a useful tool for his program of totalistic Westernization of China but they did not play a positive role in making traditional Chinese society and culture less evil from the perspective of his intellectualistic and holistic thinking. In other words, they served merely as ingredients for his pseudoreformism.[49]

48. Hu Shih, "Historical Foundations for a Democratic China," in *E. J. James Lectures on Government,* 2nd ser. (Urbana, 1941), pp. 54–55. Hu Shih's language is quite loose here. Hu quotes a statement in the *Mencius,* IVB.3., to support his interpretation: "When a ruler treats his subject like grass and dirt, then the subject should treat him as a bandit and an enemy." (This is Hu Shih's translation. A more literal rendition is: "When a ruler regards his ministers as dirt and grass, the ministers regard him as a bandit and an enemy.") Here Mencius is discussing the principle of reciprocity between the ruler and his ministers in government. In the *Mencius,* the subjects are indeed entitled to revolt against a despotic ruler, but this "right" does not entail a concept of popular sovereignty. The legitimacy of the universal king is based on the mandate he receives from Heaven. But "Heaven does not speak"; "Heaven sees as my people see, Heaven hears as my people hear" (*Mencius,* VA.5). The Mandate of Heaven manifests itself through the acceptance of the king's rule by the people. Revolt may be regarded as a sign of the king's losing the mandate; but only after a successful revolt, when another ruling house is securely established, can one be sure that the former king has actually lost it. If the revolt is suppressed, it can only be regarded as a disturbance of the harmony of the Middle Kingdom. The notion that political illegitimacy is determined by the success of the people's revolt is still within the bounds of the conception of universal kingship; it does not alter the fact that the Mandate of Heaven can be transmitted only to a new king, not to the people. The people have no right to govern themselves, and there is no way to institutionalize the Mandate of Heaven except within the framework of the Chinese universal kingship.

49. In his theory of literary revolution, Hu maintained that the history of traditional Chinese literature was a record of the vitality of vernacular language in shaping the evolution of literary forms and hence literary revolution consisted not in rejecting this prevailing trend of the past but in further developing it. See Hu Shih, "Wen-hsüeh kai-liang ch'u-i," "Li-shih ti wen-hsüeh kuan-nien lun," and "Chien-she ti wen-hsüeh ke-ming lun," *HSWT,* 1st coll., 1:7–24, 45–49, 71–96. This theory, while it served as a foundation for the literary revolution at the time, is too simplistic to recommend itself now. But it poses two questions vis-à-vis Hu's totalistic iconoclasm, when that iconoclasm is literally maintained. First, how could Hu have clung to a stance of totalistic rejection of the Chinese past while accepting and developing a prevailing trend in Chinese literature from the past? Secondly, if the Chinese mind was so holistically diseased, how could it have been receptive to the vitality of the vernacular language? Yet, if he was aware of these questions, they did not constitute a serious challenge to his totalistic iconoclasm, although they reveal a formal or logical difficulty in it. Hu's theory of the development of Chinese

On another occasion, Hu qualified the anti-Confucianism expressed in his preface to the *Collected Essays of Wu Yü* with the following statement: "Many reactionary things in China hung out signboards of Confucius. In order to overthrow these reactionary things, it is natural that we should knock down these signboards. This is different from overthrowing Confucius."[50] This statement suggests that what he did was attack the image of Confucius or what people made out of Confucius, but not Confucius the man and presumably also not the ideas of Confucius. Yet what Hu said here was precisely *not* what he implied in the celebrated introduction to Wu Yü. As I have shown

---

literature was advocated more to fit his Deweyan idea of historical evolution than to interpret viably the complex history of Chinese literature. A committed instrumentalist, Hu took as a point of departure the Deweyan idea that change should be evolutionary. Seeking some traditional sources for constructing his theory of literary revolution, a theory which was formally supported by his knowledge that in the West, at the time of the Renaissance, vernacular languages had been used to compose new literature, such as Dante's *Divine Comedy,* Hu, differing from some literary critics, came to perceive the vernacular language used, he maintained, by the past Chinese men of letters and the content of traditional Chinese literature as not being organically interrelated. Consequently, he could advocate following a prevailing trend from the past (that is, using the living speech) in expressing the ideas and values of modernity and modernization inspired by the West. To engage in a totalistic cultural iconoclasm was for Hu to reject totally the *substance* of traditional Chinese ideas and values; the literary medium of vernacular language was now regarded as being not organically related to this substance. It was therefore not difficult for Hu to accept the prevailing trend he found in the evolution of Chinese literature as a means for expressing categorically new ideas and values without feeling a challenge to his totalistic iconoclasm. Moreover, it was clear to him that, although the vernacular literary style had been a vital force in the development of Chinese literature, it had not had any positive influence on the evil or useless substantive ideas and values of the Chinese past. There were, to be sure, aesthetic and moral features in Chinese literature that Hu appreciated, and they were expressed in particularly Chinese literary forms, but he could easily have assumed—in the same way that he reduced the good moral values and ideas in traditional China to common denominators of all civilizations— that they were common elements of world literature and hence not peculiarly Chinese. Insofar as the holistically diseased Chinese mind could express some common elements of world literature, the mind was receptive to the vernacular language for expressing them. This of course raises the questions why there were some common elements of world literature in the Chinese tradition and why the traditional Chinese mind, if holistically diseased, could be receptive to the vernacular language for expressing them. That these questions cannot be answered discloses a logical or formal difficulty in Hu's totalistic iconoclasm. But it can be readily understood that Hu did not feel an acute need to answer these questions precisely because they merely posed themselves in a formal way but were not related to the peculiarly Chinese substance of Chinese literature with which his totalistic iconoclasm was concerned. For these reasons, Hu could uphold his evolutionary theory for literary revolution without feeling that, substantively, his totalistic iconoclasm was being greatly challenged.

50. Cited in Hu Sung-p'ing, "Hu Shih hsien-sheng nien-p'u chien-pien," *Ta-lu tsa-chih,* 43.1:6 (July 15, 1971).

earlier, the statements in Hu's essay indicate plainly that he was using the same intellectualistic-holistic argument as Ch'en Tu-hsiu to attack Confucianism not in terms of substantive analysis of the content of Confucius' ideas but through the assumption that the Confucian tradition was holistically shaped by the ideas of Confucius.

In summary, instead of offering an intellectually viable revision of his earlier doctrine of totalistic antitraditionalism and totalistic Westernization, Hu Shih kept repeating his earlier ideas and sometimes insisted he was not what he really was. This kind of apologia betrayed his inability, in his later years, to deal squarely with the strain evident in his earlier doctrine. The dominance in his consciousness of the intellectualistic-holistic mode of thinking may be seen as a major factor in his lack of resources for breaking out of the confinement of his earlier doctrine of totalistic iconoclasm and Westernization.

6

THE COMPLEX CONSCIOUSNESS OF LU HSÜN

Lu Hsün's consciousness is characterized by a profound and unresolved tension between an iconoclastic totalism and an intellectual and moral commitment to some traditional Chinese values. I shall here, in the interest of brevity, delineate only one such value—the principle of *nien-chiu* (roughly, "cherishing old ties")—and Lu Hsün's commitment to it, but I believe that my discussion of this issue will demonstrate the intensity of this tension, and its indelible effects on him.

The tension cannot fruitfully be analyzed in terms of a formal contradiction between a totalistic rejection of the Chinese tradition and an appreciation of certain elements in that tradition. Nor is it appropriate to apply Joseph Levenson's well-known dichotomy between "history" and "value"—the tension between an intellectual commitment to Western values and an emotional attachment to China's past. (I must, indeed, take issue with those who seem unable or unwilling to perceive the consciousness of modern Chinese intellectuals in any other terms.[1]) There existed in Lu Hsün a tension not between the two spheres of emotion and intellect but within the same intellectual and moral sphere. In other words, this tension inevitably occurred because, owing to rational consideration and moral concerns, Lu Hsün both rejected Chinese tradition in toto and found some elements in traditional Chinese culture and morals meaningful. His positive attitude toward some traditional elements did not, however, lead him to look for the possibility of a creative transformation of Chinese tradition. Rather, it caused him great agony—indeed, a sense of guilt—in the face of an iconoclastic totalism in which he also deeply believed.

In delineating the complex consciousness of Lu Hsün, it is convenient, for analytical purposes, to distinguish three levels: the explicit, conscious level, another level that is also conscious but is unexplicated, and the subconscious level. An inquiry into the significance of this last category would lead me far afield and I shall not treat it in detail, apart from occasional references to some pieces in the collection of Lu Hsün's prose poems, *The Wild Grass* (*Yeh-ts'ao*), which is, among other things, an important source for fathoming the nature of his subconscious during 1924-25.

What I shall focus on are the two conscious levels, the explicit and the implicit (I shall define the latter below). The explicit level of Lu Hsün's consciousness can, itself, be viewed under four aspects: the polemical, the scholarly, the stylistic, and the personal and aesthetic. The polemical aspect of his consciousness can be understood by an exposition of the concerns overtly expressed in his essays and of the ideas to be inferred from those creative writings, ideas that generically and structurally take the mode of his explicit polemical concerns. I shall begin with an exploration of the origins and development of these concerns during his student days in Japan.

A CATEGORY OF ANALYSIS AND EARLY CONCERNS

Lu Hsün went to Japan to study in 1902 after his graduation from the School of Railways and Mines in Nanking. After two years at Kōbun Institute in Tokyo for language training, he went to Sendai Medical School in the autumn

---

1. This chapter is, among other things, an attempt to deal with subject matter in modern Chinese intellectual history with which Levenson was not concerned. Levenson's thesis represents an approach to problems of quite a different kind, and I do not believe that it was originally intended as an analytical category to explain the complex consciousness of such a creative figure as Lu Hsün. While I assume that Levenson would not have claimed that his way of understanding

of 1904. Medicine was then not a popular subject among Chinese students in Japan, and Lu Hsün's decision to study it in Sendai—a remote provincial town in northeast Honshu where no Chinese student had ever gone before—was particularly unusual. According to his own account, his decision to become a physician arose from the traumatic experience of helplessly witnessing the suffering of his mortally ill father under the mistreatment of traditional Chinese herb doctors, coupled with his later knowledge that the modernization of Japan had originated, to a large extent, with the introduction of Western medical science. "I dreamed a beautiful dream," recalled Lu Hsün, "that on my return to China I would cure patients like my father, who had been wrongly treated, while if war broke out I could serve as an army doctor. At the same time I would strengthen my countrymen's faith in modernization."[2] However, although he did adequately well and was very much liked by a professor named Fujino Genkurō, about whom he reminisced warmly in one of his later writings,[3] in 1906 he gave up his medical studies and committed himself to literary endeavors. The incident associated with this decision has been frequently mentioned in books and articles about Lu Hsün according to what he described himself. A microbiology instructor, having ended his lecture early, was showing slides taken during the Russo-Japanese War (1904–5). One in particular provoked the laughter of Lu Hsün's Japanese classmates:

> I saw a slide showing a number of my fellow Chinese, whom I had not seen for quite some time. One of them was bound, while the others stood around him. They were all strong fellows but appeared completely apathetic. According to

---

had exhausted all possible perspectives for future research, his relentless, though brilliant, ramifications of a dichotomous thesis did restrict his understanding of the complex realities of modern Chinese intellectual history. Cf. Joseph R. Levenson, *Liang Ch'i-ch'ao and the Mind of Modern China* (Cambridge, Mass., 1959) and *Confucian China and Its Modern Fate,* 3 vols. (Berkeley, 1958–65).

2. Lu Hsün, "Tzu-hsü," *Na-han, LHCC,* 1:4. In translating this and subsequent passages from Lu Hsün's writings, I have consulted whenever possible available translations such as *Selected Works of Lu Hsün,* tr. Yang Hsien-yi and Gladys Yang, 4 vols. (Peking, 1956–61); *Ah Q and Others,* tr. Chi-chen Wang (New York, 1941); *Silent China: Selected Writings of Lu Xun [Lu Hsün],* ed. and tr. Gladys Yang (London, 1973), among others. Lu Hsün's own account of his father's illness and death is in his "Fu-ch'in te-ping," *Chao-hua hsi-shih, LHCC,* 2:257–62. Hsü Shou-shang (*Wo-so jen-shih ti Lu Hsün* [Peking, 1952], p. 19) said that Lu Hsün's decision to become a physician was also motivated by his desire to help Chinese women who had let out their bound feet. There was another personal reason that prompted Lu Hsün to decide to become a physician. See note 11 below.

3. Lu Hsün, "T'eng-yeh [Fujino] hsien-sheng," *Chao-hua hsi-shih, LHCC,* 2:271–77.

the commentary, the one with his hands bound was a spy working for the Russians, who was to have his head cut off by the Japanese military as a warning to others. The other Chinese had come to enjoy the spectacle.

Before the academic year was over, I had already left for Tokyo; for, I felt henceforward that medicine was not such an important matter. An ignorant and weak people, however strong and healthy they may be, can be no more than senseless raw material or audience for the executioner; and it is not necessarily deplorable that many of them should die of illness. Thus, the first work of importance is to transform their spirit. Since I was certain at the time that literature was the best means to this end, I decided to promote a literary movement.[4]

Although this experience in Lu Hsün's life dramatized his commitment to working toward intellectual and cultural change in China, it was by no means the major reason for his decision to embark on a literary career. The event was a catalytic rather than a decisive factor in his giving up medical studies. The roots of this decision lay much deeper. Lu Hsün's personal preference had always been for literary and artistic matters. He was an avid reader from early adolescence. Apart from the *Four Books,* the *Five Classics,* some standard collections of poems, and orthodox histories, which were required texts in the school he attended in his home town, Shaohsing, he did a great deal of "unorthodox" reading—traditional novels, folklore, Taoist texts and commentaries, heterodox historical works, local histories, and treatises on painting. These "miscellaneous readings" (*tsa-lan*), as his brother Chou Tso-jen called them,[5] did much to expose him to the realities of Chinese society and culture, and led him to transcend narrow orthodoxies in sociopolitical and cultural matters. Later, this background contributed substantially to Lu Hsün's ability as a social critic, for he could draw on an immense knowledge, accumulated from his formative years, of Chinese social, cultural, and literary history. Lu Hsün also had a lifelong interest in graphic art, which evolved from his hobby in childhood and adolescence of copying pictures from books in traditional woodblock or lithographic editions.[6] Furthermore, Lu Hsün's

4. Lu Hsün, "Tzu-hsü," *Na-han, LHCC,* 1:4–5.

5. Chou Tso-jen, "Kuan-yü Lu Hsün," in his *Kua-tou chi* (Shanghai, 1937), p. 225.

6. Ibid., pp. 212–26. A partial list of Lu Hsün's collection of books at this early stage appears on pp. 217–8. Lu Hsün also enjoyed copying rare or interesting texts, and this later led to the publication of his compilations of old literary records and notes relating to Shaohsing, as well as his meticulously edited *Hsi K'ang chi (Complete works of Hsi K'ang).* See Chou Hsia-shou (Chou Tso-jen), *Lu Hsün ti ku-chia* (Hong Kong, 1962), pp. 50–51 and 77–78, and the reminiscence of another brother, Ch'iao Feng (Chou Chien-jen), *Lüeh-chiang kuan-yü Lu Hsün ti shih-ch'ing* (Peking, 1954), pp. 3–5.

"Notes of Chia-chien-sheng," written at seventeen, and his classical poems, "Parting with My Brothers" ("Pieh chu-ti") and "Pity for Flowers" ("Hsi-hua"), written at nineteen and twenty, reveal that he had already become an accomplished essayist and poet.[7] His youthful poems are especially notewor-thy for their thoughtful content and supple style.[8]

Thoroughly equipped by his knowledge and technical training to become a writer, and awakened to ardent patriotism by the plight of his country and by the translations and essays of Yen Fu and Liang Ch'i-ch'ao, which he en-thusiastically read in Nanking in 1898–1902, Lu Hsün already was deeply concerned about the fate of China when he went to study in Japan. An old friend, Hsü Shou-shang, recalls that he was greatly impressed by Lu Hsün's searching concerns when they came to know each other at Kōbun Institute in 1902. As Hsü emphasizes in his reminiscences, Lu Hsün was preoccupied with such questions as: What is the ideal nature of man? What is the greatest deficiency in the nature of the Chinese people? What is the root of the sickness of the Chinese people?[9] In their discussions they found the greatest deficiency in the nature of the Chinese people to be "the lack of sincerity and love—in other words, the Chinese had been too deeply infected by hypocrisy, shamelessness, and suspicion."[10]

In this way, Lu Hsün, prior to his medical studies, had already defined the central problem of China's crisis in terms of the defective nature of the Chinese people. Such an attitude implied that the transformation of the nature of the Chinese people was the fundamental solution for the various problems of China. But a distinction must be made here between the recognition of the problem and a decision to make the solution of it a personal task. It would have been too presumptuous for a young man of twenty-three, who had a skeptical disposition and disdained his fellow students' boastful talk, to think that it was his personal mission to change the nature of his people. Lu Hsün selected the limited but more tangible role of the physician not only for the

---

7. These writings are collected in Lu Hsün, *Chi-wai chi shih-i*, *LHCC*, 7:709–21.

8. See the appreciative remarks about Lu Hsün's "Pity for Flowers" by Chou Tso-jen in his *Lu Hsün ti ku-chia*, p. 173.

9. Lu Hsün's frequent discussions of these questions made such a deep impression on Hsü Shou-shang that he repeatedly mentions them in his reminiscences of Lu Hsün. See Hsü Shou-shang, *Wo-so jen-shih ti Lu Hsün*, pp. 8 and 18, and Hsü Shou-shang, *Wang-yu Lu Hsün yin-hsiang chi* (Peking, 1953), p. 20.

10. Hsü Shou-shang, *Wo-so jen-shih ti Lu Hsün*, pp. 18–19.

personal reasons earlier mentioned[11] but also to demonstrate conscientiously the value of modern scientific knowledge; in this way he would contribute to the reconstruction of China. Activity of this sort could hardly by itself lead to the transformation of the nature of the Chinese people, yet it would at least not contravene that goal or give him a bad conscience, in view of his awareness of the fundamental problem.

Lu Hsün's choice of a provincial town far away from Tokyo for his medical studies was dictated by his contempt for the shallowness and sometimes downright hypocrisy of his fellow students. Most Chinese students came to Tokyo in the name of patriotism, but for all their talk, they were too ready to conform to current fads, and too often opportunistic in their selection of profitable subjects to study, such as politics, law, and police administration. Lu Hsün's decision to go to Sendai rather than to a medical school near Tokyo (which he could have entered had he so wished) was motivated by a desire to dissociate himself from the Chinese student community.[12] He has provided a vivid description of his feeling at the time:

> Tokyo was not so extraordinary after all. When cherry blossoms shimmered in Ueno, from the distance it really resembled light, pink clouds; but under the flowers you would always find groups of short-term "students from the Ch'ing Empire," their long queues coiled on top of their heads, pushing up the crowns of their student caps to look like Mount Fuji. Others had undone their queues and arranged their hair flat on their heads, so that when their caps were removed it glistened for all the world like the lustrous locks of young ladies; and they would toss their heads too. It was really a charming sight.
>
> In the gatehouse of the Chinese Students' Union there were some books on sale, and it was worth going there sometimes. In the mornings you could sit and rest in the foreign-style rooms inside. But toward the evening the floor of one

---

11. In addition to witnessing his father's suffering, Lu Hsün himself had had a shattering experience with traditional Chinese medicine when he suffered severely from toothache at fourteen and fifteen. Not only was the medicine of the herb doctors ineffective but Lu Hsün was humiliated by their theories, according to which men's teeth were physiologically related to the kidneys, which were considered male sex organs—toothache therefore implied sexual weakness, presumably as a result of self-indulgence. When Lu Hsün complained of his toothache he was promptly told that he should be ashamed of himself for mentioning it. Henceforward he endured his pain in silence. This experience, he told Sun Fu-yüan, also had something to do with his decision to become a doctor of Western medicine. Sun Fu-yüan, *Lu Hsün hsien-sheng erh-san shih* (Shanghai, 1945), pp. 66–67. For Lu Hsün's own account, see his "Ts'ung hu-hsü shuo-tao ya-chih," *Fen, LHCC*, 1:338–39.

12. See Chou Hsia-shou (Chou Tso-jen), *Lu Hsün hsiao-shuo li-ti jen-wu* (Shanghai, 1954), p. 6.

room would often be shaken by a deafening tramp of feet, and dust would fill
the whole place. If you questioned those in the know, the answer would be:
"They are learning ball-room dancing."
   Then why not go somewhere else?
   So I went to the medical school in Sendai.[13]

After Lu Hsün arrived in Sendai, where he no longer found "students from
the Ch'ing Empire" to be ashamed of, his sense of estrangement from them
receded into the background. On the other hand, his experience in the lantern
slides session once again brought to the fore a notion implicit all along: the
fundamental task in rejuvenating China, to be accomplished before anything
else, was the transformation of the nature of the Chinese people. Theoretically, there could have been many alternative proposals for the realization of
this goal. Lu Hsün's decision to engage in literature to attain this end resulted,
however, from the coalescence of his personal propensities and talent with the
cultural-intellectualistic approach that was deeply ingrained within him.
Moreover, the sense of urgency stimulated by the slide-viewing session dispelled whatever reservations he might have had about personally taking up the
task. The spiritual sickness was so serious that he felt compelled to do whatever he could then and there.
   After returning to Tokyo, Lu Hsün launched with Chou Tso-jen and a few
friends a project for a literary magazine with the avowed purpose of changing
the spirit of the Chinese people. This youthful effort proved abortive through
lack of support. In 1907 he wrote a number of essays in the classical style for
other student journals, which went largely unnoticed at the time. But they are
important for understanding his evolutionist and reformist ideas, and an
analysis of their implications reveals both the dominance of his cultural-
intellectualistic approach and his presupposition that some Chinese cultural
elements in the traditional framework remained viable.
   In "On Extremities in Cultural Development" ("Wen-hua p'ien-chih
lun"), probably his most important essay of this period, Lu Hsün began with
an excoriation of the various prevailing modes of response to the West. Since
China's defeats at the hands of the foreign powers, Lu Hsün observed, there
had been those who, being merely able to scratch the surface of China's
problems, had advocated strengthening the military power of the country.

---

13. Lu Hsün, "T'eng-yeh [Fujino] hsien-sheng," *Chao-hua hsi-shih, LHCC,* 2:271. See also
Chou Hsia-shou (Chou Tso-jen), *Lu Hsün hsiao-shuo li ti jen-wu,* p. 230.

Many returned students, without understanding either China's situation or the substance of Western civilization, echoed this idea with ideas picked up abroad, ideas Lu Hsün scorned as the rubbish of the West. Their attitude that military strength per se was a sign of civilization particularly irritated Lu Hsün, who reminded his readers that acquiring armaments could be justified only in terms of self-defense. "Furthermore, even if one grants the importance of military strength, could China acquire it," he asked, "if the people are still weak and backward?"[14] A nation should not set military might as its ultimate goal. Lu Hsün recognized the necessity of acquiring modern weapons for national defense, but without a new spiritual and cultural foundation, he argued, they could not be practically effective.

As to those who advocated industry and commerce as well as constitutionalism and popular rule for China, Lu Hsün detected disguised, self-seeking motives among many of them, as he had among those who espoused strengthening China's military power. However, there were other advocates of constitutionalism and popular rule "who, for want of enough intelligence to seek a real solution for China's problems and yet being deeply pained by her defeats at the hands of the foreign powers, could only adopt a remnant of a former popular trend in the West [the belief in popular rule] and came to argue for the rise of the masses as a means of resisting foreign encroachments."[15] While unwittingly disclosing his evolutionist ideology—popular rule, he believed, was already anachronistic in the West—Lu Hsün maintained not only that the belief in the power of the majority was as superstitious as the belief in a charm or panacea but also that popular rule might easily degenerate into tyranny by the majority.

Lu Hsün's diatribes against the advocates of military power and his insistence on a cultural and spiritual transformation of the Chinese people were not particularly unusual; such views were shared by many sensitive Chinese intellectuals. But his idea of the obsolescence of popular rule deserves special note. Amidst the clamor for democracy by the majority of the Chinese intelligentsia, it was a very independent view influenced by his evolutionist interpretation of Western history and his reading of Nietzsche at this time. But this view entails an unresolved logical difficulty of which Lu Hsün himself was not aware.

14. Lu Hsün, "Wen-hua p'ien-chih lun," *Fen, LHCC,* 1:180.
15. Ibid.

"Civilizations," Lu Hsün observed, "are unbalanced developments of extremes because they are the consequences of evolution in which this kind of extreme reaction always occurs."[16] So the rule of the majority in Europe emerged out of the revolutionary era, which was an extreme reaction against the previous autocracy, and material progress based on scientific research came to a head as a result of the extreme reaction against the dominance of Christian orthodoxy in the Middle Ages. But civilization can never reach a state of equilibrium. Its natural tendency toward excess always brings about sharp reactions in the process of its evolution. The rule of the majority and material progress had already gone too far by the end of the nineteenth century, and in reaction there arose what Lu Hsün called "neo-idealistic thought" (shen-ssu-tsung chih chih-hsin che).[17] Extreme material progress had evolved into materialism; the worship of the rule of the majority in society led to the exaltation of the lowest common denominator of its members, and to intolerance of individuality and genius. In the course of his exposition Lu Hsün cited Schopenhauer, Kierkegaard, Nietzsche, and Ibsen, among others, to illustrate the role and the meaning of the free development of individuality.[18]

Lu Hsün claimed that the rise of "neo-idealistic thought" constituted evidence that material progress and the rule of the majority were already passé. Furthermore, he questioned the validity of China's following prevalent trends in the West, for they were the results of Western internal social and cultural evolution, and might be irrelevant to a country whose problems had emerged out of the indigenous process of its own evolution and could hardly be resolved by an arbitrarily borrowed foreign recipe. He urged a reformist adaptation of elements from the West, so that China would not be left behind in the evolution of world civilization in an era of close contact among different countries. He also urged preserving elements of the indigenous civilization so that China "would not lose its own blood vessels."[19] In short, he thought his countrymen should find a workable solution to China's problems on the basis of a clear understanding of their nature and through a creative integration of certain indigenous and Western elements.

Although disclaiming any comprehensive plans for leading China to attain the goals he saw as desirable, Lu Hsün attacked materialism and the rule of

16. Ibid., p. 184.
17. Ibid., p. 185.
18. Ibid., pp. 185–91.
19. Ibid., p. 192.

the majority as obstacles to the development of individuality, and stressed the nurturing of a vigorous individualistic spirit as a primary means for China's regeneration. He argued that the most basic and fundamental change was a change in the spirit and character of the Chinese people. As it happened, his denunciations and his positive emphases coincided with the newest trend in Europe—the "neo-idealistic thought" that he had just described. At the end of his long essay, Lu Hsün even went so far as to reduce the complex origins of the splendor and power of European civilization to a monistic factor, saying that the foundation of European civilization lay in the nature of European man.[20]

These conclusions raise a number of questions. In the first place, Lu Hsün himself appeared to be falling into the attitude he had disdained in others— that of adopting the prevailing trends in Europe for implementation in China. Secondly, he had argued that European civilization was an evolutionary process, that its origins were complex, and that its course consisted of a series of extremes and the reactions to them; how in the end could he reach the monistic conclusion that he did?

The influence, albeit unconscious, of the cultural-intellectualistic approach can clearly be seen in Lu Hsün's conclusion that the origins of European civilization lay in the character of the European people, which presumably was shaped by the European spirit and mind. Likewise, he argued for the need to generate, through new ideas, a vigorous individualistic spirit, without noticing the logical difficulties in his argument. His historicist description of "neo-idealistic thought" as the most up-to-date trend in Europe was, in fact, transformed by his underlying mode of thinking into a normative demand. One can, of course, argue that China could not be isolated from world trends in the twentieth century, and that Lu Hsün adopted "neo-idealistic thought" not simply because it was the newest trend in Europe but because it seemed pertinent to the particular problems of China. But it was the cultural-intellectualistic approach lying at the root of his thinking that led him to regard the "neo-idealistic" emphasis on the power of spirit and ideas as pertinent.

One should also note that in this early essay, in sharp contrast to the totalistic attack on China's past which he was to make in the May Fourth period, Lu Hsün was highly critical of those who followed the waves of Western fashions and rejected Chinese tradition. He realized that China had to change in order to survive, but he maintained that such a change should

20. Ibid., p. 193.

involve not a total rejection of Chinese tradition and total acceptance of the West, but a blending of elements from both. Lu Hsün did not feel the need to justify this reformist stance explicitly. Traditional Chinese culture had not yet totally disintegrated, and he could still take for granted some elements from China's past. He did not at that point see the crisis of China as involving a total crisis of Chinese culture.

TOTALISTIC ANTITRADITIONALISM AND "DIARY OF A MADMAN"

Apart from writing essays, Lu Hsün collaborated with his brother Chou Tso-jen in 1908 in introducing Western literature, especially stories by Russian and Eastern European writers such as Leonid Andreyev and Henryk Sien-kiewicz, for the purpose of portraying the spirit of revolt against suppression in the West. Their efforts resulted in the publication in 1909 of two collections of translations entitled *Stories from Other Lands* (*Yü-wai hsiao-shuo chi*). Like his other literary endeavors, these volumes also elicited virtually no response.[21] Lu Hsün's youthful ambition to awaken the Chinese people by literature ended, then, in total failure. This experience gave him an over-whelming feeling of loneliness, which he later described: "If a man's pro-posal met with approval, it should encourage him; if it met with opposition, it should make him fight back; but the real feeling of helplessness for him was to lift up his voice among the living and meet with no response, neither approval nor opposition, just as if he were left in a boundless desert."[22]

It was in this bitter and lonely mood that Lu Hsün returned to China in August, 1909. He first taught at a normal school in Hangchow and a year later went back to Shaohsing to teach in a middle school. The 1911 revolution came as a surprise; locally it took the form of a melodramatic takeover by a secret society chief with *Kuang-fu hui* (Restoration Society) connections, who proclaimed himself the military governor. Still, Lu Hsün was delighted with the change and agreed to serve as the principal of Shaohsing Normal School. But difficulties soon arose out of his disagreement with the arbitrary policies of the new governor. At this juncture he received and accepted an invitation from Ts'ai Yüan-p'ei to join the staff of the Ministry of Education. Although

21. The first volume of *Stories from Other Lands* was available for sale in Tokyo and Shanghai from February, 1909, and the second volume from June the same year. Only twenty-one copies of the first volume (of which one copy was purchased by Lu Hsün's friend Hsü Shou-shang for the purpose of checking whether the bookseller had raised the price) and twenty copies of the second volume were sold in Tokyo. Similar numbers were sold in Shanghai. See Chou Tso-jen, "Kuan-yü Lu Hsün chih-erh," in his *Kua-tou chi*, pp. 235–36.

22. Lu Hsün, "Tzu-hsü," *Na-han, LHCC*, 1:5–6.

he had already learned that at the local level the revolution had not led to any substantial change, he could not but feel elated when he saw signs of a fresh start at the national level during his first few months in Nanking.[23] But after he moved to Peking in May, 1912, along with other staff members of the Ministry of Education, it did not take him long to realize that his joy was ill-founded. He later wrote: "I had seen the 1911 revolution, the second revolution, Yüan Shih-k'ai's assumption of the imperial title, and Chang Hsün's restoration of the Manchu house, and all this had made me rather cynical. I gave up hope, and lost heart completely."[24] He was overtaken by a mood of profound despair, resulting from his frustration at the national failure of the 1911 revolution and the loneliness born of his personal failure to change the spirit of Chinese people through literature.

Beginning in 1912, while serving in a routine position as a counselor in the Ministry of Education, he withdrew almost completely from the outside world and occupied himself with such activities as copying inscriptions, collecting stone rubbings, collating corrupted texts of literary works, searching for lost texts of traditional stories, folk tales, and local histories of his home town. In retrospect, these activities prepared him to become a pioneer historian of traditional Chinese fiction and folk art, and perhaps also served as a psychological "moratorium" which enabled him to achieve the mental distance from his surroundings necessary for the breakthrough of his later creativity. Whatever the ultimate value of these activities, he engaged in them at the time, in his own words, for their "insignificance" and "as a means to anesthetize my soul."[25]

Lu Hsün's self-imposed aloofness from society after 1912 indicated not indifference to the grave problems of China so much as his sense of the futility of attempting to change the current situation. When Ch'ien Hsüan-t'ung, an old friend and an associate of New Youth, came in August, 1917, to persuade him to contribute to the magazine, not primarily for the promotion of a literary revolution but rather to help it attain its fundamental goal of bringing about a revolution of thought and morals, Ch'ien's words touched Lu Hsün's long-standing and deep conviction.[26] He agreed to write, not because his sense of despair was completely dispelled by Ch'ien, but because he was moved by the

23. Lu Hsün, Liang-ti shu, LHCC, 9:26.

24. Lu Hsün, "Tzu-hsüan-chi tzu-hsü," Nan-ch'iang pei-tiao chi, LHCC, 4:347.

25. Lu Hsün, "Tzu-hsü," Na-han, LHCC, 1:6,7.

26. As Chou Tso-jen attested later, Lu Hsün was not particularly enthusiastic about the literary revolution launched by New Youth but he took the "revolution of thought" (ssu-hsiang ke-ming) to heart. See Chou Hsia-shou (Chou Tso-jen), Lu Hsün ti ku-chia, pp. 221–22.

discovery of a group of kindred spirits who also believed in the priority of intellectual and cultural change. Whatever reservations he might have had about whether the *New Youth* group would be able to attain its goals, he saw it as a tangible place to contribute his efforts to the colossal task of changing the consciousness of the Chinese people.

The first piece born of Lu Hsün's agreement to write was his famous "Diary of a Madman" ("K'uang-jen jih-chi"), written in the vernacular and published in the May 15, 1918, issue of *New Youth*. An attack on Chinese culture and society as a whole, it revealed a categorical departure from the reformist stance he had taken before the 1911 revolution. The reasons for this categorical change in Lu Hsün's consciousness may be seen to lie in his response to the simultaneous breakdown of the sociopolitical and cultural-moral orders and to the bleak realities of post-1911 China: under these circumstances his traditionally derived intellectualistic-monistic mode of thinking evolved into a holistic category of analysis which pushed him toward totalistic cultural iconoclasm. He now perceived the traditional Chinese society and culture as totally corrupted by the rotten nature of the Chinese people, which was, he wrote in 1918, molded by their "dark and confusing ideas" (*hun-luan ssu-hsiang*).[27]

It is significant that when Lu Hsün talked about the "intellectual disease"

27. Lu Hsün, "Sui-kan lu san-shih-pa," *HCN*, 5.5:517 (October [*sic;* should read November] 15, 1918), reprinted in Lu Hsün, *Je-feng, LHCC*, 1:389. This piece was published six months later than "K'uang-jen jih-chi" in *HCN*. It explicitly articulated the reasons for his totalistic antitraditionalism, which was first revealed in "K'uang-jen jih-chi." Chou Tso-jen mentioned in a letter to Ts'ao Chü-jen, when he reread Ts'ao's *Lu Hsün p'ing-chuan* (Hong Kong, 1956) and saw that Ts'ao had quoted from "Sui-kan lu san-shih-pa" ("Random thoughts, no. 38"), that this piece had actually been written by him. He did not suggest, however, that the ideas in it were not Lu Hsün's. He merely said that its style was slightly different from that of Lu Hsün but that the difference had hardly been noticed by others. Chou Tso-jen and Ts'ao Chü-jen, *Chou Ts'ao t'ung-hsin chi* (Hong Kong, 1973), 1:51–52. Nevertheless, this piece was originally published under the name [Lu] Hsün in *HCN*, and has ever since been included in all the printings of Lu Hsün's *Je-feng*. At the time when it was written, Chou Tso-jen was living together with Lu Hsün at the Shaohsing Hostel in Peking. The two brothers worked closely in their literary endeavors and shared many convictions. Each of them published most of his essays, translations, creative writings, and "Sui-kan lu" under his own name or pseudonyms. That Tso-jen published several items of "Sui-kan lu" in 1918 under his own name ("Sui-kan lu erh-shih-ssu," *HCN*, 5.3:286–90 [September 15, 1918]; "Sui-kan lu san-shih-ssu," *HCN*, 5.4:409–12 [October 15, 1918]) but let "Sui-kan lu san-shih-pa" be published under Lu Hsün's name, although it was, as he said, written by him, and that Lu Hsün himself allowed it to be included in his *Je-feng*, which was originally published in 1925 in Peking after Tso-jen had already broken with him, indicate clearly that the ideas in it were essentially Lu Hsün's, even though it was, for whatever reasons, drafted or written by Tso-jen, who most certainly at that time shared with Lu Hsün the ideas expressed in

(*ssu-hsiang shang ti ping*)[28] in this essay, he used as an analogy the most terrible congenital disease of the human body—syphilis. The image may seem crude, unfair, and even quite bizarre to one not involved in the May Fourth iconoclastic movement, but to Lu Hsün it not only conveyed, through the analogy of the organic effect of syphilis on the human body, his conception of the organismic effect of the intellectual disease on the Chinese people, but also expressed his horror and disgust about the very nature of the Chinese people. The intellectual disease had, like syphilis, infected every sphere of activity and made Chinese tradition, which is itself the product of these activities, totally abhorrent. It was distressing to realize, Lu Hsün noted, that even if this generation of the Chinese people wished for a new start, it was quite uncertain whether or not they would be able to get rid of the deeply rooted "dark and confusing elements in the blood vessels."[29] For the character of a people, once formed, is difficult to change. However, "606" (arsphenamine) had been invented to treat syphilis, and science should also be used to find a treatment for the intellectual disease of the Chinese people.[30] If a step were to be made, one could not definitely deny that it would lead to success in the future. The important thing was the will to work for change; and change, according to Lu Hsün, ought to be started by "wiping out the dark and confusing ideas in the minds [of the Chinese people] and the books of Confucianism and Taoism which have helped [to spread] darkness and confusion."[31]

It should be noted that Lu Hsün's uncertainty about whether the evils of the past could be eliminated by the iconoclastic movement crept into this essay, although it was specifically intended to serve the cause of totalistic rejection of the past. This pessimistic undertone was echoed in the "Diary of a Madman," and permeated almost all of his later writings in the May Fourth period.

it. Tso-jen broke with Lu Hsün in July, 1923. See *Lu Hsün jih-chi* (Peking, 1959), 1:453–55, 490, the entries for July 14, 19, August 2, 1923; June 11, 1924.

28. Lu Hsün, "Sui-kan lu san-shih-pa," *HCN*, 5.5:517, or *Je-feng, LHCC*, 1:389.

29. Ibid.

30. Looking at Lu Hsün's thought from a broader perspective, one notices that he is incisive in his criticism of Chinese tradition but is quite unable to offer an equally incisive and unequivocal formula for China's reconstruction. Time and again he confesses that he does not know the proper road to a brighter future. See *LHCC*, 1:362–63; 3:40–42; 9:11–14, 312–14. "Science" is offered here in line with the popularity of scientism at this time in China, but it is used in a polemical context and can hardly be regarded as a well thought-out conviction of Lu Hsün's.

31. Lu Hsün, "Sui-kan lu san-shih-pa," *HCN*, 5.5:517, or *Je-feng, LHCC*, 1:390.

Sensitive and skeptical by disposition, Lu Hsün had come to believe that the nature of his people was so diseased and their tradition so corrupt as to make it questionable whether or not the disease could be cured and the influence of tradition abolished. This skepticism was reinforced by his melancholy and despondent mood at the time, and was expressed in the very conversation during the course of which Ch'ien Hsüan-t'ung persuaded him to write:

> Imagine an iron house without windows, absolutely indestructible, with many people fast asleep inside who will soon die of suffocation. Since they will die in their sleep, they will not feel any of the pain of death. Now if you cry aloud to wake a few of the lighter sleepers, making those unfortunate few suffer the agony of irrevocable death, do you think you are doing them a good turn?[32]

He finally agreed to write because, although he "still had his conviction," he "could not blot out hope, for [whether or not] hope [is realizable] lies in the future."[33] He noted that he refrained from expressing his pessimism in the stories of *Call to Arms* (*Na-han*) because, as a foot soldier, he wanted to obey the leaders of the *New Youth* group, who were opposed to pessimism—and because he did not intend to "infect with the loneliness I had found so bitter those young people who were still dreaming pleasant dreams."[34] Nowhere does he say that he had discarded his pessimism. Despite these skeptical and pessimistic tendencies, Lu Hsün's commitment to the Chinese nation led him to do his part in the face of uncertainty. Directed by his cultural-intellectualistic approach, he was convinced that if there was to be any liberation from the shackles of Chinese tradition, it could only be achieved through an intellectual movement that attacked China's past in toto. Since Chinese tradition had been essentially shaped by its fundamental ideas, this antitraditionalism, which must not be confined to any particular aspect of the tradition, must strike first of all at its roots—the intellectual and cultural system of the past.[35]

"Diary of a Madman" set forth the general theme of Lu Hsün's explicit concerns during his most creative period (1918–26). Lu Hsün took his title from Nikolai Gogol's "Diary of a Madman," the translated title in Japanese and German of the original "Notes of a Madman." He enjoyed reading Gogol

32. Lu Hsün, "Tzu-hsü," *Na-han, LHCC*, 1:7.
33. Ibid.
34. Ibid., p. 8.
35. In 1925 he still maintained the primacy of "intellectual revolution" (*ssu-hsiang ke-ming*). Lu Hsün, "T'ung-hsün," *Hua-kai chi, LHCC*, 3:17.

while in Japan, and he was susceptible to the influence of Gogol's satiric style and technique in portraying the darker side of human life because of the sardonic humor for which he was well noted among his contemporaries.[36] But the motifs in this story are original, and Lu Hsün employs an allegorical technique absent from Gogol's piece to give the madman's words a double meaning.[37] The modern psychological concept of schizophrenia is used to portray the madman's systematic and highly developed delusion, and hence on the surface the story provides a sense of fidelity to reality. Yet there can be no mistaking that the story is an allegorical device for the author's indictment of the Chinese tradition, and that his indictment is not confined to any particular aspect of that tradition but extends to the whole of Chinese history. In the following well-known passage, for instance, Lu Hsün sees Chinese history as a record of cannibalism:

> Everything requires careful investigation if one is to understand it. In ancient times, as I recollect, people often ate human beings, but I am rather hazy about it. I tried to look this up, but my history has no chronology, and scrawled all over each page are the words: "Virtue and Morality." Since I could not sleep anyway, I carefully went over it for half the night until I began to see the words between the lines, the whole book being filled with these words—*ch'ih jen* ("eat people").[38]

The words "*ch'ih jen*" are blunt and offensive, as they are meant to be in order to convey the "deep sense of outrage" which Lu Hsün later explicitly acknowledged.[39]

Two points should be noted here. First, Lu Hsün suggests no exploration of the social and political causes of the "cannibalism" of traditional China. On the contrary, he strongly implies the determining role of ideas in Chinese history. The evolution toward humanity among primitive men began with ideas: "In the beginning, primitive men probably all ate a little human flesh. Later on, some of them gave up this practice because their *thoughts* were different. They tried their best to improve themselves and they became real

---

36. For instances, see Chou Hsia-shou (Chou Tso-jen), *Lu Hsün ti ku-chia*, pp. 188–89, 205–6; Shu T'ien, "Fang Lu Hsün hsien-sheng," reprinted in Ts'ao Chü-jen, *Lu Hsün nien-p'u* (Hong Kong, 1967), pp. 262–64.

37. See J. D. Chinnery, "The Influence of Western Literature on Lü Xùn's 'Diary of a Madman'," *Bulletin of the School of Oriental and African Studies,* 23:309–22 (1960).

38. Lu Hsün, "K'uang-jen jih-chi," *Na-han, LHCC,* 1:12.

39. Lu Hsün, "*Chung-kuo hsin-wen-hsüeh ta-hsi* hsiao-shuo erh-chi hsü," *Ch'ieh-chieh-t'ing tsa-wen erh-chi, LHCC,* 6:190.

human beings, while others continued to eat human flesh.''[40] Secondly, hope is alluded to, conditionally based on a change of ideas, which is "just one step to take."[41] However, the theme of the "Diary of a Madman" does not provide real hope. The last statement—"Save the children"[42]—is a desperate cry; but no inference can be drawn from the internal logic of the piece to indicate a realistic hope of saving the children. On the contrary, the madman feels that the children whom he has encountered all harbor cannibalistic intentions. This is not surprising, since they have all been brought up and socialized in a cannibalistic society—in the words of the madman, "They must have learned [it] from their parents.''[43]

Chinese society was an enmeshing net: no one, once born into it, could escape the infection of its culture. Whether consciously or unconsciously, every member of Chinese society was a cannibal, and there existed no inner resources that could generate an intellectual and cultural change toward a more humane society. Ironically, only by becoming "insane" could a man grasp the true nature of Chinese culture and the society in which he lived. But precisely because he was awakened, he was dismissed as a "madman" by "normal" members of the society. Although the madman was portrayed as a singularly courageous figure who defied the whole society—an image that may have resulted from Lu Hsün's Nietzschean pathos[44]—he was a tragic

40. Lu Hsün, "K'uang-jen jih-chi," Na-han, LHCC, 1:16–17. Italics mine.

41. Ibid., p. 16.

42. Ibid., p. 19.

43. Ibid., p. 10.

44. Lu Hsün was fond of reading Nietzsche when he was in Japan. See Chou Tso-jen, "Kuan-yü Lu Hsün chih-erh" in his Kua-tou chi, pp. 239–40. Lu Hsün mentioned some of Nietzsche's ideas of individuality on several occasions in his writings of 1907. Lu Hsün, "Wen-hua p'ien-chih lun," Fen, LHCC, 1:184–85, 187–88, and "Mo-lo shih-li shuo," Fen, LHCC, 1:195. Early in 1919 he published a piece in the series "Random Thoughts" (Sui-kan lu) in the New Youth in which he quotes Nietzsche to emphasize the need for the individual to strive for perfection. T'ang Ssu (Lu Hsün), "Sui-kan lu ssu-shih i," HCN, 6.1:68–69 (January 15, 1919). In 1920 Lu Hsün published a translation of the prologue of Nietzsche's Thus Spake Zarathustra: T'ang Ssu, "Ch'a-la t'u-ssu t'e-la ti hsü-yen," Hsin-ch'ao, 2.5:954–73 (June 1, 1920). However, this affection for Nietzsche did not constitute a commitment on Lu Hsün's part to the whole Nietzschean Weltanschauung, nor, as Benjamin Schwartz has rightly observed, "did he share all the preoccupations and exasperations of Nietzsche. What seems to have attracted him, above all, was a certain emotion-charged image of the sensitive, spiritual hero confronting a stupid and vicious world—confronting 'the mob.' This pathos which can be found in Nietzsche, but which can also be found in others with quite different views, seems to have struck a sympathetic chord in the sensitive and somewhat bitter young man. It has been reported that at the same time he was also very much enamored of Byron's poetry. Thus what Lu Hsün found in Nietzsche was not a whole body of doctrine but a certain welcome pathos." Benjamin I. Schwartz, "The Intellectual

figure too. His very awakening made him useless, for he was unable to communicate with other members of his society, and his criticism became completely ineffective. Without awareness of the nature of Chinese society and culture, and without liberation from the effects of them, one could not break through the cannibalism of Chinese tradition; yet, paradoxically, that very awareness and liberation nullified one's capacity to change the Chinese society and culture.

The ramifications of the iconoclastic totalism conveyed in the "Diary of a Madman" are spelled out by Lu Hsün in his polemical essays. Once he characterized the distinctive features of the Chinese people as "concealment and deceit."[45] On another occasion he described Chinese history in terms of two alternating periods: "first, the age in which the Chinese people longed in vain to be slaves; second, the age in which the Chinese people succeeded in becoming slaves for a time."[46]

Furthermore, the Chinese people are worse than stupid, weak, hypocritical, and self-deceiving. They have established a society and a culture where goodness has no place, and they in turn are shaped by this society and culture. In "Benediction" ("Chu-fu"), for example, the sturdy and good-hearted peasant woman, Hsiang-lin-sao, is driven to death by the interplay of human malice and callousness, corrupt culture and unjust social institutions. The unredeemable suffering and desolate loneliness of this good person is nowhere more vividly shown than in the episode in which she is deprived, by the folk religion of Chinese society, of even the hope of meeting her child and husband in hell.[47]

The existence of the good-hearted Hsiang-lin-sao reveals an obvious contradiction. If the Chinese tradition was totally evil, why and how could there emerge good persons—not only Hsiang-lin-sao but also Shan-ssu-sao-tzu in "Tomorrow"[48] ("Ming-t'ien") and Yün-t'u in "My Native Place"[49] ("Ku-hsiang")? All these were traditional Chinese who embodied particular elements of Chinese-ness in their personalities.

History of China: Preliminary Reflections," in John K. Fairbank, ed., *Chinese Thought and Institutions* (Chicago, 1957), p. 17.

45. Lu Hsün, "Lun cheng-le yen k'an," *Fen, LHCC,* 1:329.
46. Lu Hsün, "Teng-hsia man-pi," *Fen, LHCC,* 1:312.
47. Lu Hsün, "Chu-fu," *P'ang-huang, LHCC,* 2:5–22.
48. Lu Hsün, "Ming-t'ien," *Na-han, LHCC,* 1:35–42.
49. Lu Hsün, "Ku-hsiang," *Na-han, LHCC,* 1:61–71.

Lu Hsün's writings do not provide an adequate answer in intellectual terms to this question. But he was certainly prepared to overthrow the tradition in toto: those good persons may have been its products but they were also its victims, and he was willing to look forward without regret to a future in which good persons, although they could not resemble Hsiang-lin-sao or others he had described, would no longer become victims.

Sometimes Lu Hsün's concrete observation of some positive facts in Chinese history, such as in "Thoughts before the Mirror" ("K'an-ching yu-kan") written in 1925, appears to constitute a certain qualification of his iconoclastic totalism. Noticing that foreign plants and animals were used as engraving designs on bronze mirrors of the Han dynasty, and that the tombstone of Emperor T'ai-tsung of the T'ang dynasty had an ostrich (a foreign bird) and a horse pierced with an arrow carved in relief on it, Lu Hsün observed that the people of the Han were broad-minded and those of the T'ang stout-hearted because they, unlike the people of later dynasties, made use of foreign things without inhibition.[50] However, these qualities of the Han and T'ang were features of strength and self-confidence vis-à-vis the "barbarian" challenge. Lu Hsün, of course, recognized that there had been ups and downs in China's long history, and that during the height of certain dynasties a sense of self-confidence naturally emerged out of political and military strength. But nowhere did he imply that the moral (or immoral) nature of the Chinese people was in any way changed or modified in these high periods of imperial grandeur.

Lu Hsün did indicate that the Chinese people lost their boldness and confidence in the post-T'ang periods when one after another the Khitans, the Jürched, and the Mongols invaded. Looking solely at that comment, one might be tempted to argue that in his view the nature of the Chinese people was to a large extent influenced—perhaps even profoundly changed—by the "barbarian" invasions and hence our understanding of his concept of the determining role of ideas should be qualified. Lu Hsün's notion entailed a certain conception of the influence of the strength of the state and of the "barbarian" invasions. But two questions arise: In what sense, if at all, did he consider that these factors changed the nature of the Chinese people? Or did external vicissitudes, in his view, change the ways the Chinese people responded to certain external environments but did not necessarily change their basic nature?

50. Lu Hsün, "K'an-ching yu-kan," *Fen, LHCC,* 1:300–303.

On the basis of this piece alone, it is not clear which answer he would have offered. In order to bring the notion of "barbarian" influence in line with his persistent stress on the validity and viability of the cultural-intellectualistic approach, it is likely, however, that he would have confirmed his essentialistic and holistic concept of the nature of the Chinese people by taking the second view. However, even if he recognized at this point that certain external factors, such as the "barbarian" invasions, constituted independent agents in determining the basic nature of the Chinese people, he was not moved to add a new variable to his view of what was required for a fundamental change, and his thinking continued to be dominated by his view of the priority of intellectual change.

In another piece written in the same year, Lu Hsün argued in the context of his discussion of the meaning of a statement from the *Tso-chuan* that the "cannibalism" of the Chinese people had started as early as the sixth century B.C.:

> Let us have a look at the excellent system devised by the ancients: "There are ten suns in heaven, ten degrees among men; so those below serve those above, and the ruler waits on the gods. Thus princes are subject to the king, ministers to the princes, knights to the ministers . . . [and so on down to the lowest slave]."
> [From the record of the seventh year of Duke Chao (535 B.C.) in the *Tso-chuan.*]
>
> The lowest slaves have no subjects, which seems rather hard on them. But we need not worry on this score, for they have wives and children who rank even lower. And there is hope for the children too, for when they grow up and rise to be slaves, they will have wives and children below to serve them. Thus in this cycle everyone is all right, and whoever dares to object is condemned for trying to rise above his station.
>
> Although this happened very long ago, in the seventh year of Duke Chao of Lu in the Spring and Autumn period, those who hanker after the past need not feel pessimistic. . . . China's ancient spiritual civilization has not been destroyed by the "Republic." The only difference is, the Manchus have just left the [cannibalistic] banquet. . . . China is nothing but the kitchen where these feasts are prepared.[51]

This piece indicates that the basic feature of the nature of the Chinese people—"cannibalism"—had long been generated from within rather than effected by any forces from without; a superficial reading might suggest that the ancient sociopolitical system of hierarchical oppression had caused this "cannibalism." However, the advantages and disadvantages that most people

51. Lu Hsün, "Teng-hsia man-pi," *Fen, LHCC,* 1:314–15.

derived from that system in fact cancelled each other out. There was, therefore, no reason for them to enjoy the "feasts" which were made possible by the system in which they were also victims. This piece highlights, among other things, Lu Hsün's call for the destruction of social inequality. But the class structure itself does not provide the explanation for the characteristic nature of the Chinese people. In the final analysis, it was the "dark and confusing ideas" of the Chinese people that led them to be so blind as to enjoy oppressing others in the midst of their own undoing.

"THE TRUE STORY OF AH Q"

Now that the broad general outline of Lu Hsün's totalistic antitraditionalism have been sketched, we must ask just what was his view of the *substantial* nature of the Chinese people? What were the fundamental characteristics of the Chinese people that were concretely expressed in traditional China? What were their defining characteristics—those constituents that made them Chinese?

One way to answer this question is to examine the themes and implications of Lu Hsün's major work—"The True Story of Ah Q." Although written in satirical form, it has distinctive features that can hardly be understood in terms of conventional satire. It was intended, as Lu Hsün himself attested, to present a portrait of "the soul of the Chinese people" and "life in China."[52] But the character of the Chinese people was so incredibly rotten and outrageous as to be absurd; hence satire was the appropriate form of expression. Lu Hsün took great pains with the technical aspects of this story (such as avoiding specific names for its characters, avoiding local dialects, etc.), so that his readers could not misinterpret it as referring to particular persons or a particular place. "I take these precautions not because I am afraid of giving offense but to avoid ridiculous complications, so that the impact of the work may be more concentrated and powerful. . . . My method is to make the reader unable to tell who this character can be apart from himself, so that he cannot back away to become a bystander but rather suspects that this is a portrait of himself as well as of everyone [in China]. Therefore, a road to self-examination may open up for him."[53] The effort to depict the common features of the Chinese people

---

52. Lu Hsün, "E-wen i-pen *Ah Q cheng-chuan* hsü chi chu-che tzu-hsü chuan-lüeh," *Chi-wai chi, LHCC*, 7:78. Lu Hsün also says that "it does not aim at mockery or pity." Hsü Kuang-p'ing, ed., *Lu Hsün shu-chien* (Shanghai, 1946), p. 249.

53. Lu Hsün, "Ta '*Hsi*' chou-k'an pien-che hsin," *Ch'ieh-chieh-t'ing tsa-wen, LHCC*, 6:114.

through this story was very successful; that it was a composite portrait of the Chinese people was recognized by critics soon after its publication.[54]

While "The True Story of Ah Q" is not without its flaws, it is nevertheless an original and brilliant piece of work distinguished for its distinctive and vivid characters, its ingenious use of the Chinese vernacular, and its effortless style.[55] Above all, the general features of the Chinese people are embodied in the particular behavior and the distinctive personalities of Ah Q and the people around him in such a manner that they have become an integral part of the twentieth-century Chinese imagination: "Ah Q" has become a defining category in modern Chinese thought, an image which many Chinese in the May Fourth period and later have used to express the traditional nature of the Chinese people. Such expressions as "Ah Q-ism," "Ah Q logic" and "Ah Q-like" have become part of the living speech. In short, the strength of this piece consists in its fusion of generality and particularity. It is through the particular features of Ah Q's personality and behavior that the general features of the Chinese people found a concrete channel of expression; it is through the general features of the Chinese people, embodied in the particular behavior and personality of Ah Q, that this piece gains its potent literary and historic meaning.

Ah Q was an illiterate peasant day-laborer, living just before the collapse of the Ch'ing dynasty. He had no family, and nobody knew where he came from. He was called "Ah Quei," which was shortened to Ah Q because the author claimed not to know to which Chinese character the sound "quei"

---

54. Chou Tso-jen, "Ah Q cheng-chuan," reprinted in Ts'ao Chü-jen, *Lu Hsün nien-p'u,* pp. 193–96; Mo Tun, "Lu Hsün lun," reprinted, ibid., pp. 197–229, esp. pp. 221–22; Su Hsüeh-lin, "Ah Q cheng-chuan chi Lu Hsün ch'uang-tso ti i-shu," reprinted, ibid., pp. 230–53, esp. pp. 230–40; Chang Ting-huang, "Lu Hsün hsien-sheng," reprinted, ibid., pp. 278–90, esp. pp. 285–86.

55. The structure of the story is less than perfect and its tone occasionally incongruous. These flaws may be attributable to the particular circumstances under which the writing was initially undertaken. "The image of Ah Q had appeared in my mind for quite a few years," recalled Lu Hsün, "but I had no intention of putting it down on paper." However, late in 1921 Sun Fu-yüan, a former student of Lu Hsün's and an editor of the literary supplement of the *Peking Morning Gazette (Ch'eng-pao)* asked Lu Hsün to contribute something to the humorous section of the literary supplement. That was the occasion for Lu Hsün's writing the first chapter, the tone of which, because it was intended to fit a humorous context, is somewhat at odds with that of the later chapters. (The later chapters were moved to the section devoted to new literature in the supplement.) The story was published as a serial in the literary supplement from December 4, 1921, to February 12, 1922. For Lu Hsün's own criticism of its structure and incongruous tone, and his recollection of how he came to write the story, see his "Ah Q cheng-chuan ti ch'eng-yin," *Hua-kai-chi hsü-pien, LHCC,* 3:279–86.

referred. He was poor, and was often treated as a laughing-stock by the villagers, but in general he moved quite happily within traditional Chinese culture and society. This was not simply because he took the existing social and cultural framework for granted and willingly accepted his lot. The substance of the matter was, his happiness derived from the mutual reinforcement of the particular quality of his consciousness and the general mode of his thinking.

The particular quality of his consciousness was characterized by vileness, cowardice, cunning, and megalomania, the interplay of which gave him the ability to survive when bullied and motivated him to bully others when he was in a position to do so.[56] The general mode of his thinking—what Lu Hsün calls "the method of securing spiritual victory"[57]—consisted of a process by which he would rationalize the results of his humiliations so that they appeared advantageous to him. A vile, cowardly, cunning, and megalomaniacal person may often not be happy, especially when the result of his action is not favorable to him. But Ah Q was usually happy, regardless of the outcome of his encounters. If the outcome happened to give him pleasure personally, his native instinct would recognize and enjoy it. But more often than not he was taken advantage of, either by the gentry who wielded social, cultural, and economic power, or by other villagers who were simply physically stronger. Under these circumstances, he was able to resolve his various problems by rationalizing the consequences in such a way as to make them a source of spiritual pleasure to him. Despite the physical discomfort of a slap or of hunger, he was blessed by the "lucidity" of his mind, which lacked the capacity for real tension and conflict.

Ah Q had a high opinion of himself, habitually looking down on all others in the village. When engaged in quarrels, he would say, "We used to be much better off than you. Who do you think you are anyway?" (p. 75). After he had been to the city several times, he became more proud of himself, though he had no use for city folks either: he thought many of their ways absurd and laughable. But the villagers were, according to Ah Q, really ignorant rustics who had never seen how fish was fried in the city!

56. For the editor of the magazine *Drama (Hsi)*, who adapted "The True Story of Ah Q" as a play in 1934, Lu Hsün described the appearance of Ah Q as follows: "To my mind, Ah Q should be about thirty, quite ordinary-looking, with a peasant's simplicity and stupidity, but also a touch of roguish cunning." Lu Hsün, "Chi '*Hsi*' chou-k'an pien-che hsin," *Ch'ieh-chieh-t'ing tsa-wen, LHCC*, 6:117.

57. Lu Hsün, "Ah Q cheng-chuan," *Na-han, LHCC*, 1:77. Further page references to the text of the story will be given in parentheses in the text.

When teased about the ringworm scars on his head—he was not proud of these—Ah Q would either curse or fight, according to whether the offender was slow of words or weak in strength. When he came out the loser, he changed his tactics. He would angrily glare at whoever was taunting him, and he sometimes retorted: "You don't even deserve . . . ," as though the scars on his scalp were noble and honorable, something to be envied.

> As the idlers still would not let him alone, a fight usually followed. Ah Q inevitably lost and ended up by being held by the queue while his head was thumped against the wall four or five times. The idlers would walk away, satisfied at having won. Ah Q would stand there for a second, thinking to himself, "I have been beaten by my son. What a world we live in today!" He too would go off satisfied and spiritually victorious. [P. 77.]

But the combination of Ah Q's cowardice and "method of securing spiritual victory" sometimes did not work. They then were reinforced by another special feature of his nature—vileness—so as to make him happy.

One spring day when Ah Q was walking along the street, he saw Whiskers Wang sitting against a wall in the sun, catching lice in the lining of his coat. Ah Q felt an infectious itch and sat down by his side, taking off his ragged coat to begin to catch his. Had it been anyone else, Ah Q might have hesitated. But Ah Q held Whiskers in great contempt, and was not afraid of him. But after a long search, Ah Q only found three or four lice, while Whiskers caught one after another in swift succession. Ah Q felt disappointed at first, but his feeling soon gave way to indignation. Ah Q swore at Whiskers, who thereupon beat him up. In Ah Q's memory this was the first humiliation of his life, because he had always scoffed at Whiskers on account of his ugly whiskered cheeks, but had never been scoffed at, much less beaten, by him. In this emotionally unstable state, Ah Q ran into the Imitation Foreign Devil, the son of a gentry family in the village, whom Ah Q despised because he had gone abroad, cut his queue, and wore a false one after his return to the village. In the past Ah Q had only cursed him under his breath; but today, because he was in a bad temper and wanted to work off his feelings, the curse words inadvertently slipped out. This drew a beating from the Imitation Foreign Devil, despite Ah Q's prompt excuse that the words were meant for someone else. As far as Ah Q could remember, this was the second humiliation of his life. Fortunately, after the beating was over, it seemed to him that the matter was closed, and he felt somewhat relieved. Moreover, the precious "ability to forget" handed down by his ancestors stood him in good stead. He walked slowly away, and by the time he approached the village tavern he again felt quite happy.

Just then a little nun from the local convent went by. Ah Q was cowardly only before people who were either physically or socially superior to him. But he took delight in hurling an insult at the little nun even when he was in a good mood. Now all the resentment that he had felt for his recent defeats turned against the helpless nun:

> "I was wondering why I've been so unlucky all day, now I see that it's because I had to see you!" he thought.
>
> He went up to her and spat noisily. "Ugh!... Pah!"
>
> The nun paid not the least attention, but walked on with lowered head. Ah Q went up to her, thrust out his hand to rub her newly shaved head, saying with an idiotic grin, "Baldhead! Hurry home, your monk is waiting for you. . . ."
>
> "What has possessed you that you dare to touch me!" the nun said hurrying on, her face flushed.
>
> The people in the tavern laughed. Seeing that his feat had won their admiration, Ah Q felt elated.
>
> "Since the monk can touch you, why not I?" he said, pinching her cheek.
>
> The people in the tavern laughed again. Ah Q became more pleased with himself, and gave the nun another pinch before letting her go, just for the benefit of the onlookers.
>
> This encounter drove the memory of Whiskers Wang and the Imitation Foreign Devil out of his mind, and avenged all the misfortunes of the day, so that, strange to relate, he was even more relaxed than after the beating. He felt light and buoyant, as if he were floating on air.
>
> "May Ah Q never have any offspring!" the little nun's voice sounded tearfully in the distance.
>
> "Ha! ha! ha!" laughed Ah Q triumphantly.
>
> "Ha! ha! ha!" echoed the tavern. [Pp. 83–84]

There is a sexual factor in this encounter which gives Ah Q an added feeling of excitement after he has touched the nun's cheek. But the vileness so clearly evident here cannot be reduced to a matter of Ah Q's sexual response, for sexuality in itself is not vile. Lu Hsün once discussed the nature of the Chinese people with a friend, who said that they were particularly noted for their laziness, the manifestation of which consisted mainly in "resignation to fate and following the middle course."[58] Lu Hsün replied,

> These kinds of behavior are, I'm afraid, not simply due to laziness. They actually originated from vileness and cowardice. When the Chinese are confronted with the powerful, they dare not resist but use the words "taking the

---

58. Hsü Ping-ch'ang's letter to Lu Hsün (dated March 16, 1925) quoted in Lu Hsün, "T'ung-hsün," *Hua-kai chi, LHCC,* 3:17.

middle course'' to put a good face on their real behavior so that they feel consoled. If they have power and realize that others cannot interfere with them, or they are supported by the "majority," most of them are cruel, heartless, and tyrannical, just like despots; they then do not take the middle course. When they have lost power and cannot help taking the "middle course," they readily talk about its wisdom. As soon as they are totally defeated, they are ready to resign themselves to fate. By the time they become slaves, they do not feel moved by their plight. No matter what happens they would not then go astray from "the path of the sages." These traits can lead the Chinese people to perish, regardless of whether or not there is an enemy from without. If we want to remedy them, we must first of all expose them by tearing off their attractive masks.[59]

If we probe further into the theme of this story and the implications of Ah Q's nature, it is difficult to avoid coming to an even more negative conclusion, that Ah Q's vileness, cowardice, cunning, megalomania, and his despicable method of securing spiritual victory are merely surface features, while a more fundamental characteristic is his lack of an interior self, making him almost completely incapable of drawing inferences from experience. If we include the elements of the traditional social and cultural systems adopted by Ah Q through socialization (i.e., his second nature) as parts of his nature, then Ah Q may be called a creature who lives and behaves mostly by natural instinct. An instinctive creature can adjust to his environment and is capable of conditioned reflex. But he does not have self-awareness, nor does he have the ability to change himself. Herein lay Lu Hsün's despair of the Chinese people, of whom Ah Q was the epitome. If man, to follow Pascal, is a frail reed which thinks, then Ah Q is almost ahuman. Although his mind is "lucid" by virtue of his method of securing spiritual victory, he does not really think in Pascal's sense.

Lu Hsün graphically illustrated Ah Q's lack of an interior self in the episode where Ah Q begged the widowed housemaid Amah Wu to sleep with him. Amah Wu was dumbfounded the instant she saw Ah Q kneel before her to make the request. She trembled and rushed out of the kitchen, shrieking and sobbing. The eldest son of Ah Q's employer soon came in, cursed Ah Q, and beat him with a big bamboo pole. Ah Q fled to the threshing-floor. "After this cursing and beating it seemed that something was over and done with, and he felt free from anxieties" (p. 87). He set to work pounding rice, and shortly afterwards heard a commotion outside. Ah Q always liked to join in any excitement, so he went out in the direction of the noise. He saw Amah Wu

59. Ibid., p. 21.

wailing in shame and despair and some other people trying to persuade her not to think of committing suicide. But not until Ah Q saw the eldest son rushing at him with the big bamboo pole, which reminded him of the physical pain he had just suffered, did he realize that something he had done was somehow connected with this commotion.

Ah Q's lack of self-awareness, his inability to infer from experience and to change, are finally presented in a portrait of his grotesque involvement in the 1911 revolution.[60] Mainly because of his lack of an interior self, Ah Q drifted along with the trends of the day in such a way as to become a "revolutionary." That his "revolution" could not but fail, and that he ended up being executed by members of the traditional ruling class, who were able to continue to maintain their power during and after the "revolution," was because there was no real revolution at all.

The literary historian Cheng Chen-to once criticized the ending of "The True Story of Ah Q" as hasty and improbable: "Not wanting to go on writing, [the author] casually gave it the 'Grand Finale.' When the author began to write the story he probably did not expect that a man like Ah Q would eventually want to become a revolutionary.... At the least, Ah Q would seem to have had a dual personality."[61] To these comments Lu Hsün replied, "In my opinion, if China had not undergone the [1911] revolution, Ah Q would not have turned out to be a revolutionary. But the revolution did occur, so Ah Q did become a revolutionary. This was the only fate possible for my hero Ah Q, and I would not say that he had a dual personality.... As a matter of fact, the 'Grand Finale' was not thrust 'casually' upon Ah Q."[62] The implications of Lu Hsün's remarks are plain enough: since the Chinese people went through the experience of the 1911 revolution, Ah Q, the epitome of the Chinese people, had to go through it too. The things that happened (and that did not happen) to Ah Q and the other characters in the story, as well as to their society, were carefully intended as an allusion to the reasons for the

60. Lu Hsün had sometimes felt that he might have condemned the Chinese people too strongly in "The True Story of Ah Q"; but he said in 1926 that he no longer thought so. A realistic portrayal of events in China, he said, would look grotesque to people from another country or to the Chinese in the future if China were to be changed for the better. "I often have fancies which strike me as utterly bizarre, until I come across similar events, even more incredible. With my shallow views and limited knowledge, I could never foresee that they would happen." Lu Hsün, "Ah Q cheng-chuan ti ch'eng-yin," *Hua-kai-chi hsü pien, LHCC*, 3:284.

61. Hsi Ti (Cheng Chen-to), "Na-han," in Li Ho-lin, ed., *Lu Hsün lun* (Shanghai, 1930), p. 198. See also Lu Hsün, "Ah Q cheng-chuan ti ch'eng-yin," *Hua-kai-chi hsü pien, LHCC*, 3:279.

62. Lu Hsün, "Ah Q cheng-chuan ti ch'eng-yin," *Hua-kai-chi hsü pien, LHCC*, 3:282–83.

failure of the 1911 revolution and, by implication, to the possible way of breaking through the inhibiting barriers that made the 1911 revolution fail.

As the story progressed, after the "tragedy of love," Ah Q found that no one in the village came to hire him for odd jobs any more, so he drifted into the city and joined a gang of thieves. There he had the pleasure of watching the public beheading of a revolutionary, whom Ah Q, like most of the others, detested, because he instinctively felt "the revolutionaries were rebels, and a rebellion would make things difficult for him" (p. 99).

When he returned to the village, he was loaded with stolen goods, pretending that he had acquired them by having worked in the household of the *chü-jen* (who was the highest degree-holder in the area and thus called by the name of his degree). Members of the Chao family, which had barred Ah Q from its gates because he had brought shame on its housemaid, breached their own rule without the slightest embarrassment at their hypocrisy in order to gain an immediate advantage. Like the other villagers, they were now eager to be friendly with Ah Q in order to purchase goods from him at a bargain. Later, when he was suspected of stealing, he was held at a "respectful" distance by the villagers, who feared he might rob them. When he told them that his real role in the burglary was merely to wait outside for things to be passed to him, and that he now did not dare to venture into the city again, his prestige sank once more: he was too low to inspire fear.

Shortly afterwards, along with the rumor that the *chü-jen* had sent some old trunks to the Chao family for safekeeping, the news that the revolutionaries were about to occupy the city reached the village, causing great uneasiness and fear. Ah Q had an instinctive dislike not only of the gentry but also of others in the village. While he also detested the revolutionaries, he felt pleased that the revolution had frightened the highly prestigious *chü-jen* and caused fear among the villagers. Without understanding what a revolution was all about, or how to become a part of it, he was deluded into the belief that revolution could fulfill his instinctive desire not to be bullied by others but instead to bully as he pleased, and after a few too many cups of wine, he "became" (or claimed to be) a revolutionary.

The cost of Ah Q's delusion was his arrest by members of the ruling class, who had become "real" revolutionaries by giving new titles to their old positions, for his supposed role in the robbery of a gentry family in the village. In the village, some other "changes" also occurred. The number of those who coiled their queues on top of their heads increased day by day; Ah Q joined reluctantly in this act out of fear. The two sons of two gentry families, one of them the Imitation Foreign Devil and the other a lower-level degree-holder, had previously not gotten along together; but on the day they heard that the revolutionaries had entered the city, they joined hands in smashing the tablet inscribed "Long Live the Emperor" in the local convent.

Even in prison, even on his way to the execution ground, Ah Q still did not have a clear, personal awareness of the horror of his own death. He felt a brief panic, but his lack of an interior self and his way of thinking led him to "rationalize," in general terms, that "in this world probably it was the fate of some people at some time to have their heads cut off" (pp. 112–13). After this thought Ah Q regained his "composure" and lost himself in playing the conventional role of the condemned prisoner that the watching crowd expected.

The experience that genuinely disturbed him takes place in the courtroom when he is ordered to sign his name on a document admitting his "guilt":

> A man in a long gown approached Ah Q with a sheet of paper and a writing brush which he was about to put into Ah Q's hand. At this moment Ah Q was nearly frightened out of his wits, because this was the first time in his life that his hand had ever come into contact with a writing brush. He was pondering how it should be held, when the man pointed to a place on the sheet of paper and told him to sign. "I—I—can't read," Ah Q said with terror and shame as he grasped the brush in his hand. "In that case, to make it easy for you, draw a circle!" Ah Q was willing but in spite of himself the brush shook in his hand; so the man spread the paper on the ground. Ah Q bent down and tried with all his might to draw the circle. Fearful of people laughing at him, he determined to make the circle round; however, the wretched brush was not only heavy but also unruly. Just as he was about to close the circle with his trembling hand, it jerked with a centrifugal motion with the result that the circle was shaped like a melon seed. [P. 111.]

Under the shaping influence of traditional Chinese culture, life was less important than the medium for the transmission of that culture. The successful transmission of that culture had led to ignorance in the Chinese people about what life was and how it should be lived. Here Lu Hsün's iconoclasm reaches its most mordant heights.

Nevertheless, by the time Ah Q approached death, he began to have a true awareness of reality:

> Ah Q turned to take another look at the shouting crowd.
> At that instant his thoughts whipped about like a whirlwind. Four years ago he had met a hungry wolf at the foot of a mountain; it had followed him with

dogged persistence, never too near and never too far, its mouth watering for his flesh. He was scared to death, but fortunately had had with him a woodcutter's axe, which gave him the courage to get back to Weichuang. Yet he could never forget those eyes of the wolf, fierce and yet slinking, gleaming like two will-o'-the-wisps, as though piercing right through his skin and flesh. And now he beheld eyes such as he had never seen before, even more horrible than those of the wolf: dull and lusterless yet glinting with greediness; already devouring his words and still more eager to devour something beyond his flesh and blood. These eyes followed him, never too near and never too far.

These eyes seemed to merge into one, gnawing at his soul. [Pp. 113–14.]

At this instant he could not rationalize and be happy any longer. He wanted to shout "Help, . . ." But it was too late for Ah Q to utter the word. "All became black before his eyes, there was a buzzing in his ears, and he felt as if his whole body were being scattered like light dust" (p. 114).

From his earliest iconoclastic writings, the horror of Chinese cannibalism was a constant theme of Lu Hsün's antitraditionalism. Ah Q's pleasure in watching the beheading of a revolutionary is one case in point; but since his personality has an element of naïveté, his vileness in this episode is coated with a certain insensibility, and the immediate shock to the reader is somewhat mitigated. When Ah Q's pleasure is echoed by the pleasure of the common people in watching his own execution, the cannibalistic motif is expressed by Lu Hsün with genuine horror. Even among unself-conscious creatures there are those which instinctively care for life, at least that of their own species, and those which do not. According to Lu Hsün here, the Chinese must be classified among the latter.

In other societies too the public execution of a criminal has been treated as a spectacle. While Lu Hsün was not a student in the comparative study of mass culture and mass psychology, challenged on this ground he would probably have argued that there was something uniquely Chinese in the cruel enjoyment of the suffering and destruction of life as such. The particular way in which the Chinese enjoyed watching the spectacle expressed this trait, which cannot be related to the universal nature of man but to the nature of the Chinese tradition, under whose influence the natural man had become the Chinese man.

The cannibalistic theme reappears time and again in Lu Hsün's writings. "Since the dawn of the Chinese civilization," he wrote in 1925, "countless feasts—large and small—of human flesh have been spread, and those at these feasts eat others and are eaten themselves; but the anguished cries of the weak, to say nothing of the women and children, are drowned in the senseless clamor of the murderers.''[63]

A dark, pessimistic view of the Chinese people emerges as a major motif of "The True Story of Ah Q." Nevertheless, there are some innocent and naïve aspects of Ah Q that cannot be regarded as unequivocally deplorable. In comparison with some of the other conspicuous characters in the story, such as the members of the Chao family, the Imitation Foreign Devil, the *chü-jen,* Ah Q seems more likeable because of this trace of innocence. For instance, after losing all his money in gambling and being obliged to watch from the back of the crowd, he "became worried for the other participants" (p. 78). When questioned insistently by the idlers, he proudly recounts his experience in the city as a thief without any attempt at concealment. In the courtroom scene in which he was ordered to sign his name, he makes a sincere effort to draw a circle. While the second instance might not be merely a reflection of his naïveté, but also an indication of his desire to show off, the first and third instances do suggest a strain of innocence.

What are the implications of this side of Ah Q for the iconoclasm of Lu Hsün? Lu Hsün's consciousness is dialectical in that while he attacks the Chinese tradition in toto, he is committed to some values derived from it; the other side of the dialectic, however, cannot be inferred from this aspect of Ah Q's character. Though Ah Q's sense of innocence can be appreciated in and of itself, it can hardly be understood as a possible source for generating intellectual and moral change from within, or for receiving the stimulus for such change from without. Ah Q's lack of an interior self prevents that, for without self-awareness he could not consciously cultivate and develop this good element in any way. Living mostly by instinct, he could not be inspired by external stimulation, even if it were available. His innocence is in fact a peculiar manifestation of his lack of an interior self, rather than being a moral strength in his personality. The function of this innocence toward the end of the story is to entrap him in the evil systems of traditional society and culture and let him be killed by the ruling class without knowing why. Not until the last moment of his life does he have any self-awareness. But it is brought to him by death; as long as he was alive, it was always beyond his reach. Living without an interior self was the very nature of his existence.

It is thus a totally dark view of the Chinese people that the story of Ah Q conveys. Nothing in the village—the microcosmic China—could be taken as a

63. Lu Hsün, "Teng-hsia man-pi," *Fen, LHCC,* 1:316.

positive source of hope. The 1911 revolution, instead of changing anything, only revealed the abhorrent nature of the Chinese people. Aside from the formal change in the titles of official posts, the destruction of some tokens of the old society, and so on, the old cultural and social system (superstitions, ethos, the hierarchical order of Chinese society) remained in substance intact.

This view is dark enough; still it does not fully reflect the profound pessimism of Lu Hsün. One cannot say that the 1911 revolution accomplished nothing: it did put Ah Q to death. In a sense, Ah Q was killed by the ruling class that embodied the traditional Chinese social and cultural systems. But why was he not killed before the revolution, when the ruling class was as malicious as it was in the revolution? Ah Q, Lu Hsün indicated, could not help becoming a "revolutionary": the interplay of his inclination to follow the prevailing trend, his instinctive dislike of the ruling class, his naïveté, his cunning, and his desire to take advantage of others saw to that. In the old days, Ah Q had sometimes disliked the ruling class, and had also been vile, cunning, and naïve, but his cowardice had prevented him from becoming a robber, although for a short while he had been a petty thief. He would not have been killed even if he had been caught. But his eagerness to become a "revolutionary" put him in a position where he could readily be condemned as a robber—he became more liable to manipulation by the ruling class. Two important implications emerge from this. First, although the 1911 revolution did not change anything for the better, it had, in Lu Hsün's retrospective view, unleashed the evil forces of Chinese society from the restraints of its traditional framework and made them even more active and effective. Secondly, by showing the relationship between Ah Q's eagerness to become a "revolutionary" without knowing what revolution was and his consequent death for becoming a "revolutionary," Lu Hsün offers a lesson to the Chinese of the future if they wish to work for revolutionary change. Ah Q had not known the goals and the method of revolution, and moreover was incapable of acquiring such knowledge, for he did not have an interior self. In the final analysis, a fundamental and categorical change in China could be achieved by the Chinese people only if their nature had already been fundamentally and categorically changed to enable them to understand the goals and the method of revolutionary change. This, then, was the primary task for China's regeneration.

Theoretically, of course, there are many possible routes to such change. And it is also possible that one might be at a loss in trying to find a viable way to accomplish it. However, under the shaping influence of the cultural-

intellectualistic approach, reinforced by his bitter experience in the failure of
the 1911 revolution, Lu Hsün, like other May Fourth intellectuals, believed
the intellectual revolution to be the necessary precondition. Talking with a
friend in 1925 about ways of change, he said that he still believed in what *New
Youth* had advocated: the necessity and priority of intellectual revolution
("*ssu-hsiang ke-ming*"), "without which there can be no way at all"[64] to
reach the goal.

But Lu Hsün faced an agonizing dilemma: he did not consider that the route
he believed, intellectually, to be correct was, in practice, viable. If Ah Q
epitomized the Chinese people, then they clearly lacked even the minimum of
self-awareness that would seem mandatory for a successful intellectual revolution; there were no resources within the Chinese people for such a change.
Quite consistently, then, on this level of his consciousness, Lu Hsün de-
spaired of the future.

Despite his pessimism about the future, Lu Hsün nevertheless was prepared
to engage in "a war of resistance in despair."[65] The imperative of his
nationalism committed him, in spite of his despair, to work for a better China,
which, his fundamental assumptions dictated, had to be built on a new intellectual and cultural foundation. Forces at work on a level quite different
from that of the forces leading to his despair called for hope. Although hope
could not be suggested by a realistic assessment of the nature of the Chinese
people, it could rest on the formal notion of the unpredictability of the future.
Since the future had not arrived, no one could, logically speaking, know what
it would be. Thus, as long as there is a future, there exists a possibility for
hope.

Lu Hsün's hope, in this restricted sense, was frequently expressed in his
writings. We have already noted it in the preface to his *Call to Arms*. In
another piece, sighing over the fact that the China of his day was similar to
previous ages, he yet continued, "Fortunately, no one can say with certainty
that the nature of the [Chinese] people will never change. Although this
'uncertainty' implies that we may experience something we have never experienced before—the horror of annihilation—it also means there is hope for
regeneration, which would also be an exception to our past experience."[66]

64. Lu Hsün, "T'ung-hsün," *Hua-kai-chi, LHCC*, 3:17.
65. Lu Hsün's letter to Hsü Kuang-p'ing dated March 18, 1925: "My works are too dark
because I often feel that only 'darkness and emptiness' are 'reality.' However, I am determined to
launch a war of resistance in despair against them." Lu Hsün, *Liang-ti shu, LHCC*, 9:18.
66. Lu Hsün, "Hu-jan hsiang-tao," *Hua-kai chi, LHCC*, 3:14.

Nevertheless, his hope was a corollary of his despair; it was against the background of his despair that this sense of hope had arisen. This sense of hope had a built-in ambivalence; he sometimes felt that the hope was vain because it was unrealistic. "My heart," wrote Lu Hsün in one of his celebrated prose poems, "once overflowed with sanguinary songs: blood and iron, fire and poison, resurgence and revenge. Then suddenly they all became empty. But I sometimes deliberately filled my heart with vain, self-deluding hope. Hope, hope—I took this shield of hope to withstand the invasion of dark night in emptiness, although behind this shield there was still dark night in emptiness."[67]

Yet, in the same poem, quoting the Hungarian poet Sándor Petőfi, Lu Hsün concludes that "despair, like hope is [also] but vanity";[68] it is a surrender to the past, or more precisely, to rational calculation based on past experience. His agonized tension between hope and despair led him to emphasize will— the will to strive to answer the calling in life.[69] Here his thought is characterized by an existentialist stress on the meaning of will in human nature and history without entailing the existentialist conception of the absurdity of life.

THE SCHOLARLY, THE STYLISTIC,
AND THE PERSONAL AND AESTHETIC

One of the ironies in the life of Lu Hsün was that, although he was among the foremost in calling for total rejection of the Chinese tradition, he spent a good deal of time in scholarly research on various aspects of that tradition, and there are other aspects at the explicit level of his consciousness that were positively linked to it. He made use of some traditional stylistic techniques in his creative writings. Personally and aesthetically, he appreciated a number of elements in the tradition. We should, therefore, investigate the implications of these attitudes for his iconoclastic totalism. Was it seriously undermined by them, or merely contradicted in a formal (or logical) sense?

Lu Hsün was one of the eminent scholars in the history of Chinese literature.[70] His pioneer work on the history of Chinese fiction, based on his lecture notes at National Peking University and originally published in 1923–24, was

---

67. Lu Hsün, "Hsi-wang," *Yeh-ts'ao, LHCC,* 2:170.

68. Ibid., p. 171.

69. This is forcefully shown in Lu Hsün, "Kuo-k'o," *Yeh-ts'ao, LHCC,* 2:179–85.

70. His eminence is generally recognized. For instance, the late Professor Tsi-an Hsia wrote of him: "At one time a professor of Chinese literature, he was probably as learned in his field as any scholar of his time." Tsi-an Hsia, *The Gate of Darkness* (Seattle, 1968), p. 102.

the first treatment by a Chinese scholar of the general history of Chinese prose fiction from its ancient beginnings through the Ch'ing period.[71] He edited, in the best tradition of Chinese textual criticism, several anthologies of traditional tales, a collection of historical materials about his native city, Shaohsing, and the works of the poet Hsi K'ang (A.D. 223–62). He also accumulated a notable collection of rubbings of early inscriptions and carvings and worked on an as yet unpublished listing of Han stone portraits and Buddhist carvings and tomb inscriptions of the Six Dynasties (A.D. 420–589) period.[72]

His *Brief History of Chinese Fiction* (*Chung-kuo hsiao-shuo shih-lüeh*), although containing a number of iconoclastic remarks about the practice and effects of the Confucianist ethos, was in the main a judicious treatment of the evolution of traditional Chinese fiction. He particularly singled out *Chin P'ing Mei* and *The Scholars* (*Ju-lin wai-shih*) for approval on account of their realistic humanism.[73]

From a formal or logical point of view, Lu Hsün's scholarly treatment of traditional Chinese fiction and his iconoclastic totalism are incompatible. If everything in China's past was abhorrent, how could he express appreciation

71. Cheng Chen-to, an authority on the history of Chinese fiction, states that Lu Hsün's pioneer work ''has pointed out the general direction for later research for thirty years.'' Cheng's remarks are cited in Wang Yao, *Lu Hsün yü Chung-kuo wen-hsüeh* (Shanghai, 1952), p. 54. Wang Yao is eager to establish a positive relationship between Lu Hsün's works and the Chinese literary tradition, but his discussion is confused; in it he often quotes passages from Lu Hsün out of context and fails to distinguish elements of traditional Chinese literature as literary techniques, which Lu Hsün used, from traditional Chinese literary form and content, which he discarded.

72. Hsü Kuang-p'ing, ed., "Lu Hsün i-chu shu-mu," in *Lu Hsün hsien-sheng chi-nien chi* (Shanghai, 1937), pp. 1–11.

73. Lu Hsün, *Chung-kuo hsiao-shuo shih-lüeh, LHCC*, 8:146, 181–82: "The writer [of *Chin P'ing Mei*] shows a perspicacious understanding of the life of his time; his descriptions are clear yet subtle, highly lucid yet implicitly satirical, and for the sake of contrast he sometimes portrays two quite different aspects of life. His writing displays such a variety of human interest that no novel of that period could surpass it. . . . It is not true to say that *Chin P'ing Mei* deals only with the profligates and loose women of urban society, for Hsimen comes from a wealthy family and his friends include nobles, influential men, and scholar-officials. Hence the presentation of such a family is in effect a condemnation of various kinds of people, [and the novel is] not simply a story disparaging low society. . . . Wu Ching-tzu's *The Scholars* is the first novel in which a writer criticizes social abuses without any personal malice, directing his attack mainly on the literati. The style is warm and humorous, gentle and ironical. This must rank as China's first novel of social satire. . . . Since he based his characters mainly on cases he had seen or heard of himself and succeeded in bringing these figures to life in his book, it is like a candle lighting up the dark, leaving nothing hidden. Officials, literati, scholars, hermits, sometimes humble townsfolk too, all stand vividly revealed in these pages, while a panorama of the whole country is unfolded before the reader's eyes.''

for works of traditional fiction? From a substantive point of view, however, this formal contradiction did not constitute a serious tension in Lu Hsün's consciousness, for he saw the positive features of some works of traditional Chinese fiction as reflecting a standard of realistic humanism which claimed a general (universal) applicability to literature, including foreign literature.[74] These features were, according to this view of literature, not particularly Chinese. They were, then, quite inconsequential to the Chinese quality of the rest of the Chinese cultural tradition.

This of course still leaves unanswered the question why some positive elements, albeit cross-cultural ones, could arise in a Chinese past that was perceived holistically as a total evil. One's inability to find an answer to this question discloses a logical fallacy in Lu Hsün's iconoclastic totalism (and for that matter, in that of Ch'en Tu-hsiu and Hu Shih, who, as previous chapters have shown, also recognized some general and cross-cultural positive elements in the Chinese tradition). Lu Hsün never faced this fallacy squarely: the possibility of his doing so was remote because of its merely formal nature. Lu Hsün would probably not have felt greatly disturbed if he had been conscious of it. For the positive features in the tradition discovered by applying a general and cross-cultural category such as realistic humanism could not be taken as affecting, or being affected by, the particularly Chinese nature of the Chinese tradition. They could, indeed, be regarded as accidental to that tradition. Thus his iconoclastic rejection of all things generically Chinese in China's past was not, in any substantive sense, challenged.

On the explicit level of consciousness, Lu Hsün drew on traditional Chinese artistic techniques, but the form (or structure) and content of his creative writings were categorically new.[75] It is also well-known that he freely used the

74. Whether literature should be approached from this point of view is of course a different question. This pattern of treatment also occurs in Lu Hsün's *Outline of a History of Chinese Literature (Han wen-hsüeh shih kang-yao)*, originally his lecture notes at Amoy University in 1926, and published posthumously. He singles out a number of features in the *Book of Odes*, the *Li-sao*, and other writings for appreciation in terms of his general categories of aesthetic standards and realistic humanism. See *LHCC*, 8:255–309.

75. For Lu Hsün's own account of his use of traditional artistic techniques, see his "Wo tsen-mo tso-ch'i hsiao-shuo lai," *Nan-ch'iang pei-tiao chi, LHCC*, 4:393. Jaroslav Průšek holds similar views in many of his writings. Průšek maintains that the modern Chinese literary revolution was a qualitative change that cannot be traced to earlier evolutionary changes in Chinese literature. The literary revolution, he holds, was the result of a revolution in the mind of the Chinese writer and a revolutionary transformation in the relationships among the shaping factors of literary art. See Jaroslav Průšek "A Confrontation of Traditional Oriental Literature with

vocabulary of the *Chuang-tzu* and the writings of Ch'ü Yüan.[76] Some contemporary literary critics have stressed the organic nature of the relationship between form and content in literature; in Lu Hsün's creative writings, form and content are organically integrated and qualitatively different from those in traditional Chinese literature. For Lu Hsün, traditional Chinese literary elements served merely as some of the raw materials upon which he drew for the form and content of his literary art. They were related to that art only in a technical sense and had no essential bearing on his ideology and moral judgment. Hence, they also did not pose a serious challenge to his iconoclastic totalism.

Lu Hsün's interest in Chinese woodblock engravings constituted an expres-

---

Modern European Literature in the Context of the Chinese Literary Revolution," in Leon Edel, ed., *Literary History and Literary Criticism* (New York, 1965), pp. 168–70. But Průšek indicates that Lu Hsün, while abandoning the traditional Chinese literary forms, used the traditional Chinese lyrical method to organize many of his creative writings. The subjective, impressionistic, nonparticular nature of the lyric, with its lack of a story line and structured plot, was removed from its rigidly prescribed traditional form and was freely used by Lu Hsün to express a revolutionary perception of social reality. Jaroslav Průšek "Some Marginal Notes on the Poems of Po Chü-i," in his *Chinese History and Literature* (Prague, 1970), pp. 80–81: "The Chinese lyric has for centuries striven by a juxtaposition of several elements selected from Nature and saturated with high emotion to create a picture capable of communicating a supreme experience, an insight, a complete yielding to, and immersion in, the *mysterium* of Nature. The basic presumption for such a procedure was the artist's power of accurate observation, an acute perception of traits that may be small, but are characteristic, that would go to the core of the situation which the author wishes to communicate to the reader.... This method taught the artist to pick out what was typical in every phenomenon and, by reducing it to its most essential traits, to express its substance as concisely as possible. It is not difficult to imagine what this method implied when the artist applied it to social reality. Excessively refined perceptivity gave him the ability to select from the chaos of phenomena the most significant—that dominant in the picture to which we referred above—and render it in a few pregnantly revealing brush-strokes. Thus does the poet build up pictures which not only give the substance of individual events, but a résumé of whole epochs. It seems to me that this method enabled the artist to render more incisively and cogently the horrors of social evil than could any epic procedure. In the individual story, light and shade must necessarily alternate and often the subjective factor excuses and obscures the workings of social evils, whereas in the lyrical poem the facts stand out in their stark, naked and unalterable frightfulness. With the removal of all additive detail, everything vanished that might modify the horror of the phenomenon presented.... That is also the reason why this artistic method—the rendering of the substance of a certain social situation in a single, typical picture, vibrating with emotion and stripped of all that is secondary and accidental—was employed by modern artists such as Lu Hsün, in his attempt to express *in a new way* his revolutionary attitude to reality." (Italics mine.)

76. See Kuo Mo-jo, "Chuang-tzu yü Lu Hsün," in his *Chin-hsi p'u-chien* (Shanghai, 1947), pp. 275–96, and Hsü Shou-shang, "Ch'ü Yüan yü Lu Hsün," in his *Wang-yu Lu Hsün yin-hsiang chi*, pp. 5–8.

sion of personal, aesthetic, and scholarly aspects of his explicit consciousness. He had had an interest in traditional Chinese graphic art since childhood,
and had been greatly impressed by the artistic quality of woodblock prints of
drawings by Chinese painters, printed on traditional-style stationery, when he
saw them in Peking. Later, under the shadow of the Japanese invasion, he
took great pains, in collaboration with Cheng Chen-to, to collect and publish
such prints, fearing that this indigenous tradition, combining the art of the
literati and of craftsmen, might be destroyed by the imminent war.[77]

He had also been intrigued since childhood by the mystery of some aspects
of folk theatre and folklore. Of his fondness for the ghosts of folk theatre in
particular the late Tsi-an Hsia once observed:

> For some of [the ghosts] he could even harbor a secret love. His attitude towards
> the ghostly figures [*Wu-ch'ang* (Life-is-transient [The infernal agent]) and *Nü-
> tiao* (The ghost of the hanged woman)] in the *Mu-lien-hsi* (Cycle of the legends
> of Saint Mu-lien) was that of doting fondness. Few authors are able to discuss a
> macabre subject with so much zest. These two essays [about the two ghosts] are
> especially precious since they are from Lu Hsün, a social reformer surprisingly
> sympathetic to popular superstitions. Whereas Chou Tso-jen wrote a number of
> witty but rather dispassionate studies of Chinese folklore, Lu Hsün's interest
> was not purely scholarly. He took a fascinated look at and then made fun of the
> ghosts' horrible looks. He let his fancy run freely over the subject, and, in good
> humor, he tried to find if there were some reason that we should all love these
> ghosts. With his vivid imagination he called them back to life, as it were, and
> affectionately showed them around to his readers.[78]

Lu Hsün's interest in these kinds of traditional art, folklore, and folk theatre
was directed to their particular modes of expression. In other words, it was
precisely their particularly Chinese qualities that fascinated him, not their
reflection of some universal, cross-cultural aspect of art or their technical
possibilities. Lu Hsün's attraction to these aspects of traditional culture indicates the complexity of his consciousness and suggests some countermotifs in
his totalistic iconoclasm. Still, these countermotifs, while challenging it in a
substantive way, did not seriously undermine his totalistic stance of iconoclasm as a moral judgment, for the elements of Chinese tradition he appreciated were accepted primarily on an aesthetic basis in the private realm of

77. See Lu Hsün and Hsi Ti (Cheng Chen-to), eds., *Peiping chien-p'u* (Peking, 1934). The
Harvard-Yenching Library holds a copy of this beautiful book. Lu Hsün's preface is reprinted in
his *Chi-wai-chi shih-i*, *LHCC*, 7:664–65. Lu Hsün's collaboration with Cheng Chen-to in publishing this book is detailed in his letters to Cheng in Hsü Kuang-p'ing, ed., *Lu Hsün shu-chien*,
pp. 519–84.
78. Tsi-an Hsia, *The Gate of Darkness*, pp. 155–56.

his consciousness. Had he felt the need to align all aspects of his consciousness in a consistent manner, he should have modified his iconoclastic totalism in the light of this interest. Without additional countermotifs, however, one can say that Lu Hsün was totally repelled by the moral (or immoral) aspects of the Chinese tradition but felt aesthetically at home with some parts of traditional folklore and theatre in the private realm of his consciousness. Since these were primarily his private aesthetic concerns, he did not make a public cause out of them. His connoisseur-like interest in traditional Chinese woodblock prints was more than private, but its public nature was scholarly and sentimental rather than moral.

THE IMPLICIT LEVEL OF CONSCIOUSNESS

The most serious challenge to Lu Hsün's totalistic rejection of traditional Chinese morality and culture lay in his implicit intellectual and moral commitment to some traditional Chinese values. Owing to the complexity of Lu Hsün's consciousness, these two aspects of his thought have to be explained and differentiated with care. His totalistic iconoclasm was clearly, not to say polemically, expressed in many of his essays and creative writings. In the latter, such as "The True Story of Ah Q," the motif of totalistic iconoclasm and the referents of totalistic attacks, though subtly presented, can hardly be missed. The demand for total rejection of the Chinese tradition was, in fact, Lu Hsün's most prominent explicit polemical concern in the May Fourth era. We can, therefore, regard this iconoclasm as belonging to the explicit, polemical level of his consciousness. On the other hand, however, Lu Hsün was intellectually and morally committed to some traditional Chinese values. He was fully aware of these traditional values in his consciousness, and some of his creative writings were involved in articulating them. Yet since he was intellectually and morally committed, in an explicit fashion, to iconoclastic totalism, he was reluctant to expound the reasons for his commitment to some of the traditional values, which remained implicit, though conscious. In the interest of brevity I shall henceforward refer to the explicit polemical level as the explicit level, and the conscious but unexplicated level as the implicit level.

Lu Hsün's simultaneous intellectual and moral commitments to iconoclastic totalism and to some traditional Chinese values gave rise to an intense tension, no mere formal or logical contradiction, in his consciousness. Under the pressure of this tension, Lu Hsün might have responded in a number of ways. He might have reached creatively another stage of awareness that transcended this tension. Or, for lack of a genuine solution, he might have been torn asunder, his creativity paralyzed, by the divided vision and the resultant sense of guilt. An inquiry into exactly how he responded is, then, of pivotal significance to an understanding of his complex consciousness.

It is appropriate to my purpose here to elucidate this tension through a close look, in one of his stories, at one of the traditional values to which Lu Hsün was committed. The story is a freer vehicle for this purpose than the essay: the author can express different and even irreconcilable ideas and evoke different moods through different people and settings, feeling less pressure toward consistency.

"In the Tavern" ("Tsai chiu-lou shang") is written in the form of personal reminiscence. The narrator encounters his former classmate and colleague Lü Wei-fu, whom he has not seen for many years. The two episodes that Lü Wei-fu recounts in the story concern, respectively, the reinterment of a much-loved younger brother and a visit to the daughter of a former neighbor, both done in fulfillment of the expressed wishes of Lü's mother. These two episodes, Chou Tso-jen wrote in 1952, "were [experienced by] the author [Lu Hsün] himself, although the poetry (shih) is not entirely identical with the actual facts."[79]

In the first instance, the facts of the story and those of Lu Hsün's life are substantially the same, with only minor and inconsequential differences in detail. Lu Hsün's fourth younger brother, Chou Ch'un-shou, died of acute pneumonia on December 20, 1898, when he was about five and a half years old, to the great grief of the family.[80] Lu Hsün's mother, in particular, grieved profoundly over the death of her child. She asked Chou Tso-jen to have a picture of Ch'un-shou painted from his description. The picture hung on the wall of her room in Shaohsing and, later, in Peking throughout her life.

Ch'un-shou was buried near the edge of a public burial ground. The soil nearby was over the years excavated by local people, and Ch'un-shou's grave was in danger of collapse. When Lu Hsün came back to Shaohsing in 1919, his mother, greatly worried, asked him to move the grave to a burial ground that the family had later purchased, where his father was buried. The family

---

79. Chou Hsia-shou (Chou Tso-jen), *Lu Hsün hsiao-shuo li-ti jen-wu*, p. 163.

80. Lu Hsün was taking the preliminary district civil service examination in his hometown when Ch'un-shou died. He had returned home from Nanking, where he had been attending the Kiangnan Naval Academy, for the purpose of taking the examination. But Lu Hsün was so saddened by the sudden death of his brother that he had no heart to continue the examination, which was to last several more days, and abruptly left home for Nanking on December 24.

was too sad to question Lu Hsün about the reinterment of Ch'un-shou; but Chou Tso-jen believes that what Lü Wei-fu had experienced and done in the story were what Lu Hsün himself had experienced and done.

There is some confusion about the second episode of "In The Tavern"—Lü Wei-fu's delivery, at the express command of his mother, of artificial flowers to the daughter of a former neighbor. We have two comments about this by Chou Tso-jen: the one, already cited, to the effect that the episode was "experienced by the author himself," and a later one in which he claimed that the episode was fictitious but that the daughter in the story was modeled upon the daughter of a neighbor of Lu Hsün's family, who died not of consumption, as in the story, but of typhoid fever.[81]

The discrepancy is probably more apparent than real. Chou Tso-jen wrote his account of the life of Lu Hsün when he was sixty-seven, and it is not particularly surprising that his statements are not strictly consistent. He seems to have meant that Lu Hsün's feelings toward the daughter of their neighbor were similar to those of Lü Wei-fu in the story; he therefore regarded the second episode as having been "experienced" by Lu Hsün himself.

Whatever the exact meaning of Chou Tso-jen's words, his account provides enough solid evidence for us to infer that Lu Hsün used Lü Wei-fu's words and deeds to articulate his own consciousness. In short, the conversation in the story between Lü Wei-fu and the narrator may be considered a dialogue which takes place in the mind of Lu Hsün himself.

The story begins with the narrator's account of a journey from the north to the southeast during which he visited his native place and then went to a nearby city where he had taught school for a year. Indolence and nostalgia made him put up at an inn. He went round to call upon former colleagues he thought might still be in the city, but none were to be found. To escape from the dismal feeling of disappointment and loneliness he went to a tavern he had formerly frequented. Sipping wine alone, he unexpectedly met Lü Wei-fu, an old classmate and a colleague in his teaching days in this city, whom he had not seen for many years. Wei-fu now bore little resemblance to the vigorous and iconoclastic young man he once had been. Since they had parted, Wei-fu had done a number of insignificant things; he now lived with his mother in Taiyüan and, to earn his living, taught Confucian classics to the children of a

81. The above account is based on Chou Hsia-shou (Chou Tso-jen), *Lu Hsün hsiao-shuo li-ti jen-wu*, pp. 163–75, and *Lu Hsün ti ku-chia*, pp. 108–9. See also Chou Tso-jen, *Chih-t'ang hui-hsiang-lu* (Hong Kong, 1970), pp. 46–53, 592–99.

fellow provincial. The narrator asked Wei-fu why he had returned to this city, which was his native place. Wei-fu said:

"For a few things quite inconsequential." In one gulp he emptied his cup, then took several pulls at his cigarette and his eyes widened somewhat. "Inconsequential—but we may as well talk about them. . . . Perhaps you knew that I had a little brother, who died when he was three and was buried in the country here. I can't even remember clearly what he looked like, but my mother tells me that he was a very lovable child, and very fond of me. Even now it brings tears to her eyes to speak of him. This last spring a cousin of mine wrote that water was beginning to approach his grave and that unless something was done, it might soon be washed into the river. My mother became very distressed when she learned about it—I couldn't keep it from her as she knows how to read—and could hardly sleep for several nights. But what could I do? I had neither time nor money for the trip. I could not do a thing at the time.

"It was put off until now. The New Year vacation gave me the opportunity to come back South to move his grave. . . . It was the day before yesterday. I brought a small coffin—for I thought that the original one must have rotted away long ago—and some new bedding and cotton batting, and went out to the country with four laborers to attend to the reinterment. I suddenly had an exalted feeling, and was eager to dig up the grave and see the remains of the little brother of mine who had been so fond of me. I had never had any experience with such things before. When we reached the grave, I found that the river was indeed eating into the bank and was already less than two feet away from it; it was in a pitiful state, almost level with the ground, as no earth had been heaped upon it for two years. I stood in the snow and, pointing to it, said to the laborers: 'Dig it up!' . . . When they had reached the enclosure, I went over to look, and found, as I expected, that the coffin had rotted almost completely away, leaving only a heap of splinters and small fragments of wood. With my heart beating violently, I carefully removed the heap of wood so as to get a look at my little brother. But there was nothing—bedding, clothes, bones—nothing! I thought that if these things had all perished, there might at least be some hair left, since I had been told that hair is the most imperishable part of the human body. I leaned over and searched carefully where his head should have been. There was nothing, not a single hair! . . .

"Really there was no need of reinterment. One could have flattened the ground, sold the coffin, and considered the matter ended. . . . But that was not what I did. Instead, I spread out the bedding, took some earth from where his body had been, wrapped it up in the cotton, put it in the new coffin, had it carried to my father's grave, and buried it beside him. Because I used bricks for the enclosure of the coffin, I was busy most of yesterday supervising the work. Well, I have done what had to be done, at least enough to deceive my mother and set her mind at peace. Ah, are you looking at me like that because you are surprised that I am so different from what I used to be? Yes, I still remember the time when we went together to the Tutelary God's Temple and pulled off the idols' beards; how we used to discuss methods of changing China all day long until we came to blows. But now I am like this, willing to let things slide and to compromise. I have sometimes thought that my old friends probably would no longer consider me a friend when they see the way I am—nevertheless (*jan-erh*), this is the way I am now.'"[82]

Lü Wei-fu told the narrator further that just before he came to the tavern he did another "inconsequential thing, which he was *nevertheless* glad to do" (p. 29; italics mine). When he was about to set out on this journey, his mother had remembered that Ah Shun, the eldest daughter of their neighbor the boatman, had once longed for an artificial flower made of red velvet; she saw someone wear it and cried a long while because she couldn't get one and was spanked by her father. This particular kind of flower was made in another province and was not procurable in his native city; his mother had asked him to buy some on his way and give them to Ah Shun. Lü Wei-fu said that he did not consider this errand irksome: he had a sincere wish to do something for Ah Shun, who had capably and diligently taken care of her younger brother and sister and attended to the wants of her father after her mother died when she was about ten. She had earned praise from her neighbors and gratitude from her father.

Wei-fu had not known about the episode of the artificial flower, but when his mother spoke of it he recalled with fondness another episode in which he was moved by Ah Shun's pureness of heart. He was, therefore, very enthusiastic about what he was asked to do. After searching all over Taiyüan without success, he finally found the flowers in Tsinan, where he made a stop for that particular purpose. "I don't know that they were the same kind of flowers for which she was spanked, but they were made of the same material," continued Lü Wei-fu. "I did not know whether she liked deep or light colors, so I bought one of brilliant red and one of pinkish red and brought them here with me" (p. 31). He stayed over for another day just to deliver these flowers to Ah Shun. But when he got to her house, neither she nor her father was there. Wei-fu found out from a neighbor that she had died of consumption the preceding autumn. "Well, that was that," said Lü Wei-fu. He then asked the neighbor to give the flowers to Ah Shun's sister; he intended, he said, to tell his mother that Ah Shun was too happy for words

---

82. Lu Hsün, "Tsai chiu-lou shang," *P'ang-huang, LHCC*, 2:26–28. Further page references to the text of this story are given in parentheses in the text.

when she got the flowers. "But, what do these inconsequential things matter
anyway?" he immediately added.

> "When I have muddled through the New Year vacation, I shall again begin to
> teach 'The Master says' and 'The *Book of Odes* says.'"
> "Is that what you teach?" I asked with astonishment.
> "Of course, did you think that I was teaching English? I had only two pupils
> at first, one studying the *Book of Odes,* the other the *Mencius.* Recently
> another one was added, a girl, studying *Precepts for Women* (*Nü-erh ching*). I
> do not even teach any arithmetic; not that I don't want to, but because their
> parents don't."
> "I really did not think that you would be teaching such books...."
> "That's what their father wants them to read. I am an outsider, so it's all the
> same to me. What do these inconsequential things matter anyway? One need not
> be too serious about them." [P. 33.]

This story of Lu Hsün's is pregnant with complex ambiguities that give rise
to a genuine intellectual tension between his explicit iconoclastic totalism and
his intellectual and moral commitment to a traditional Chinese value at the
implicit level of his consciousness. On the surface, it would seem that Lü
Wei-fu's seeming retreat from his youthful iconoclasm might be explained in
terms of a tension between an intellectual commitment to Western values and
an emotional attachment to China's past. Actually, this is not the case. Before
Lü Wei-fu recounts the two episodes in the story, he prefaces them with
apologies, saying that they are "inconsequential matters" and that he "is now
much more obtuse than before" (pp. 28–29). These statements suggest that
what he did in the two episodes was in conflict with what he still believed. He
apologizes because he believes that what he did is not justifiable in the face of
his iconoclastic rejection of tradition—a commitment which he apparently
still holds.

Actually, only one iconoclastic act of Wei-fu's is mentioned in the story,
his pulling off the beards of the idols in the Tutelary God's Temple. One
symbolic act, directed against the idols of a tradition, need not imply a
totalistic rejection of everything in that tradition, in the substantial sense. One
can well imagine a kind of iconoclasm that attacks the idols of a tradition and
what they represent but does not attack every substantive aspect of that tradition. It is also conceivable that the idols of a tradition are distorting symbols of
its positive features or do not represent its totality. But Lü Wei-fu is largely
modeled upon Lu Hsün himself, and the May Fourth iconoclasm was not
given to differentiating among the elements in China's past. It is, therefore,

quite certain that Lü Wei-fu's iconoclasm is a totalistic one, which makes any positive link with, or appreciation of, any part of the Chinese tradition look like a compromise of one's explicit intellectual and moral commitments. Hence the apologies.

However, Lü Wei-fu is related positively to Chinese tradition, as it is manifested in the two episodes of the story. This positive relationship does not constitute a psychological counterbalance that serves to assuage the sense of intellectual inferiority resulting from commitment to Western values. It is a reflection of an implicit but conscious adoption of a traditional Chinese cultural norm and of an intellectual and moral commitment to a traditional Chinese value. Thus, a genuine tension exists, intellectually; and to explain this tension in terms of a dichotomy between emotional attachment to China's past and intellectual commitment to Western values is to impose a rigid category of explanation at the expense of the complexity of concrete historical sources.

Lü Wei-fu insists that he does not take his actions seriously because they were inconsequential. But were they really so inconsequential? He has wanted to please his mother, but he clearly shares her genuine human concerns, channeled through a typically traditional Chinese pattern of person-to-person expression—her anxiety over the condition of her youngest son's grave and her long-held memory of the seemingly small matter of the boatman's daughter's desire for an artificial flower and her suffering for it. He has come back to his native place as soon as he possibly could. He has carried out his tasks with singular intensity and painstaking care. In this regard, his identity of spirit with his mother cannot be described as merely emotional; it is a reflection of the traditional Chinese moral value of *nien-chiu* (roughly, "cherishing old ties"). Hence, Lü Wei-fu feels, at the implicit level of his consciousness, that to move the grave of his little brother and to buy an artificial flower for the boatman's daughter are intellectually and morally meaningful acts in life. Indeed, it was in the spirit of making contact with the noble side of humanity through the moral value of *nien-chiu* that he had moved the earth from the place where the body of his little brother had lain and carried out the reinterment. For, even though he found no remains of his little brother, the reinterment, as an act for the sake of the memory of his little brother, has a symbolic meaning for him. Also under the moral imperative of *nien-chiu,* he took pains in finding an artificial flower for the boatman's daughter—even stopping on his way at another city for that particular purpose.

The two episodes, then, reveal Lü Wei-fu's genuine intellectual and moral commitment to *nien-chiu*; it would appear that Lu Hsün, upon whom Lü Wei-fu was modeled, was himself never intellectually and morally alienated from this traditional value in his life. Wei-fu's apologies for his behavior in the two episodes merely *appeared* to indicate a retreat from his youthful iconoclasm; they were in fact uttered out of a sense of guilt arising from the tension between two incompatible intellectual and moral commitments that he simultaneously holds.

Lu Hsün's continuing commitment to the value of *nien-chiu* throughout his life can be amply illustrated. His lifelong, warm relationship with his mother was existentially based upon his adaptation of a traditional filial norm to the modern context of his life, but intellectually subsumed under the idea of *nien-chiu*.[83] In the story, this existential adaptation of a filial norm accounts for Wei-fu's decision not to tell his mother the true result of his trip, so as to please her and set her mind at ease. Lu Hsün took pride in having a number of lifelong friends, such as Hsü Shou-shang and Shao Ming-chih, with whose opinions he had not always or entirely been in agreement.[84] Moreover, among his earliest writings there are six poems entitled "Parting with My Brothers" ("Pieh chu-ti"), three composing a set written when he was about twenty, depicting his nostalgia for the company of his brothers; his poems also include an elegiac couplet (written at twenty) in memory of a deceased friend.[85] During the last ten days of his life, extremely weak from consumption, he summoned up enough energy to write two essays about his former teacher Chang Ping-lin (who had died a few months earlier); among other reasons for his undertaking to write these essays, they were undoubtedly inspired by his moral commitment to *nien-chiu*.[86]

It is clear from the above account of "In the Tavern" that Lü Wei-fu's *nien-chiu* is culturally influenced and logically deduced but not psychologically imputed; it is therefore a traditional value implicitly held by him. By

83. This can be attested to by the extant fifty letters written by Lu Hsün to his mother during the last five years (1932–36) of his life. Hsü Kuang-p'ing, ed., *Lu Hsün shu-chien*, pp. 267–313.

84. See Lu Hsün's letter to Ts'ao Chü-jen dated February 21, 1936, ibid., pp. 472–73.

85. Lu Hsün, "Pieh chu-ti," *Chi-wai chi shih-i*, *LHCC*, 7:713, 720; "Wan Ting Yao-ch'ing lien," ibid., p. 721.

86. Lu Hsün, "Kuan-yü T'ai-yen hsien-sheng erh-san shih," *Ch'ieh-chieh-t'ing tsa-wen mo-pien, LHCC*, 6:442–45; "Yin T'ai-yen hsien-sheng erh hsiang-ch'i ti erh-san shih," ibid., p. 449–53. The second essay was written on October 17, 1936, two days before his death—the last thing he ever wrote.

nien-chiu being logically deduced is meant that this traditional moral value, though disconnected from its traditional framework after the breakdown of the sociopolitical and cultural-moral orders, still retains a clear identity for a Chinese person like Lü Wei-fu and a power to influence, on its own merit, such a person so as to provide him with an intellectually and morally meaningful channel of expression; it deductively follows for Lü that he is holding this moral principle as a value.

As the implications of this story make plain, Lu Hsün continued to hold the value of *nien-chiu* in his private life and at the implicit level of his consciousness, but was reluctant to bring it onto the explicit level, even if only for himself; because to do so would require a fully formulated justification on the basis of a new, systematic cultural framework which was not available to him. He was, however, connected with certain elements from the Chinese tradition (whose integrated order had broken down, but some of whose elements had not necessarily lost their identity and the power to influence) in such a way that his commitment to *nien-chiu* was authentic.

On the other hand, it is clear in "In the Tavern" that Lü Wei-fu was exasperated that he was teaching some of the Confucian classics and the *Precepts for Women*. Although implicitly committed to a traditional value that he found meaningful as a private person, he would not have agreed with the policy of reviving the old orthodox curriculum for current education. Even if some traditional values could be revived through education, it cannot be said with certainty that he would have preferred this, on account of his lack of a comprehensive and systematic world view to serve as a basis for a more definite view about the future. His earlier stance of totalistic iconoclasm had apparently not become invalid for him despite his implicit commitment to a traditional value, and it is likely that he would not have approved of a revival of traditional values in the public realm, despite his commitment to a traditional value in private life. Much less would he have wanted to see that he himself, by order of his employer, was playing a role in perpetuating the old orthodox curriculum in a modern context that made such study an empty ritual for his students, while its teaching was nothing but a means for him to earn a living. These activities not only could not save the tradition but themselves violated its authenticity—they made the traditional degenerate into the traditionalistic.[87]

---

87. The term "traditionalistic" usually refers to an ideological usage of tradition for untraditional purposes without admitting its violation of the authenticity of tradition. Here it is

This analysis of the nature of the multilayered consciousness of Lu Hsün indicates that a genuine and intense intellectual tension existed between his iconoclastic totalism and his intellectual and moral commitment to a traditional value. Lu Hsün's resistance to any doctrinaire position and the complex and intense nature of his consciousness, which felt the pulse of his times and is symbolic of the unprecedented crisis of culture in twentieth-century China, bear witness to his intellectual and moral stature in a cliché-ridden age of easy generalizations. Nevertheless, his inability to transcend this tension—which might otherwise have been a fountainhead for a transformative interpretation of Chinese tradition, or might at least have led him explicitly to question the validity of a totalistic rejection of Chinese tradition—was primarily due to the dominance of his iconoclastic totalism. But why was it so dominant? In the final analysis, under the influence of his cultural-intellectualistic approach—the pressures resulting from post-1911 sociopolitical realities had shaped it into a holistic mode of thinking—he could not work towards a more viable, pluralistic way of coping with his intellectual tensions. For all his ardent desire to emancipate himself and others from the shackles of Chinese tradition, a traditionally derived mode of thinking held him in bondage, so that alternative categories of analysis could not arise in his mind. Hence the crisis of his consciousness remained unresolved.

---

stretched to cover a usage of tradition for an untraditional purpose or as a utilitarian means in life, while admitting its violation of the authenticity of tradition.

7
CONCLUSION

Looking back at the May Fourth era with some historical perspective, we realize that a novel feature of that age was its totalistic cultural iconoclasm. Modern Chinese iconoclasm had, of course, started earlier—as noted in chapter 3, some members of the first generation of the Chinese intelligentsia had already begun in the 1890s to attack certain elements of Chinese social and cultural tradition. But these intellectuals did not reach the stance of totalistic rejection of Chinese tradition largely because they still took some traditional values and beliefs for granted, in a social and cultural order that had not yet totally disintegrated.

The historical significance of May Fourth iconoclasm lies largely in the way it exhibits the nature and the effects of the crisis of Chinese consciousness—that instability and uncertainty in the sphere of culture which make impossible viable solutions or lasting settlements of new cultural and intellectual problems resulting from sociopolitical and cultural change.

A predominant factor in modern Chinese culture has been the presence of

152

various elements of Western culture. It is not pertinent to ask whether or not Western culture should be present on the Chinese scene: history is not reversible. The only relevant question is, What is a viable way for the Chinese to deal with Western culture? Iconoclastic totalism was an answer offered by some major intellectual leaders of the May Fourth era. The adoption of some Western ideas and values led them toward a new criterion for evaluating Chinese social and cultural tradition. The interplay of this new criterion with their traditionally derived, cultural-intellectualistic approach eventually led them, in conjunction with other factors, to maintain the necessity and priority of an intellectual revolution based on a totalistic rejection of China's past. The types of totalistic antitraditionalism advocated by Ch'en Tu-hsiu and Hu Shih moved them easily toward the idea of totalistic Westernization as a goal, although their conceptions of its nature and the methods for achieving it were not the same.

Their iconoclastic totalism and, for that matter, totalistic Westernism are variants of formalism or abstractionism, which, in the context of this study, can be considered a formal construction of a hypostatized understanding of culture and society. Formalism is a reified mental formulation without careful and sustained reference to the complex realities of a phenomenon; it thus inevitably results in simplification and distortion of the realities of that phenomenon. Before his totalistic rejection of China's past and advocacy of wholesale Westernization Ch'en Tu-hsiu did not examine in any substantive way the whole range of the specificities of Chinese social and cultural tradition or of modern Western culture, nor did he ponder whether each of them was meaningful for or useful to China. His organismic conception of culture made such an examination and reflection seem unnecessary and superfluous, even pedantic. If all elements of traditional China were organismically related to the whole, the disintegration of the whole meant, by definition, the loss of meaning and usefulness in all its parts. No part can survive the whole. Moreover, the Chinese could not keep the moribund elements of their tradition and still introduce new elements of the modern West to China, because the elements of Western culture were also organismically related to the whole of the Western culture. Hence the only viable way, according to Ch'en, would be both to reject Chinese tradition and to adopt the modern West in toto.

Hu Shih's totalistic iconoclasm was more elusive than that of Ch'en Tu-hsiu. I have shown how both his background and his adherence to Deweyan thought led him to insist on evolutionary and reformist cultural change. But Hu's iconoclastic totalism and undiscriminating acceptance of the early ideas and values of Dewey made his evolutionary reformism become merely a formalistic insistence. The discovery, from his Deweyan perspective, of a scientific strain in Chinese tradition was used by Hu to claim consistency with evolutionary reformism; it did not prevent him from engaging in the campaign of totalistic iconoclasm and Westernism. Hu's insistence on evolutionary reform of Chinese tradition did not inspire him to examine elements of Chinese tradition substantively before his totalistic attack.

For both Ch'en Tu-hsiu and Hu Shih, there was no need to examine the Chinese tradition in any substantive way. The discredited Chinese tradition could not be valuable, according to their intellectualistic-holistic mode of thinking. In line with this formalistic argument, those things in the Chinese tradition that could be singled out as valuable were, by definition, general features of all civilizations. They could neither explain nor contribute to the Chinese nature of the Chinese tradition.

But this argument for totalistic iconoclasm and Westernism could not effectively deal with substantive problems resulting from the confrontation of Chinese and Western culture on the Chinese scene. By its very formalistic nature, it ignored the real problems and issues arising from this confrontation. What, then, were these real problems and issues?

First, after the breakdown of the framework of Chinese tradition in 1911–12, many intellectual and moral elements of Chinese culture survived the collapse of the whole. Lu Hsün, as was pointed out, found in that tradition at least one principle which remained intellectually and morally meaningful to him, and there are others that might have been selected for discussion.[1] What Lu Hsün expressed in his works is shared by many less articulate. Indeed, the value of Lu Hsün's art lies, in part, in giving expression to what many Chinese felt to be the case. But, iconoclastic totalism excluded for many the possibility of recognizing explicitly the intellectual and moral meaning of elements of the old Chinese culture that had survived the disintegration of the Chinese tradition. Since those elements could not be explicitly recognized and dealt with, they were ignored. But ignoring them could not resolve the very real problem of finding a new framework for integrating the intellectually meaningful parts from the old culture with the new ideas and values from the West.

Secondly, in the realm of political ideology, iconoclastic totalism and

---

1. Note, for instance, the ambivalence towards the Confucian value of moral equanimity expressed in the story "K'ung I-chi" (*Na-han, LHCC,* 1:20–24).

nationalism were hardly compatible. Although iconoclastic totalism was urged in the May Fourth era for the preservation and advancement of the Chinese nation, the question of national identity could not be resolved by a militant negation of the nation's past. On the contrary, national identity calls for some sort of positive relationship with that past.

Thirdly, iconoclastic totalism created new problems that could not be resolved by its own resources. Arising from the collision of forces from Western culture with some millennial forces from Chinese tradition, it came to be a powerful movement in twentieth-century China. While it was by no means historically predetermined, it was nevertheless influenced by deep-rooted historical forces. In a situation of political and cultural disintegration, iconoclastic totalism, with its all-embracing dichotomy, caught the imagination of the majority of the intelligentsia. Modernity now rested on totalistic rejection of the past. A permanent war had to be waged, since Chinese tradition could not be totally eradicated: some of its elements survived for intellectual and moral reasons; others were clung to on nationalistic grounds. Such a situation of permanent war against Chinese tradition made its creative transformation into modernity all but impossible, yet it seems that only through such a transformation can the crisis of culture in China be, relatively speaking, settled.

Fourthly, a totalistic view of culture called also for a totalistic acceptance of foreign ideology. Underlying Ch'en Tu-hsiu's shift from an early commitment to democracy and science to his acceptance of Marxism was a consistent totalistic orientation toward the West. But such acceptance proved to be unsuitable either to the growth of democracy and science or to the Communist revolution. Hu Shih's adoption of Dewey's early experimentalism gave a specious appearance of reformism to his thought, but the link he established through his finding of a Chinese strain of science was formalistic, not genuine. Insisting on this link, he was able neither to investigate the substantive nature of Chinese tradition nor to apply the pragmatic method to China's concrete problems. Dewey's experimentalism, if adopted not totalistically but creatively, is in fact an open-ended method, whose application to the pressing problems in China might well have led to a conclusion that called for forsaking iconoclastic totalism and the priority of intellectual revolution. It was Hu's view of culture as an organismic entity, a view influenced mainly by a traditionally derived, intellectualistic-holistic mode of thinking, that led him to adopt Dewey's ideas and values totalistically and prevented him from making a critical and viable adaptation of the West and bringing about the reform of Chinese culture.

The great stature of Lu Hsün is due, among other things, to his dialectical involvement in articulating the intellectual and moral meaning of certain surviving elements of the Chinese cultural tradition in the midst of totalistic iconoclasm. Despite his own commitment to totalistic iconoclasm, his spiritual strength in withstanding complex and unsettling incongruities at different levels of his consciousness, his grasp of the realities of Chinese culture and society, and his resistance to formalism enabled him to face and to articulate the intellectual and moral meaning of elements of the old culture in the post-traditional Chinese society. But for all his intellectual and spiritual power, he was not able, in the end, to transcend the formalistic dichotomy of tradition and modernity, nor did he further utilize his "discovery"—which was in fact a specific and material transcendence over the dichotomy in question—of the intellectual and moral value of surviving parts of the traditional culture.

In the aftermath of the disintegration of the Chinese cultural-moral order, Lu Hsün was, in the final analysis, influenced in his own way by the intellectualistic-holistic mode of thinking. In the context of iconoclastic totalism, it seems that his recognition of the survival of old elements of Chinese culture reached the outer limits of his artistic perception. Instead of probing further into the possibility of transcending iconoclastic totalism, he was, however, torn asunder by the "discovery" and suffered the agony of spiritual and intellectual conflicts.[2]

The findings of this study have indicated that it was relatively less difficult for Chinese intellectuals to change many elements in the content of their thought, on the basis of the adoption by some or the adaptation by others of various Western ideas and values, than it was for them to change their patterns of thought and modes of thinking, particularly those which had persisted through thousands of years and had been deeply rooted in the Chinese consciousness. And if many leading figures of the May Fourth intelligentsia were dominated by their conception of the unity of political and cultural orders and by a traditionally derived, intellectualistic-holistic mode of thinking, several pertinent questions arise. Are the same traditional forces still at work in contemporary China? Was Mao Tse-tung influenced by the cultural-

---

2. A statement by Lu Hsün in 1926 reveals his agony over these conflicts vividly: "But I myself suffer from carrying these old ghosts, which I cannot cast off, and thus often feel a stifling weight. . . . Because I feel that I also often have those hateful thoughts contained in books written by the ancients." Lu Hsün, "Hsieh-tsai *Fen* hou-mien," *Fen, LHCC,* 1:364.

intellectualistic approach? Was Mao's simultaneous call for transforming the nature of the Chinese man and for placing "politics in command" a reflection of a traditional pattern of thought that takes for granted close integration of the cultural-moral and sociopolitical orders? Was his recurring iconoclastic urge related to the totalistic iconoclasm of the May Fourth era?

It lies beyond the scope of this study to enter into a comprehensive discussion of Mao's consciousness or his ideology. I find it suggestive, however, that in the cultural sphere Mao repeatedly stressed ideas that distinguished the May Fourth movement: the urge for a cultural revolution that involves first of all a radical attack on Chinese tradition. Yet one need not subscribe to the simplistic theories of those who fanatically insist that Mao was more or less a Chinese emperor in new garb, or accept the ideas of the more sophisticated theoreticians who claim stronger links with the past for Communist China than she actually has, to realize that there was in Mao's thought a certain measure of continuity with Chinese tradition. It seems very likely that the tenacious Maoist ideas of cultural revolution and radical iconoclasm are closely related to the radical heritage of the May Fourth movement, which, as we have seen, was related in its own way to Chinese tradition. This does not imply that these Maoist ideas had origins identical in all respects with those of the May Fourth iconoclasts; the recurrent Maoist calls for cultural revolution and radical rejection of the "high culture" of China's past undoubtedly originated from the complex interaction of politics, economics, culture, international relations, and so forth in different periods of Mao's life. But they have clearly been constant themes, surviving fluctuations, shifts, and turns of the party line.

As a Marxist-Leninist, Mao in his explicit statements modified the cultural-intellectualistic approach at times. It would be quite naïve to think that his acceptance of Marxism-Leninism did not produce any basic changes in his consciousness, that it provided only rhetorical trappings. But the cultural-intellectualistic approach may well have played a considerable role in generating the initial impulse for the voluntaristic Chinese reinterpretation of Marxism, with its great stress on the element of consciousness, that was started by Mao's mentor Li Ta-chao and continued by Mao himself.[3] It is fairly accurate to say that the knowledge of Marxism gained by the first generation of Chinese Marxists was more in accord with the deterministic vein of the

3. For a perceptive analysis of Li Ta-chao's voluntaristic reinterpretation of Marxism and its influence on Mao, see Maurice Meisner, *Li Ta-chao and the Origins of Chinese Marxism* (Cambridge, Mass., 1967).

orthodox European Marxist tradition, as carried on by the later Engels and Karl Kautsky. Given their deterministic understanding of Marxism, the remarkable voluntaristic reinterpretation by Li and Mao may be understood as largely due to the interplay of indigenous factors. Their desire for action led them to be impatient with the orthodox Marxian understanding, which claimed that the historical conditions for immediate socialist revolution were lacking in China. This desire, combined with other factors, such as the chiliastic feelings about immediate transformation of the world inspired by the October Revolution in Russia, might have passed through the filter of the cultural-intellectualistic approach to arrive at the voluntaristic reinterpretation. As revolutionary activists, however, Li and Mao did not feel constrained by an approach which demanded the priority of intellectual and cultural change over sociopolitical change. To a certain extent, the cultural-intellectualistic approach in its holistic form and the totalistic iconoclasm— the May Fourth syndrome, if one may so describe it—might have at times been modified, in both scope and intensity, by the interaction between their activistic, revolutionary impulses and their orthodox, deterministic understanding of Marxism, which was different from their reinterpretation of it. Mao might have continued to feel the necessity of attacking the predominant strains of the "high culture" of China's past; but such an attack no longer involved all the elements of the "high culture" and the folk culture. He might have continued to stress the necessity of intellectual and cultural change, without holding to the absolute priority of intellectual change over sociopolitical change. It seems unmistakable, however, that the combined Maoist emphases on cultural revolution and radical iconoclasm as means to transform the nature of the Chinese people so as to guarantee the success of social and political revolution have a generic affinity with the May Fourth syndrome. Perhaps at a deep level of Mao's consciousness, a level of which he might not have been fully aware, it did not lose its gripping power, and lay at the heart of his recurring insistence on cultural revolution and the radical rejection of China's past.

When the May Fourth syndrome reasserted itself in its fundamental or essential form in Mao's consciousness at various times of his life, he readily engaged in a totalistic attack on the "high culture" of China's past. This radical antitraditionalism extended to a totalistic attack on the culture of the bourgeois West, in which at a certain point he included Soviet Russia. On the basis of this totalistic view of culture, there arises what Benjamin Schwartz has called a "sense of infinite possibility."[4] This sense of infinite possibility, which implies that China will break away from the "high culture" of her past as well as from the culture of the bourgeois West, is both an effect and a cause of the continuing crisis of consciousness in China in the years since 1911. It has arisen out of a totalistic view of culture whose form crystallized initially in the May Fourth iconoclastic movement; and it opens up in the cultural sphere a totally fluid situation that is likely to produce great and continuing ferment.

The sense of infinite possibility gave rise, in Chairman Mao and his admirers inside and outside China, to a romantic feeling of freedom and a conviction that the future lay entirely open to them. It, in fact, exacerbated the crisis of culture in China, which, as this study has suggested, can hardly be resolved or settled through formalistic ways of conceiving solutions or by underestimating the complexities of the problems of culture. It resulted, moreover, from an inability on the part of Mao to transcend the millennial forces of Chinese tradition in the aftermath of its disintegration, rather than from a creative response to the cultural anomie in post-traditional China.

Mao Tse-tung was a great hero in leading China to success in political and, to a large extent, social revolution. Some of his admirers will perhaps enjoy predicting success for the Maoist cultural revolution in the future.[5] About this

4. Professor Benjamin I. Schwartz's Hilldale Lecture, entitled "The Crisis of Culture in Twentieth-Century China," delivered at the University of Wisconsin-Madison, on April 23, 1974.

5. Since the death of Mao and the downfall of the "gang of four" in 1976, Peking's cultural and educational policies have become somewhat more flexible vis-à-vis the Chinese past. Early in 1978 reports were circulated in the news media suggesting that Confucius was being "rehabilitated." On the basis of a news dispatch about an article entitled "Kuan-yü K'ung Ch'iu chu Shao-cheng Mao" written by Yen Ling and published in the January, 1978, issue of the *Li-shih yen-chiu,* some Chinese intellectuals in Hong Kong thought that to be the case. See, for instance, Hsü Fu-kuan "Tao T'ang Chün-i hsien-sheng," *Ming pao yüeh-k'an* 13.3:14–15 (March, 1978). A dispatch by the Associated Press in June, 1978, also reported that, according to Mu Shih's "Research Work in Philosophy and Social Sciences Unshackled," *Peking Review,* 21.19:16–18, 21 (May 12, 1978), "after a decade of abuse, the Chinese Communists have rehabilitated Confucius, another demonstration of the change since the purge of the party's radical wing." *Wisconsin State Journal,* Section 5, p. 12 (June 11, 1978). But a close reading of the original sources for the rise of the story of Confucius' rehabilitation reveals no fundamental departure from the legacy of the May Fourth ideology of totalistic iconoclasm. See the article in the *Peking Review* just referred to and Yen Ling, "Kuan-yü K'ung Ch'iu chu Shao-cheng Mao," *Li-shih yen-chiu* no. 1:63–76 (1978). Within the framework of totalistic iconoclasm, positive merits of various aspects of the past can of course be acknowledged—if they are thought to accord

prediction Chairman Mao might well have been the first to express some reservations, judging from the anxiety about failure betrayed by his recurring urge for cultural revolution. It remains to be seen whether the Maoist vision of infinite possibility will be a useful guide to the solution or settlement of China's cultural crisis, or whether there will emerge a pluralist and substantive approach to the specificities of the cultural problems, an approach which the tenor of this study has suggested is likely to provide, in the long run, more realistic possibilities for creative solution or settlement of the crisis of Chinese consciousness.[6]

---

with a general or formal category—as they quite frequently were by the May Fourth iconoclasts in the past. However, as far as these recent sources indicate, the "positive" merits are not defined in any substantive terms. Actually Yen Ling's article is primarily a diatribe against the way in which "the gang of four" had handled their attack on Confucius. Instead of rehabilitating Confucius in any substantive sense, it describes the school of Confucianism as well as that of Legalism as both cruel and oppressive, with Confucianism being regarded as more cunning. It is impossible of course to foretell what will happen in the future, but it seems that, insofar as one can tell from the available evidence, the legacy of totalistic iconoclasm has not run its full course. See also Chin Ching-fang, "Lun ju-fa," *Li-shih yen-chiu,* no. 5:84–91 (1977), and Jen Chi-yü, "Ch'in Han ti t'ung-i yü che-hsüeh ssu-hsiang ti pien-ke," *Li-shih yen-chiu,* no. 6:62–70 (1977).

6. At the end of this study it is perhaps appropriate to add a note of a somewhat personal nature: Although the May Fourth iconoclastic intellectuals had their limitations, some of which were the result of their historical time and their backgrounds and were hardly avoidable, the May Fourth period was an era of hope and enlightenment in that the iconoclastic intellectuals were genuinely aroused by and indignant at the wrongs, injustice, and suffering in China's past, and sincerely believed that by emancipation through knowledge something could be done about the social and cultural heritage. In some respects, their "knowledge" turned out to be misunderstanding, and their totalistic antitraditionalism was doctrinaire; nevertheless, the genuineness and seriousness of their commitment to overthrowing the evil and the obsolete in Chinese tradition command respect. In a sense, the very fact that they were fervently committed to a radical cause, quite apart from their being limited by various objective and subjective factors, left them vulnerable to rational criticism. On the other hand, however, their radical rejection of the Chinese heritage led them to clear away many of the evil and/or useless ideas and practices that stood in the way of finding any solution to modern Chinese problems. Furthermore, from the perspective of Michael Polanyi's epistemological insight into the relationship between commitment and originality (Michael Polanyi, *Personal Knowledge: Towards a Post-Critical Philosophy* [Chicago, 1958], esp. pp. 299–324, and Michael Polanyi and Harry Prosch, *Meaning* [Chicago, 1975]), it can be seen that personal commitment to radical iconoclasm is one of the essential factors leading to great achievement in iconoclastic literature, such as that of Lu Hsün. It is in this sense of respect for some of the great figures of the May Fourth movement that I have undertaken to follow the lead of rational analysis and to draw out its implications in the hope that my study may not only serve as a basis for understanding a crucial period of modern history but also may point to the direction of a proper and viable development of the Chinese intellect and

Chinese culture in the future, a development that should involve interactions of Chinese and Western ideas and values on the basis of thorough understanding and rigorous analysis.

In comparison with other periods of twentieth-century Chinese history, intellectuals in the May Fourth period, although they were subjected to political oppression at times, were relatively free to pursue their ideas, mainly because the systematic political and ideological control and manipulation of thought were still to come. They made use of this precious period of intellectual freedom; some of their works stand as testimony to its value. In this sense the May Fourth period was the finest time in modern Chinese intellectual history. While remembering the limitations and achievements of the past, Chinese intellectuals must now work not for the totalistic rejection of the Chinese tradition but for its creative transformation. For an attempt at a structural understanding of the philosophic coherency and ambiguity of classical Confucianism, see Lin Yü-sheng, "The Evolution of the Pre-Confucian Meaning of *Jen* and the Confucian Concept of Moral Autonomy," *Monumenta Serica,* 31:172–204 (1974–75).

REFERENCE MATTER

BIBLIOGRAPHY

"Anhwei ai-kuo-hui chih ch'eng-chiu" 安徽愛國會之成就 (The achievements of the Anhwei Patriotic Society), *Su-pao,* May 25, 1903, pp. 1-2.

Balazs, Etienne. *Chinese Civilization and Bureaucracy,* tr. H. M. Wright. New Haven, Yale University Press, 1964.

Bellah, Robert. "Epilogue," in Robert Bellah, ed., *Religion and Progress in Modern Asia.* New York, Free Press, 1965.

Boorman, Howard L., ed. *Biographical Dictionary of Republican China.* 4 vols. New York, Columbia University Press, 1967 - 1971.

Chan Wing-tsit. *A Source Book in Chinese Philosophy.* Princeton, Princeton University Press, 1963.

———, tr. *Instructions for Practical Living and Other Neo-Confucian Writings* by Wang Yang-ming. New York Columbia University Press, 1963.

———, tr. *The Way of Lao Tzu.* Indianapolis, Bobbs-Merrill, 1963.

Chang Hao. *Liang Ch'i-ch'ao and Intellectual Transition in China, 1890 - 1907.* Cambridge, Mass., Harvard University Press, 1971.

Chang Ting-huang 張定璜 . "Lu Hsün hsien-sheng" 魯迅先生 (Mr. Lu Hsün), reprinted in Ts'ao Chü-jen 曹聚仁 , *Lu Hsün nien-p'u* 魯迅年譜 (Chronological biography of Lu Hsün), pp. 278 - 290. Hong Kong,

San-yü t'u-shu wen-chü kung-ssu 三育圖書文具公司 , 1967.

Ch'en, Jerome. *Mao and the Chinese Revolution.* New York and London, Oxford University Press, 1965.

——. *Yuan Shih-k'ai.* 2nd ed. Stanford, Stanford University Press, 1972.

Ch'en Ku-ying 陳鼓應 . *Lao-tzu chin-chu chin-i* 老子今註今譯 (An annotation on and vernacular translation of the *Lao-tzu*). Taipei, Commercial Press, 1972.

Ch'en Tu-hsiu 陳獨秀 (Ch'en Yu-chi 陳由己). "Anhwei ai-kuo-hui yen-shuo" 安徽愛國會演說 (Speech [recorded] at the Anhwei Patriotic Society), *Su-pao,* May 26, 1903, pp. 2-3.

——. "Ai-kuo-hsin yü tzu-chüeh-hsin" 愛國心與自覺心 (Patriotism and self-consciousness), *Chia-yin tsa-chih* 甲寅雜誌 (The tiger magazine), 1.4:1-6 (November 1914).

——. "She-kao" 社告 (Announcement), *HCN,* 1.1:1 (September 15, 1915).

——. "Ching-kao ch'ing-nien" 敬告青年 (Call to youth), *THWT,* I, 1 - 10.

——. "Ti-k'ang li" 抵抗力 (The power of resistance), *THWT,* I, 27 - 34.

——. "I-chiu i-liu nien" 一九一六年 (The year 1916), *THWT,* I, 41 - 47.

——. "Po K'ang Yu-wei chih tsung-t'ung tsung-li shu" 駁康有爲致總統總理書 (In refutation of K'ang Yu-wei's letter to the president and the premier), *THWT,* I, 95 - 101.

——. "Hsien-fa yü K'ung-chiao" 憲法與孔教 (Constitution and Confucianism), *THWT,* I, 103 - 112.

——. "K'ung-tzu chih-tao yü hsien-tai sheng-huo" 孔子之道與現代生活 (The way of Confucius and modern life), *THWT,* I, 113 - 124.

——. "Chiu ssu-hsiang yü kuo-t'i wen-t'i" 舊思想與國體問題 (The old thought and the problem of polity), *THWT,* I 147 - 151.

——. "Fu-p'i yü tsun-K'ung" 復辟與尊孔 (The monarchical restoration and reverence for Confucius), *THWT,* I, 161 - 168.

——. "Ta Ch'ang Nai-te" 答常乃悳 (Reply to Ch'ang Nai-te), *THWT,* III, 24 - 28.

——. "Ta p'ei chien ch'ing-nien" 答佩劍青年 (Reply to the young man bearing a sword), *THWT,* III, 47 - 49.

——. "Shih-an tzu-chuan" 實庵自傳 (Autobiography of Shih-an [Ch'en Tu-hsiu]), reprinted in *Chuan-chi wen-hsüeh* 傳記文學 (Biographical literature), 5.3:55 - 58 (September 1964).

Ch'en Yu-chi 陳由己 , see Ch'en Tu-hsiu.

Chiang Yung 江永 , ed. *Chin-ssu-lu chi chu* 近思錄集注 (A collected commentary on *Reflections on Things at Hand*), comp. Chu Hsi 朱熹 and Lü Tsu-ch'ien 呂祖謙 . 1844 ed.

Ch'iao Feng 喬峯 (Chou Chien-jen 周建人). *Lüeh-chiang kuan-yü Lu Hsün ti shih-ch'ing* 略講關於魯迅的事情 (A brief discussion of stories about Lu Hsün). Peking, Jen-min wen-hsüeh ch'u-pan she 人民文學出版社 , 1954.

Ch'ien Mu 錢穆 . *Chung-kuo chin san-pai-nien hsüeh-shu shih* 中國近三百年學術史 (A history of scholarship in China during the last three hundred years). Shanghai, Commercial Press, 1937.

Ch'ien Te-hung 錢德洪 . [*Wang Yang-ming*] *Nien-p'u* [王陽明]　年譜 (Chronological biography [of Wang Yang-ming]), in *Wang wen-ch'eng kung ch'üan-shu* 王文成公全書 (Complete works of Wang Yang-ming), SPTK ed.

Chih Yü-ju. "Ch'en Tu-hsiu: His Career and Political Ideas," in Chün-tu Hsüeh, ed., *Revolutionary Leaders of Modern China*, pp. 335 - 366. London and New York, Oxford University Press, 1971.

Ch'ih Kuang 赤光 . "Ch'en Tu-hsiu ti sheng-p'ing chi ch'i cheng-chih chu-chang" 陳獨秀的生平及其政治主張 (The life and political views of Ch'en Tu-hsiu), in Ch'en Tung-hsiao 陳東曉 , ed., *Ch'en Tu-hsiu p'ing-lun* 陳獨秀評論 (Discussions on Ch'en Tu-hsiu). Peiping, Tung-ya shu-chü 東亞書局 , 1933.

Chin Ching-fang 金景芳 . "Lun ju-fa" 論儒法 (On Confucianism and Legalism), *Li-shih yen-chiu,* no. 5:84-91 (1977).

Chinnery, J. D. "The Influence of Western Literature on Lǔ Xùn's 'Diary of a Madman'," *Bulletin of the School of Oriental and African Studies,* 23:309 - 322 (1960).

Chou Hsia-shou 周遐壽 (Chou Tso-jen). *Lu Hsün hsiao-shuo li-ti jen-wu* 魯迅小說裏的人物 (The characters in Lu Hsün's novels). Shanghai, 1954.

———. *Lu Hsün ti ku-chia* 魯迅的故家 (The old home of Lu Hsün). Hong Kong, Ta-t'ung shu-chü 大通書局 , 1962.

Chou Shu-jen 周樹人 , see Lu Hsün.

Chou Tso-jen 周作人 . "Sui-kan lu erh-shih-ssu" 隨感錄二十四　(Random thoughts, No. 24), *HCN,* 5.3:286-90 (September 15, 1918).

———. "Sui-kan lu san-shih-ssu" 隨感錄三十四　(Random thoughts, No. 34), *HCN,* 5.4:409-12 (October 15, 1918).

———. "Hsi-yang yeh-yu ch'ou-ch'ung" 西洋也有臭蟲 (There are bedbugs in the West, too), *Tu-li p'ing-lun* 獨立評論 (The independent critic), 107:12 (July 1, 1934).

———. "Kuan-yü Lu Hsün" 關於魯迅 (Concerning Lu Hsün), in his *Kua-tou chi* 瓜豆集 (A collection of melons and beans), pp. 212 - 226. Shanghai, Yü-chou-feng she 宇宙風社 , 1937.

———. "Kuan-yü Lu Hsün chih-erh" 關於魯迅之二 (Concerning Lu Hsün: II), *Kua-tou chi,* pp. 230 - 243.

———. *Chih-t'ang hui-hsiang-lu* 知堂回想錄 (Reminiscences of Chih-t'ang). Hong Kong, San-yü t'u-shu wen-chü kung-ssu, 1970.

———. "Ah Q cheng-chuan" 阿Q正傳 (On "The True Story of Ah Q"), reprinted in Ts'ao Chü-jen, *Lu Hsün nien-p'u,* pp. 193 - 196.

——— and Ts'ao Chü-jen. *Chou Ts'ao t'ung-hsin chi* 周曹通信集　(The correspondence between Chou [Tso-jen] and Ts'ao [Chü-jen]). 2 vols. Hong Kong, Nan-t'ien shu-yeh kung-ssu 南天書業公司 , 1973.

Chow Tse-tsung. *The May Fourth Movement.* Cambridge, Mass., Harvard University Press, 1960.

———. "The Anti-Confucian Movement in Early Republican China," in A. F. Wright, ed., *The Confucian Persuasion.* Stanford, Stanford University Press, 1960.

Chu Hsi 朱熹 . *Meng-tzu chi-chu* 孟子集注 (Collected commentaries on the *Mencius*). SPPY ed.

——. Chu-tzu *ch'üan-shu* 朱子全書 (Complete works of Master Chu), ed. Li Kuang-ti 李光地 et al. Ku-hsiang-chai 古香齋 ed.

——. Chu-tzu *wen-chi* 朱子文集 (Collection of literary works by Master Chu), comp. Chu Tsai 朱在 , Yü Shih-lu 余師魯 , et al. SPPY ed. entitled Chu-tzu *ta-ch'üan* 朱子大全 (Complete works of Master Chu).

Chu Hsi and Lü Tsu-ch'ien, comps. *Reflections on Things at Hand,* tr. Wing-tsit Chan. New York, Columbia University Press, 1967.

Ch'ü Wan-li 屈萬里 . *Hsiao-t'un (ti-erh pen): Yin-hsü wen-tzu chia-pien k'ao-shih* 小屯（第二本）：殷虛文字甲編考釋 (Hsiao-t'un [The Yin-Shang site at Anyang, Honan], volume 2: annotations of inscriptions of part 1). Taipei, Institute of History and Philology, Academia Sinica, 1961.

Conkin, Paul K. *Puritans and Pragmatists.* New York, Dodd, Mead, 1968.

Creel, H. G. *The Birth of China.* New York, Reynal and Hitchcock, 1937. reprint ed., New York, Ungar, 1954.

de Bary, Wm. T. et al., comps. *Sources of Chinese Tradition.* 2 vols. New York, Columbia University Press, 1964.

Dewey, John. *How We Think.* Boston, D. C. Heath, 1910.

——. *Essays in Experimental Logic.* Chicago, University of Chicago Press, 1916.

——. "The Sequel of the Student Revolt," *New Republic,* 21.273:380 - 382 (February 25, 1920).

——. "New Culture in China," in his *Characters and Events,* ed. Joseph Ratner. 2 vols. New York, Henry Holt, 1929.

Eisenstadt, S. N. "Transformation of Social, Political and Cultural Orders in Modernization," *American Sociological Review,* 30.5:650 - 673 (October 1965).

——. *Modernization: Protest and Change.* Englewood Cliffs, N.J., Prentice-Hall, 1966.

——. "The Protestant Ethic Thesis in an Analytical and Comparative Framework," in S. N. Eisenstadt, ed., *Protestant Ethic and Modernization.* New York, Basic Books, 1968.

——. "The Development of Sociological Thought," in *International Encyclopedia of the Social Sciences.* New York, Macmillan and Free Press, 1968.

——. "Introduction: Charisma and Institution Building, Max Weber and Modern Sociology," in S. N. Eisenstadt, ed., *Max Weber on Charisma and Institution Building.* Chicago, University of Chicago Press, 1968.

Emerson, Rupert. *From Empire to Nation.* Boston, Beacon Press, 1962.

Feng Tzu-yu 馮自由 . *Ko-ming i-shih* 革命逸史 (Fragments of revolutionary history). Shanghai, Commercial Press, 1939.

Ferguson, Adam. *An Essay on the History of Civil Society.* London, 1767.

Fung Yu-lan. *A History of Chinese Philosophy,* tr. Derk Bodde. 2 vols. Princeton, Princeton University Press, 1952-53.

————. *A Short History of Chinese Philosophy.* New York, Macmillan, 1960.

Geertz, Clifford. "Ideology as a Cultural System," in his *Interpretation of Cultures.* New York, Basic Books, 1973.

Grieder, Jerome B. *Hu Shih and the Chinese Renaissance.* Cambridge, Mass., Harvard University Press, 1970.

Haimson, Leopold H. *The Russian Marxists and the Origins of Bolshevism.* Cambridge, Mass., Harvard University Press, 1955.

Hayek, F. A. *Studies in Philosophy, Politics and Economics.* Chicago, University of Chicago Press, 1967.

HCN: Hsin ch'ing-nien 新青年 (New youth), photo-reprints of the original issues. 12 vols. Tokyo, Kyūko Shoin 汲古書院 , 1970 - 1971.

Ho Chih-yü 何之瑜 , comp. "Tu-hsiu chu-tso nien-piao" 獨秀著作年表 (A chronological list of writings by [Ch'en] Tu-hsiu), pp. 1 - 6, in *Tu-hsiu ts'ung-chu* 獨秀叢著 (Collected works of [Ch'en] Tu-hsiu). Galley proofs (gift of Hu Shih). Washington, D.C., Library of Congress.

Hofstadter, Richard. *Social Darwinism in American Thought.* 2nd ed. rev. Boston, Beacon Press, 1955.

Hou Wai-lu 侯外廬 et al., eds. *Liu Tsung-yüan che-hsüeh hsüan-chi* 柳宗元哲學選集 (Selected philosophical works of Liu Tsung-yüan). Peking, Chung-hua shu-chü 中華書局 , 1964.

Howard, Richard C. "K'ang Yu-wei (1858 - 1927): His Intellectual Background and Early Thought," in A. F. Wright and D. Twitchett, eds., *Confucian Personalities.* Stanford, Stanford University Press, 1962.

Hsi K'ang 嵇康 . *Hsi K'ang chi* 嵇康集 (Complete works of Hsi K'ang), ed. and annoted by Lu Hsün, in *Lu Hsün san-shih-nien chi* 魯迅三十年集 (The works of Lu Hsun over a period of thirty years), V. Shanghai, Lu Hsün ch'üan-chi ch'u-pan she 魯迅全集出版社 , 1941.

Hsi Ti 西諦 [Cheng Chen-to 鄭振鐸]. "Na-han" 吶喊([On] *Call to arms*), in Li Ho-lin, ed., *Lu Hsün lun*, pp. 197 - 199.

Hsia Tsi-an. *The Gate of Darkness.* Seattle, University of Washington Press, 1968.

Hsiao Kung-ch'üan 蕭公權 . *Chung-kuo cheng-chih ssu-hsiang shih* 中國政治思想史 (History of Chinese political thought). Taipei, Chung-hua wen-hua ch'u-pan shih-yeh wei-yüan-hui 中華文化出版事業委員會 , 1954.

————. "K'ang Yu-wei and Confucianism," *Monumenta Serica,* 18:173 (1959).

————. *A Modern China and a New World: K'ang Yu-wei, Reformer and Utopian, 1858-1927.* Seattle, University of Washington Press, 1975.

Hsin ch'ing-nien, see *HCN.*

Hsü Fu-kuan 徐復觀 . "Tao T'ang Chün-i hsien-sheng" 悼唐君毅先生 (In memory of Mr. T'ang Chün-i), *Ming-pao yüeh-k'an* 明報月刊 , 13.3: 14-15 (March 1978).

Hsü Kuang-p'ing 許廣平 , ed. "Lu Hsün i-chu shu-mu" 魯迅譯著書目 (A list of Lu Hsün's writings and translations), in *Lu Hsün hsien-sheng chi-nien chi* 魯迅先生紀念集 (Essays in memory of Mr. Lu Hsün), pp. 1-11. Shanghai, *Lu Hsün chi-nien wei-yüan-hui* 魯迅紀念委員會 , 1937.

——, ed. *Lu Hsün shu-chien* 魯迅書簡 (The letters of Lu Hsün). 2 vols. Shanghai, Lu Hsün ch'üan-chi ch'u-pan she, 1946.

Hsü Shou-shang 許壽裳 . *Wo-so jen-shih ti Lu Hsün* 我所認識的魯迅 (The Lu Hsün that I know). Peking, Jen-min wen-hsüeh ch'u-pan she, 1952.

——. *Wang-yu Lu Hsün yin-hsiang chi* 亡友魯迅印象記 (Impressions of my departed friend Lu Hsün). Peking, Jen-min wen-hsüeh ch'u-pan she, 1953.

——. "Ch'ü Yüan yü Lu Hsün" 屈原與魯迅 (Ch'ü Yüan and Lu Hsün), in his *Wang-yu Lu Hsün yin-hsiang chi*, pp. 5 - 8.

HSWT: Hu Shih wen-ts'un 胡適文存 (Collected essays of Hu Shih). 1st coll., 4 vols. Shanghai, Ya-tung t'u-shu-kuan 亞東圖書館 , 1921; 2nd coll., 4 vols., 1924; 3rd coll., 4 vols., 1930.

Hu Hou-hsüan 胡厚宣 . "Shih 'Yü I-Jen' " 釋余一人 (Explaining "I, the One Man"), *Li-shih yen-chiu*, no. 1:75-78 (1957).

Hu Shih 胡適 . "The Confucianist Movement in China," *The Chinese Students' Monthly*, 9.7:533 - 536 (May 1914).

——. "Wen-hsüeh kai-liang ch'u-i" 文學改良芻議 (A preliminary discussion of literary reform), *HSWT*, 1st coll., I, 7-24.

——. "Li-shih ti wen-hsüeh kuan-nien lun" 歷史的文學觀念論 (On the historical concept of literature), *HSWT*, 1st coll., I, 45-49.

——. "Chien-she ti wen-hsüeh ke-ming lun" 建設的文學革命論 (On a constructive literary revolution), *HSWT*, 1st coll., I, 71-96.

——. "Kuei-kuo tsa-kan" 歸國雜感 (Miscellaneous reflections after returning to my country), *HCN*, 4.1:20 - 27 (January 15, 1918); or *HSWT*, 1st coll., IV, 1 - 12.

——. "Chieh-shao hsin ch'u-pan-wu" 介紹新出版物 (Introducing new publications), *Mei-chou p'ing-lun* 每週評論 (The weekly review), 36:4 (August 24, 1919). Microfilm. Stanford, Hoover Liberary.

——. "Ch'ing-tai hsüeh-che ti chih-hsüeh fang-fa" 清代學者的治學方法 (The method of study of Ch'ing-period scholars), *HSWT*, 1st coll., II, 205 - 246.

——. *The Development of the Logical Method in Ancient China.* Shanghai, Ya-tung t'u-shu kuan, 1922.

——. "K'e-hsüeh yü jen-sheng-kuan hsü" 科學與人生觀序 (Preface to *Science and View of Life*). *HSWT*, 2nd coll., II, 1 - 28.

——. "Tu Liang Sou-ming hsien-sheng ti *Tung Hsi wen-hua chi ch'i che-hsüeh*" 讀梁漱溟先生的東西文化及其哲學 (On reading of Mr. Liang Sou-ming's *The Culture of East and West and Their Philosophies*), *HSWT*, 2nd coll., II, 57 - 85.

——. "Wo ti ch'i-lu" 我的歧路 (My unsettled path), *HSWT*, 2nd coll., III, 91 - 101.

——. "Ching-hua-yüan ti yin-lun" 鏡花緣的引論 (Introduction to *Flowers in the Mirror*), *HSWT*, 2nd coll., IV, 119 - 168.

——. "The Civilizations of the East and the West," in C. A. Beard, ed., *Whither Mankind.* New York, Longmans, Green, 1928.

———. "Ming-chiao" 名教 (The worship of names), *HSWT*, 3rd coll., I, 91-107.

———. "Conflicts of Cultures," *The China Christian Year Book, 1929*, pp. 112 - 121. Shanghai, Christian Literature Society, 1930.

———. "My Credo and Its Evolution," in *Living Philosophies*. New York, Simon and Schuster, 1931.

———. "Ch'en Tu-hsiu yü wen-hsüeh ke-ming" 陳獨秀與文學革命 (Ch'en Tu-hsiu and the literary revolution), in Ch'en Tung-hsiao, ed., *Ch'en Tu-hsiu p'ing-lun.*

———. *Hu Shih lun-hsüeh chin-chu* 胡適論學近著 (Recent scholarly writings of Hu Shih). Shanghai, Commercial Press, 1935.

———. "Hsin-hsin yü fan-hsing" 信心與反省 (Faith and reflection), *Hu Shih lun-hsüeh chin-chu*, pp. 479 - 485.

———. "Tsai lun hsin-hsin yü fan-hsing" 再論信心與反省 (Another discussion of faith and reflection), *Hu Shih lun-hsüeh chin-chu*, pp. 486 - 492.

———. "San-lun hsin-hsin yü fan-hsing" 三論信心與反省 (Third discussion of faith and reflection), *Hu Shih lun-hsüeh chin-chu*, pp. 493 - 499.

———. "Shih-p'ing so-wei 'Chung-kuo pen-wei ti wen-hua chien-she' " 試評所謂「中國本位的文化建設」 (A critique of so-called "Cultural Reconstruction on a Chinese Base"), *Hu Shih lun-hsüeh chin-chu*, pp. 552 - 557.

———. Unpublished diaries, 1921-1935. Microfilm. New York, Archives of the Oral History Project, Columbia University.

———. "The Indianization of China," *Independence, Convergence and Borrowing in Institution, Thought and Art*, pp. 219 - 247. Harvard Tercentenary Publications. Cambridge, Mass., Harvard University Press, 1937.

———. "Historical Foundations for a Democratic China," in *E. J. James Lectures on Government*, 2nd series, pp. 53 - 64. Urbana, University of Illinois Press, 1941.

———. *Ssu-shih tzu-shu* 四十自述 (Autobiography at forty). Taipei, Yüan-tung t'u-shu kung-ssu 遠東圖書公司 , 1954.

———. "Dr. Hu Shih's Personal Reminiscences," interviewed, compiled and edited by Te-kong Tong, with Dr. Hu's corrections in his own hand-writing, 1958. Typescript. New York, Department of Special Collections, Butler Library, Columbia University.

———. *Hu Shih liu-hsüeh jih-chi* 胡適留學日記 (Hu Shih's diary while studying abroad). Taipei, Commercial Press, 1959.

———. "The Scientific Spirit and Method in Chinese Philosophy," in Charles A. Moore, ed., *Philosophy and Culture—East and West*. Honolulu, University of Hawaii Press, 1962.

———. "The Chinese Tradition and the Future," *Sino-American Conference on Intellectual Cooperation: Reports and Proceedings*, pp. 13 - 22. Seattle, Department of Publications and Printing, University of Washington, 1962.

Hu Shih wen-ts'un, see *HSWT.*

Hu Sung-p'ing 胡頌平 . "Hu Shih hsien-sheng nien-p'u chien-pien" 胡適先生 年譜簡編 (A brief chronological biography of Hu Shih), *Ta-lu tsa-chih* 大陸雜誌 , 43.1:1 - 33 (July 15, 1971).

Jen Chi-yü 任繼愈 . "Ch'in Han ti t'ung-i yü che-hsüeh ssu-hsiang ti pien-ke" 秦漢的統一與哲學思想的變革 (The unification [of China] in the Ch'in and Han and the changes in philosophical thought), *Li-shih yeh-chiu,* no. 6:62-70 (1977).

Kagan, Richard C. "Ch'en Tu-hsiu's Unfinished Autobiography," *The China Quarterly,* 50:295 - 314 (April - June 1972).

———. "The Chinese Trotskyist Movement and Ch'en Tu-hsiu: Culture, Revolution, and Polity." Ph.D. diss., University of Pennsylvania, 1969.

K'ang Yu-wei 康有爲 "Nan-hai K'ang hsien-sheng tzu-pien nien-p'u" 南海 康先生自編年譜 (Chronological autobiography of K'ang Yu-wei), in *K'ang Yu-wei: A Biography and a Symposium,* tr. and ed. Lo Jung-pang. Tucson, University of Arizona Press, 1967.

———. *K'ang-tzu nei-wai p'ien* 康子內外篇 , 1886 - 1887 (The inner and outer books of the philosopher K'ang). Microfilm. Stanford, Hoover Library.

Karlgren, Bernard, tr. *The Book of Odes.* Stockholm, reprinted from Bulletin No. 22, Museum of Far Eastern Antiquities, 1950.

———, tr. *The Book of Documents.* Stockholm, Museum of Far Eastern Antiquities, 1950.

Keightley, David N. "Legitimation in Shang China." Mimeographed. Conference on Legitimation of Chinese Imperial Regimes, Asilomar, June 15 - 24, 1975.

Ko Hung 葛洪 . *Pao-p'u tzu* 抱扑子 . SPPY ed.

Ku Yen-wu 顧炎武 . *Jih-chih lu* 日知錄 (Daily notebook of knowledge). Taipei, Shih-chieh shu-chü 世界書局 , 1962.

Kuo Ch'ing-fan 郭慶藩 , ed. *Chiao-cheng Chuang-tzu chi-shih* 校正莊子集釋 (Collected commentaries on the *Chuang-tzu).* Taipei, Shih-chieh shu-chü, 1962.

Kuo-min jih-jih pao 國民日日報 ("The China National Gazette").

Kuo Mo-jo 郭沫若 . "Chuang-tzu yü Lu Hsün" 莊子與魯迅 (Chuang-tzu and Lu Hsün), in his *Chin-hsi p'u-chien* 今昔蒲劍 (The present and the past, and the rush-sword), pp. 275 - 296. Shanghai, Hai-yen shu-tien 海燕書 店 , 1947.

Kuo, Thomas C. *Ch'en Tu-hsiu (1879 - 1942) and the Chinese Communist Movement.* South Orange, N.J., Seton Hall University Press, 1975.

Langer, Susanne K. *Philosophy in a New Key.* 4th ed. Cambridge, Mass., Harvard University Press, 1960.

Lasker, Bruno, ed. *Problems of the Pacific, 1931.* Proceedings of the Fourth Conference of the Institute of Pacific Relations, Hangchow and Shanghai, China, October 21 to November 2. Chicago, University of Chicago Press, 1932.

Lau, D. C. "Theories of Human Nature in *Mencius* and *Shyuntzyy," Bulletin of the School of Oriental and African Studies,* 15:541 - 565 (1953).

———, tr. *Lao Tzu Tao Te Ching.* Harmondsworth, England, Penguin Books, 1963.

Legge, James, tr. *Chinese Classics.* 2nd ed. rev. Oxford, Clarendon Press, 1895; 3rd ed. Hong Kong, Hong Kong University Press, 1960.

Levenson, Joseph R. *Confucian China and Its Modern Fate.* 3 vols. Berkeley, University of California Press, 1958 - 1965.

————. *Liang Ch'i-ch'ao and the Mind of Modern China.* Cambridge, Mass., Harvard University Press, 1959.

LHCC: Lu Hsün ch'üan-chi 魯迅全集 (Complete works of Lu Hsün). 10 vols. Peking, Jen-min wen-hsüeh ch'u-pan she, 1956.

Li Chien-nung 李劍農. *Chung-kuo chin-pai-nien cheng-chih shih* 中國近百年政治史 (A political history of China during the last hundred years). Shanghai, Commercial Press, 1947.

Li Ho-lin 李何林, ed. *Lu Hsün lun* 魯迅論 (On Lu Hsün). Shanghai, Pei-hsin shu-chü, 1930.

Li Ju-chen 李汝珍. *Ching-hua-yüan* 鏡花緣 (Flowers in the mirror). Shanghai, Ya-tung t'u-shu-kuan, 1923.

Li Jui 李銳. *Mao Tse-tung t'ung-chih ti ch'u-ch'i ke-ming huo-tung* 毛澤東同志的初期革命活動 (Comrade Mao's early revolutionary activities). Peking, Chung-kuo ch'ing-nien ch'u-pan she 中國青年出版社, 1957.

Li-shih yen-chiu 歷史研究 (Historical studies).

Li Ta-chao 李大釗. *Li Ta-chao hsüan-chi* 李大釗選集 (Selected works of Li Ta-chao). Peking, Jen-min ch'u-pan she, 1959.

Liang Ch'i-ch'ao 梁啓超. *Yin-ping-shih ho-chi* 飲冰室合集 (Complete works of the Ice-Drinker's Studio). Shanghai, Chung-hua shu-chü, 1936. *Chuan-chi* 專集 (Special collection), 24 vols.; *Wen-chi* 文集 (Literary collection), 16 vols.

————. "Pien-fa t'ung-i" 變法通議 (A general discussion on reform), in his *Yin-ping-shih ho-chi, Wen-chi*, I.

————. *Intellectual Trends in the Ch'ing Period,* tr. Immanuel C. Y. Hsü. Cambridge, Mass., Harvard University Press, 1959.

Lin Ch'en 林辰. "Lu Hsün ti hun-yin sheng-huo" 魯迅的婚姻生活 (The married life of Lu Hsün) in his *Lu Hsün shih-chi k'ao* 魯迅事蹟考 (A study of some events in Lu Hsün's life). Shanghai, K'ai-ming shu-tien 開明書店, 1948.

Lin Yü-sheng. "Radical Iconoclasm in the May Fourth Period and the Future of Chinese Liberalism," in Benjamin I. Schwartz, ed., *Reflections on the May Fourth Movement.* Cambridge, Mass., East Asian Research Center, Harvard University, 1972.

————. "The Evolution of the Pre-Confucian Meaning of *Jen* and the Confucian Concept of Moral Autonomy," *Monumenta Serica,* 31:172-204 (1974-75).

————. "The Suicide of Liang Chi: An Ambiguous Case of Moral Conservatism," in Charlotte Furth, ed., *The Limits of Change: Essays on Conservative Alternatives in Republican China.* Cambridge, Mass., Harvard University Press, 1976.

Lo Chia-lun 羅家倫. "I-nien-lai wo-men hsüeh-sheng yün-tung ti ch'eng-kung shih-pai ho chiang-lai ying-ch'ü ti fang-chen" 一年來我們學生運動底成功失敗和將來應取的方針 (The victories and defeats of our student movement during the past year and the orientation that should be adopted in the future), *Hsin-ch'ao* 新潮 (New tide), 2.4:846 - 861 (May 1, 1920).

Lovejoy, Arthur O. *The Great Chain of Being: A Study of the History of an Idea*. New York, Harper and Row, Harper Torchbooks, 1960.

Lu Hsün 魯迅 . "Tzu-hsü" 自序 (Preface), *Na-han* 吶喊 (Call to arms), *LHCC*, I, 3 - 8.

———. "K'uang-jen jih-chi" 狂人日記 (Diary of a madman), *Na-han*, *LHCC*, I, 9 - 19.

———. "Ming-t'ien" 明天 (Tomorrow), *Na-han*, *LHCC*, I, 35 - 42.

———. "Ku-hsiang" 故鄉 (My native place), *Na-han*, *LHCC*, I, 61 - 71.

———. "Ah Q cheng-chuan" 阿Q正傳 (The true story of Ah Q), *Na-han*, *LHCC*, I, 72 - 114.

———. "Wen-hua p'ien-chih lun" 文化偏至論 (On extremities in cultural development), *Fen* 墳 (The grave), *LHCC*, I, 179-193.

———. "Mo-lo shih-li shuo" 摩羅詩力說 (The power of Mara poetry), *Fen*, *LHCC*, I, 194 - 234.

———. "K'an-ching yu-kan" 看鏡有感 (Thoughts before the mirror), *Fen*, *LHCC*, I, 300 - 303.

———. "Teng-hsia man-pi" 燈下漫筆 (Some notions jotted down by lamplight), *Fen*, *LHCC*, I, 309 - 316.

———. "Lun cheng-le yen k'an" 論睜了眼看 (On looking facts in the face), *Fen*, *LHCC*, I, 328 - 332.

———. "Ts'ung hu-hsü shuo-tao ya-chih" 從胡鬚說到牙齒 (A discussion ranging from beard to tooth), *Fen*, *LHCC*, I, 333 - 341.

———. "Hsieh-tsai *Fen* hou-mien" 寫在「墳」後面 (Postscript to *Grave*), *Fen*, *LHCC*, I, 360 - 365.

———. "Sui-kan lu san-shih-pa" 隨感錄三十八 (Random thoughts, No. 38), *HCN*, 5.5:515-518 (October [*sic*; should read November] 15, 1918), reprinted in Lu Hsün, *Je-feng* 熱風 (Hot wind), *LHCC*, I, 387-390.

———. "Chu-fu" 祝福 (Benediction), *P'ang-huang* 徬徨 (Hesitation), *LHCC*, II, 5 - 22.

———. "Tsai chiu-lou shang" 在酒樓上 (In the tavern), *P'ang-huang*, *LHCC*, II, 23 - 34.

———. "Hsi-wang" 希望 (Hope), *Yeh-ts'ao* 野草 (Wild grass), *LHCC*, II, 170 - 171.

———. "Kuo-k'e" 過客 (The passer-by), *Yeh-ts'ao*, *LHCC*, II, 179 - 185.

———. "Erh-shih-ssu hsiao t'u" 二十四孝圖 (Illustrations of twenty-four examples of filial piety), *Chao-hua hsi-shih* 朝花夕拾 (Morning flowers plucked at dusk), *LHCC*, II, 232 - 238.

———. "Fu-ch'in te-ping" 父親的病 (Father's illness), *Chao-hua hsi-shih*, *LHCC*, II, 257 - 262.

———. "T'eng-yeh hsien-sheng" 藤野先生 (Mr. Fujino), *Chao-hua hsi-shih*, *LHCC*, II, 271 - 277.

———. "Hu-jan hsiang-tao" 忽然想到 (Sudden notions), *Hua-kai chi* (Bad luck), *LHCC*, III, 10 - 15.

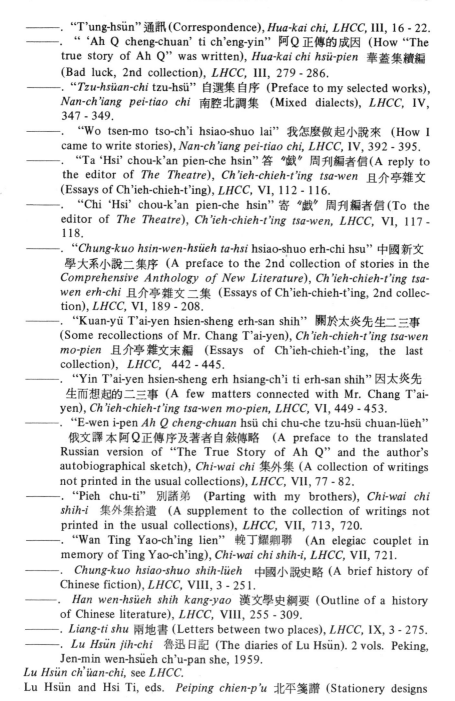

———. "T'ung-hsün" 通訊 (Correspondence), *Hua-kai chi, LHCC,* III, 16 - 22.

———. "'Ah Q cheng-chuan' ti ch'eng-yin" 阿Q正傳的成因 (How "The true story of Ah Q" was written), *Hua-kai chi hsü-pien* 華蓋集續編 (Bad luck, 2nd collection), *LHCC,* III, 279 - 286.

———. "*Tzu-hsüan-chi* tzu-hsü" 自選集自序 (Preface to my selected works), *Nan-ch'iang pei-tiao chi* 南腔北調集 (Mixed dialects), *LHCC,* IV, 347 - 349.

———. "Wo tsen-mo tso-ch'i hsiao-shuo lai" 我怎麼做起小說來 (How I came to write stories), *Nan-ch'iang pei-tiao chi, LHCC,* IV, 392 - 395.

———. "Ta 'Hsi' chou-k'an pien-che hsin" 答 "戲" 周刊編者信 (A reply to the editor of *The Theatre*), *Ch'ieh-chieh-t'ing tsa-wen* 且介亭雜文 (Essays of Ch'ieh-chieh-t'ing), *LHCC,* VI, 112 - 116.

———. "Chi 'Hsi' chou-k'an pien-che hsin" 寄 "戲" 周刊編者信 (To the editor of *The Theatre*), *Ch'ieh-chieh-t'ing tsa-wen, LHCC,* VI, 117 - 118.

———. "*Chung-kuo hsin-wen-hsüeh ta-hsi* hsiao-shuo erh-chi hsu" 中國新文學大系小說二集序 (A preface to the 2nd collection of stories in the *Comprehensive Anthology of New Literature*), *Ch'ieh-chieh-t'ing tsa-wen erh-chi* 且介亭雜文二集 (Essays of Ch'ieh-chieh-t'ing, 2nd collection), *LHCC,* VI, 189 - 208.

———. "Kuan-yü T'ai-yen hsien-sheng erh-san shih" 關於太炎先生二三事 (Some recollections of Mr. Chang T'ai-yen), *Ch'ieh-chieh-t'ing tsa-wen mo-pien* 且介亭雜文末編 (Essays of Ch'ieh-chieh-t'ing, the last collection), *LHCC,* 442 - 445.

———. "Yin T'ai-yen hsien-sheng erh hsiang-ch'i ti erh-san shih" 因太炎先生而想起的二三事 (A few matters connected with Mr. Chang T'ai-yen), *Ch'ieh-chieh-t'ing tsa-wen mo-pien, LHCC,* VI, 449 - 453.

———. "E-wen i-pen *Ah Q cheng-chuan* hsü chi chu-che tzu-hsü chuan-lüeh" 俄文譯本阿Q正傳序及著者自敍傳略 (A preface to the translated Russian version of "The True Story of Ah Q" and the author's autobiographical sketch), *Chi-wai chi* 集外集 (A collection of writings not printed in the usual collections), *LHCC,* VII, 77 - 82.

———. "Pieh chu-ti" 別諸弟 (Parting with my brothers), *Chi-wai chi shih-i* 集外集拾遺 (A supplement to the collection of writings not printed in the usual collections), *LHCC,* VII, 713, 720.

———. "Wan Ting Yao-ch'ing lien" 輓丁耀卿聯 (An elegiac couplet in memory of Ting Yao-ch'ing), *Chi-wai chi shih-i, LHCC,* VII, 721.

———. *Chung-kuo hsiao-shuo shih-lüeh* 中國小說史略 (A brief history of Chinese fiction), *LHCC,* VIII, 3 - 251.

———. *Han wen-hsüeh shih kang-yao* 漢文學史綱要 (Outline of a history of Chinese literature), *LHCC,* VIII, 255 - 309.

———. *Liang-ti shu* 兩地書 (Letters between two places), *LHCC,* IX, 3 - 275.

———. *Lu Hsün jih-chi* 魯迅日記 (The diaries of Lu Hsün). 2 vols. Peking, Jen-min wen-hsüeh ch'u-pan she, 1959.

Lu Hsün ch'üan-chi, see *LHCC.*

Lu Hsün and Hsi Ti, eds. *Peiping chien-p'u* 北平箋譜 (Stationery designs with woodblock engravings from Peiping). Peking, 1934.

Lyell, William A., Jr. *Lu Hsün's Vision of Reality.* Berkeley, University of
California Press, 1976.

Mao Tse-tung 毛澤東. "Hsin min-chu chu-i lun" 新民主主義論 (On new
democracy), in *Mao Tse-tung hsüan-chi* 毛澤東選集 Selected works of
Mao Tse-tung), II, Peking, Jen-min ch'u-pan she, 1966. (Eng. tr.
in *Selected Works of Mao Tse-tung,* II, [Peking, Foreign Languages
Press, 1961 - 1965]).

Meisner, Maurice. *Li Ta-chao and the Origins of Chinese Marxism.* Cambridge, Mass., Harvard University Press, 1967.

Mo Tun 茅盾. "Lu Hsün lun" 魯迅論 (On Lu Hsün), reprinted in Ts'ao
Chü-jen, *Lu Hsün nien-p'u,* pp. 197 - 229.

Mu Shih. "Research Work in Philosophy and Social Sciences Unshackled,"
Peking Review, 21.19:16-18, 21 (May 12, 1978).

Ou Chü-chia 歐榘甲. "Lun Chung-kuo pien-fa pi tzu fa-ming ching-hsüeh
shih" 論中國變法必自發明經學始 (China's reforms must start from
an understanding of the hidden meaning of the classics), *Chih-hsin pao*
知新報 (New knowledge journal), No. 38 (November 1, 1897).

P'an Kuang-tan 潘光旦. "Book Review," *China Critic,* 3.9:210 - 211
(February 27, 1930).

Pao Chia-lin 鮑家麟. "Li Ju-chen ti nan-nü p'ing-teng ssu-hsiang" 李汝珍
的男女平等思想 (Li Ju-chen's thoughts on equality between man and
woman), *Shih-huo yüeh-k'an* 食貨月刊 (Food and money monthly),
n. s. 1.12:12 - 21 (March 1972).

Parsons, Talcott. *The Structure of Social Action.* Glencoe, Ill., Free Press,
1949.

Polanyi, Michael. *Personal Knowledge: Towards a Post-Critical Philosophy.*
Chicago, University of Chicago Press, 1958.

———and Harry Prosch. *Meaning.* Chicago, University of Chicago Press,
1975.

Popper, K. R. *The Open Society and Its Enemies.* 4th ed. rev. 2 vols. New
York, Harper and Row, Harper Torchbooks, 1963.

Poussin, L. de la Vallée. "Karma," in James Hastings, ed., *Encyclopedia of
Religion and Ethics,* VII. New York, Scribner's, 1915, repr. 1955.

Průšek, Jaroslav. "A Confrontation of Traditional Oriental Literature with
Modern European Literature in the Context of the Chinese Literary
Revolution," in Leon Edel, ed., *Literary History and Literary
Criticism.* New York, New York University Press, 1965.

———. "Some Marginal Notes on the Poems of Po Chü-i," in his *Chinese
History and Literature.* Prague, Academia, 1970.

Pulleyblank, E. G. "Neo-Confucianism and Neo-Legalism in T'ang Intellectual
Life, 755-805," in Arthur F. Wright, ed., *The Confucian Persuasion.*
Stanford, Stanford University Press, 1960.

Ryle, Gilbert. *The Concept of Mind.* New York, Barnes and Noble,
University Paperbacks, 1949.

Schram, Stuart. *Mao Tse-tung.* Rev. ed. New York, Simon and Schuster,
1969.

————. *The Political Thought of Mao Tse-tung.* Rev. ed. New York, Praeger, 1969.

Schwartz, Benjamin I. "Ch'en Tu-hsiu and the Acceptance of the Modern West," *Journal of the History of Ideas*, 12.1:61 - 74 (January 1951).

————. "The Intellectual History of China: Preliminary Reflections," in John K. Fairbank, ed., *Chinese Thought and Institutions.* Chicago, University of Chicago Press, 1957.

————. "Some Polarities in Confucian Thought," in D. S. Nivison and A. F. Wright, eds., *Confucianism in Action.* Stanford, Stanford University Press, 1959.

————. *In Search of Wealth and Power: Yen Fu and the West.* Cambridge, Mass., Harvard University Press, 1964.

————. "The Chinese Perception of World Order, Past and Present," in John K. Fairbank, ed., *The Chinese World Order.* Cambridge, Mass., Harvard University Press, 1968.

Shih Chün 石峻 , ed. *Chung-kuo chin-tai ssu-hsiang-shih tsan-k'ao tzu-liao chien-pien* 中國近代思想史參考資料簡編 (A concise source book in modern Chinese intellectual history). Peking, San-lien shu-tien 三聯 書店 , 1957.

Shih, Vincent Y. C. "A Talk with Hu Shih," *The China Quarterly*, 10:149-165 (April-June 1962).

Shils, Edward. "Ideology and Civility," in his *The Intellectuals and the Powers and Other Essays.* Chicago, University of Chicago Press, 1972.

————. "Center and Periphery," "Charisma," and "Charisma, Order, and Status," in his *Center and Periphery: Essays in Macrosociology.* Chicago, University of Chicago Press, 1975.

Shu T'ien 曙天 . "Fang Lu Hsün hsien-sheng" 訪魯迅先生 (Visiting Mr. Lu Hsün), reprinted in Ts'ao Chü-jen, *Lu Hsün nien-p'u*, pp. 262-264.

Snow, Edgar. *Red Star Over China.* 1st rev. and enlarged ed. New York, Grove Press, 1968.

SPPY: Ssu-pu pei-yao 四部備要 (Essentials of the four libraries) .

SPTK: Ssu-pu ts'ung-k'an 四部叢刊 (Four-library series) .

Su Hsüeh-lin 蘇雪林 . " 'Ah Q cheng-chuan' chi Lu Hsün ch'uang-tso ti i-shu" 阿Q正傳及魯迅創作的藝術 ("The True Story of Ah Q" and the art of Lu Hsün's creation), reprinted in Ts'ao Chü-jen, *Lu Hsün nien-p'u*, pp. 230 - 253.

Su-pao 蘇報 (The Kiangsu journal).

Suh Hu, see Hu Shih.

Sun Fu-yüan 孫伏園 . *Lu Hsün hsien-sheng erh-san shih* 魯迅先生二三事 (Two or three events in Mr. Lu Hsün's life). Shanghai, Tso-chia shu-wu 作家書屋 , 1945.

Tai Chen 戴震 . "Letter to Tuan Yü-ts'ai; May 30, 1777," in Hu Shih, *Tai Tung-yüan ti che-hsüeh* 戴東原的哲學 (The philosophy of Tai Tung-yüan). Taipei, Commercial Press, 1967.

T'an Ssu-t'ung 譚嗣同 . *T'an Ssu-t'ung ch'üan-chi* 譚嗣同全集 (The complete works of T'an Ssu-t'ung). Peking, San-lien shu-tien, 1954.

————. "Ssu-wei yin-yün-tai tuan-shu–pao Pei Yüan-cheng" 思緯壹壹臺
短書—報貝元徵 (A pamphlet from the Pavilion of *Ssu-wei yin-yün*
–in reply to Pei Yüan-cheng), in Shih Chün, ed., *Chung-kuo chin-tai
ssu-hsiang-shih tsan-k'ao tzu-liao chien-pien,* pp. 531-571.

T'ang Ssu 唐俟 (Lu Hsün). "Sui-kan lu ssu-shih-i" 隨感錄四十一 (Random
thoughts, No. 41), *HCN,* 6.1:68 - 69 (January 15, 1919).

————. "Ch'a-la t'u-ssu t'e-la ti hsü-yen" 察拉圖斯忒拉的序言 ([A translation of] Zarathustra's Prologue), *Hsin-ch'ao,* 2.5:954 - 973 (June
1, 1920).

Teng, Ssu-yü and John K. Fairbank. *China's Response to the West.* Cambridge,
Mass., Harvard University Press, 1954.

THWT: Tu-hsiu wen-ts'un 獨秀文存 (Collected essays of [Ch'en] Tu-hsiu).
3 vols. Shanghai, Ya-tung t'u-shu-kuan, 1922.

Ting Wen-chiang 丁文江 , ed. *Liang Jen-kung hsien-sheng nien-p'u ch'ang-pien
ch'u-kao* 梁任公先生年譜長編初稿 (The first draft of the chrono-
logical biography of Mr. Liang Ch'i-ch'ao). Taipei, Shih-chieh shu-chü,
1958.

Tocqueville, Alexis de. *Democracy in America,* ed. P. Bradley. New York,
Vintage Books, 1954.

Ts'ao Chü-jen 曹聚仁 . *Lu Hsün p'ing-chuan* 魯迅評傳 (A critical biography
of Lu Hsün). Hong Kong, Shih-chieh ch'u-pan she 世界出版社 , 1956.

————. *Lu Hsün nien-p'u* 魯迅年譜 (Chronological biography of Lu Hsün).
Hong Kong, San-yü t'u-shu wen-chü kung-ssu, 1967.

Tu-hsiu wen-ts'un, see *THWT.*

Tung Chung-shu 董仲舒 . *Ch'un-ch'iu fan-lu* 春秋繁露 (Luxuriant dew of
the spring and autumn annals). SPTK ed.

Wang Chi-chen, tr. *Ah Q and Others.* New York, Columbia University Press,
1941.

Wang Hsien-ch'ien 王先謙 , ed. *Hsün-tzu chi-chieh* 荀子集解 (*Hsün-tzu* with
collected annotations). Taipei, Shih-chieh shu-chü, 1962.

Wang Shu-ch'ien 汪淑潛 . "Hsin-chiu wen-t'i" 新舊問題 (The problem
between the new and the old), *HCN,* I, No. 1, article 4, pp, 1 - 4.

Wang Yang-ming 王陽明 . *Wang Wen-ch'eng-kung ch'üan-shu* 王文成公全書
(Complete works of Wang Yang-ming). SPTK ed.

————. *Ch'uan-hsi lu* 傳習錄 (Instructions for practical living), in *Wang wen-
ch'eng-kung ch'üan-shu.*

————. *Ta-hsüeh wen* 大學問 (Inquiry on the Great Learning), in *Wang Wen-
ch'eng-kung ch'üan-shu,* XXVI, 2-10b.

Wang Yao 王瑤 . "Lu Hsün tui-yü Chung-kuo wen-hsüeh i-ch'an ti t'ai-tu
ho t'a so-shou Chung-kuo wen-hsüeh ti ying-hsiang" 魯迅對於
中國文學遺產的態度和他所受中國文學的影響 (Lu Hsün's attitude
toward the Chinese literary heritage and the influence of Chinese
literature on him), in *Lu Hsün yü Chung-kuo wen-hsüeh* 魯迅與中
國文學 (Lu Hsün and Chinese literature), pp. 1 - 59. Shanghai, P'ing-
ming ch'u-pan she 平明出版社 , 1952.

Watson, Burton, tr. *The Complete Works of Chuang Tzu.* New York,
Columbia University Press, 1968.

Weber, Max. *The Methodology of the Social Sciences,* tr. Edward A. Shils and Henry A. Finch. New York, Free Press, 1949.

———. *The Protestant Ethic and the Spirit of Capitalism,* tr. Talcott Parsons. New York, Scribner's, 1958.

White, Morton. *Social Thought in America.* Boston, Beacon Press, 1957.

Wilhelm, Hellmut. "Chinese Confucianism on the Eve of the Great Encounter," in M. B. Jansen, ed., *Changing Japanese Attitudes Toward Modernization.* Princeton, Princeton University Press, 1965.

Wu Yü 吳虞. *Wu Yü wen-lu* 吳虞文錄 (Collected essays of Wu Yü). Shanghai, Ya-tung t'u-shu-kuan, 1921.

Yang, Gladys, ed. and tr. *Silent China: Selected Writings of Lu Xun.* London, Oxford University Press, 1973.

Yang, Hsien-yi and Gladys Yang, eds. and trs. *Selected Works of Lu Hsün.* 4 vols. Peking, Foreign Languages Press, 1956–1961.

Yen Ling 延陵. "Kuan-yü K'ung Ch'iu chu Shao-cheng Mao" 關於 孔丘 誅少正卯 (Concerning the episode in which Confucius was alleged to have killed Shao-cheng Mao), *Li-shih yen-chiu,* no. 1:63-65 (1978).

Yi Pai-sha 易白沙. "K'ung-tzu p'ing-i" 孔子平議 (An impartial discussion of Confucius), *HCN,* 1.6: (article 3) 1–6 (February 1, 1916) and 2.1: (article 4) 1–6 (September 1, 1916).

Young, Ernest P. "The Hung-hsien Emperor as a Modernizing Conservative," in Charlotte Furth, ed., *The Limits of Change: Essays on Conservative Alternatives in Republican China.*

———. *The Presidency of Yüan Shih-k'ai: Liberalism and Dictatorship in Early Republican China.* Ann Arbor, University of Michigan Press, 1977.

Yü Ying-shih 余英時. "Fan-chih-lun yü Chung-kuo cheng-chih ch'uan-t'ung" 反智論與中國政治傳統 (Anti-intellectualism and the Chinese political tradition) in his *Li-shih yü ssu-hsiang* 歷史與思想 (History and thought), pp. 1 - 46. Taipei, Lien-ching ch'u-pan shih-yeh kung-ssu 聯經出版事業公司, 1976.

CHARACTER LIST

Names and titles appearing in the Bibliography are not included in this list.

Ah Shun 阿順
ai 愛
Anhwei 安徽
Anhwei su-hua pao 安徽俗話報

Chang Hsün 張勳
Chang Kuo-t'ao 張國燾
Chang Ping-lin 章炳麟
Chang Tsai 張載
Changsha 長沙
Chao 趙
"Chao-kao" 召誥
Ch'en Huan-chang 陳煥章
"Chen-ju tao" 眞如島
Ch'en-pao 晨報
Ch'en Shu-yung 陳樹鏞

Ch'eng 誠
Ch'eng-Chu 程朱
Ch'eng I 程頤
Ch'eng Shih-ko 程師葛
chiao 敎
Ch'i 齊
ch'i 氣
Chia-chien sheng 夏劍生
"Chia-lo" 假樂
Ch'ien Hsüan-t'ung 錢玄同
chih 智
chih-hsing ho-i 知行合一
chih jen 吃人
chih-kuo 治國
chih-kuo p'ing t'ien-hsia 治國平天下
chih liang-chih 致良知

Ch'in 秦
Chin P'ing Mei 金瓶梅
Ch'ing 清
Ch'ing-nien tsa-chih 青年雜誌
Ching-yeh hsün-pao 競業旬報
Chinputang 進步黨
Chou 周
Chou Ch'un-shou 周椿壽
Chou En-lai 周恩來
Chu An 朱安
chü-jen 舉人
chü-luan shih 據亂世
Ch'ü Yüan 屈原
Chuang-tzu 莊子
ch'ün 群
Ch'ün-i shu-she 群益書社
chung 忠
"ch'ung-fen shih-chieh-hua yü ch'üan-p'an hsi-hua" 充分世界化與全盤西化
Chung-kuo kung-hsüeh 中國公學
"Chung-kuo pen-wei ti wen-hua chien-she hsüan-yen"
    中國本位的文化建設宣言
chung-shu chih tao 忠恕之道

feng-chien 封建
Fu Ssu-nien 傅斯年
Fujino Genkurō 藤野嚴九郎

Han 漢
Han-fei-tzu 韓非子
Han Wu-ti 漢武帝
Han Yü 韓愈
Hangchow 杭州
Ho Hsiu 何休
ho-p'ing 和平
Hsi 戲
"Hsi-hua" 惜花
Hsiang-lin-sao 祥林嫂
hsiao 孝
Hsimen 西門
hsin 心
hsin hai 辛亥
Hsin-hsüeh wei-ching k'ao 新學僞經考
"Hsin-min shuo" 新民說
Hsin-min ts'ung-pao 新民叢報

hsing 性
hsiu-shen 修身
hsiu-ts'ai 秀才
Hsü Ping-ch'ang 徐炳昶
Hsü Yu 許由
Hsün-tzu 荀子
Huang Tsung-hsi 黃宗羲
hun-luan ssu-hsiang 昏亂思想
Hunan 湖南
Hung-hsien 洪憲

i 義
I Jen 一人

jan-erh 然而
jang 讓
jen 仁
jen hsin 人心
Jen-hsüeh 仁學
Ju-lin wai-shih 儒林外史

"K'ai-pan *Anhwei su-hua pao* ti yüan-ku"
    開辦安徽俗話報的緣故
kang 綱
k'ao-cheng hsüeh-p'ai 考證學派
Ku K'e-kang 顧克剛
"Kua-fen Chung-kuo" 瓜分中國
Kuang-fu hui 光復會
K'ung-chiao hui 孔教會
"K'ung I-chi" 孔乙己
Kung-po Liao 公伯寮
Kung-sun lung-tzu 公孫龍子
K'ung-tzu kai-chih k'ao 孔子改制考
Kung-yang 公羊
"Kung-yang-chuan chu tzu[*sic*] hsü" 公羊傳注自序
kuo 國
kuo-chia 國家
Kuo-yü 國語

Lao-tzu 老子
li 禮
li-chiao 禮敎
Li sao 離騷
Li Ssu 李斯

Li Yüan-hung 黎元洪
liang-chih 良知
Liang Sou-ming 梁漱溟
Liu Hsin 劉歆
Liu Tsung-yüan 柳宗元
Lu 魯
Lu Chien-chang 陸建章
Lu Lung-chi 陸隴其
Lu-Wang 陸王
Lü Wei-fu 呂緯甫
Lun-yü 論語

Manchu 滿洲
Mao-shih 毛詩
Meng-tzu 孟子
Meng-tzu tzu-i shu-cheng 孟子字義疏證
Ming 明
ming 命
Mo-tzu 墨子
Mu-lien-hsi 目連戲

nien-chiu 念舊
Nü-erh ching 女兒經
Nu-li chou-pao 努力週報
Nü-tiao 女吊

Pao Ching-yen 鮑敬言
Pi Yün-ch'eng 畢雲程
ping-hsü 丙戌
Po Chü-i 白居易
Po Wen-wei 柏文蔚
Pu-jen 不忍
Pu-yi 溥儀

san-kang 三綱
Shan-ssu-sao-tzu 單四嫂子
Shang-shu 尚書
Shaohsing 紹興
Shao Ming-chih 邵銘之
Shao Yung 邵雍
shen-ssu-tsung chih chih-hsin che
    神思宗之至新者
sheng-chih-shih-che-yeh 聖之時者也
sheng-jen 聖人
sheng-p'ing shih 昇平世
Shih-ching 詩經

Shih-wu pao 時務報
Shu-sun t'ung 叔孫通
Shun 舜
"Shuo-ch'ün hsü" 說群序
ssu-hsiang ke-ming 思想革命
ssu-hsiang shang-ti p'ing 思想上的病
ssu-yü 私欲
sui 歲
Sun Yat-sen 孫逸仙
Sung 宋
Sung Chiao-jen 宋教仁

ta-tan chia-she, hsiao-hsin ch'iu-cheng
    大膽假設，小心求證
Tai Chen 戴震
t'ai chi 太極
t'ai-p'ing shih 太平世
T'ai-tsung 太宗
Taiyüan 太原
Tan 旦
T'ang 唐
tao 道
Ti 帝
t'ien 天
t'ien-hsia 天下
t'ien-li 天理
t'ien-tao 天道
"To-fang" 多方
"To-shih" 多士
tsa-lan 雜覽
Ts'ai O 蔡鍔
Ts'ai Yüan-p'ei 蔡元培
Ts'ao-fu 巢父
Tsinan 濟南
Tso-chuan 左傳
Tsou 鄒
tsui-hsin yüeh-tu 醉心閱讀
Tuan Ch'i-jui 段祺瑞
Tuan Hsi-p'eng 段錫朋
Tuan Yü-ts'ai 段玉裁
T'ung-meng-hui 同盟會

wang 王
Wang An-shih 王安石
Wang Fu-chih 王夫之
Wang Yung-kung 王庸工

Weichuang 未莊
wei-yen ta-i 微言大義
Wu 吳
Wu-ch'ang 無常
Wu Ching-tzu 吳敬梓
Wu-li t'ung-k'ao 五禮通考
wu-wei 無爲

yang 陽
Yang Chu 楊朱
Yao 堯

Yeh Shih 葉適
Yen Fu 嚴復
yin 陰
Yin 殷
yin-yang 陰陽
Yü I-Jen 余一人
Yü Sung-hua 俞頌華
Yü-wai hsiao-shuo chi 域外小説集
Yüan Shih-k'ai 袁世凱
Yün-t'u 閏土
Yunnan 雲南

INDEX

COMPILED BY THOMAS C. PIERSON

185

DESIGNED BY RON FENDEL
COMPOSED BY THE COMPOSING ROOM, INC., GRAND RAPIDS, MICHIGAN
MANUFACTURED BY THOMSON-SHORE, INC., DEXTER, MICHIGAN
TEXT IS SET IN TIMES ROMAN, DISPLAY LINES IN OPTIMA

Library of Congress Cataloging in Publication Data
Lin Yü-sheng, 1934-
The crisis of Chinese consciousness.
Bibliography: p. 165-179.
Includes index.
1.   China—Intellectual life.
2.   May fourth movement.   I.   Title.
DS721.L567   951.05   77-91057
ISBN 0-299-07410-2